SMART MOVES

WHY LEARNING IS NOT ALL IN YOUR HEAD

BY CARLA HANNAFORD, PH.D.

GREAT OCEAN PUBLISHERS
ARLINGTON, VIRGINIA

Permission for use of the following is gratefully acknowledged:
Brain Gym® is a Registered Trademark of the Educational Kinesiology Foundation. Frances Park Stryk kindly loaned me the name of her exercise and physical training company, *Smart Moves*. Illustration on page 65 is from Anthony Trowbridge's model. Illustration on page 67, "Caution: Children Not at Play" is copyright American Heart Association. Illustration on page 80 is copyright Great Ocean Publishers. Photographs on pages 118-125 and 127 are by Cherokee Shaner.

Book and cover design by M. M. Esterman
Cover painting by Paige Billin-Frye

For information contact:

Great Ocean Publishers
1788 Queens Way
Atlanta, Georgia 30341

Library of Congress Cataloging in Publication Data

Hannaford, Carla
Smart Moves : why learning is not all in your head / Carla Hannaford
p. cm.
Includes bibliographical references and index.
ISBN 0-915556-26-X (alk. paper). — ISBN 0-915556-27-8 (pbk. : alk. paper)
1. Learning — Physiological aspects . 2. Mind and body. I. Title
QP408.H36   1995   95-32775
612.8—dc20   CIP

Printed in the United States of America   10   9

To my mother, Minnie Foote, for life, tenacity,
and her model of excellence and flexibility

To my father, Jim Foote, for giving me the courage
to risk and make life an adventure

To my daughter, Breeze, for her deep love, wisdom, insights,
and being my teacher, co-teacher and traveling partner

Acknowledgements

I would like to acknowledge and thank the following individuals:

James Lindsey for his love, patience, creative suggestions and computer expertise

Mark and Margaret Esterman for their dedication and absolute support

Cherokee Shaner, Sandra Zachary, Linda Grinde, Johanna Bangeman, Chris Brewer, Angela Spain, Peggy Spencer and families and my other friends in Hawaii and Montana for working and playing with me so we could all learn together

Brian Nakashima and Francis Shimatsu, who through their concern for children in the Hawaiian schools, were willing to support my work

Paul and Gail Dennison for their profound work, and Olemara Peters for her timely suggestions

Paul MacLean, Fran Woolard, Cal Hashimoto and Jeff Low for their inspiration

Rose Harrow, Jessica Thayer, Victoria Lennon, Judy Metcalf, Ruth Knight, Ann Bogdavich, Jim Lieb, Carol Hunter, Lloyd Walker, Martha Denny, Mary and Billy O'Donnell for their undying faith in me and reading the manuscript at various stages

Barbara Given and Paul Messier for their expansive vision and timely connections

Arney Langburg and his pro-active vision of academic success against all odds

Dee Coulter for presenting a model for my life in her work with youth

Anthony Trowbridge for his friendship and brilliant insights

Svetlana Masgutova, Anne Marie Nel, Esta Steenekamp, Laurette Metcalfe, Marilyn Stewart, Andre Vermeulen, Andrzej Wieckowski, Renata Wennekes, Irene Kirpichnikov, Alfred Schatz, Rosemary Sonderregger, Tanya McGregor and all the other remarkable people throughout Russia, Southern Africa, Poland, Europe, Canada, Australia and New Zealand for sharing their understanding with me

Karl Nel, Shirley Bell, Hanna and Anthony Scott, Helen and Glen Jansen, Truss Gaerts and Faruk Hoosain for making it possible to deeply know many wonderful African people and their way of life

Dawn Gilchrist and Harley Hayward who as Australian Aborigines enlightened me on their rich culture

Karen Faurfelt, Jörgen Lerche and Metta Nielsen for introducing me to the Danish school system

John and Ros Harding for encouraging and allowing me to work with the Down's Syndrome and Cerebral Palsy children at the Sunfield Home School

Jim Butler for his help and information on EMFs

Penelope Mathes, first grade teacher, for sharing the figure in chapter seven showing the writing improvement of one of her students

All the children who so touched my life, in my work with them and their work with me

Charles Harter, M.D., for his love and the final perturbation to finish the book.

Contents

WAYS OF KNOWING

SMART MOVES

NURTURING AND PROTECTING OUR LEARNING SYSTEMS

Illustrations

1. ≈

Learning Is Not All In Your Head

The mind, the unfathomable generator of reality, culture, history and all human potentiality, continues to intrigue and baffle us in our quest to understand ourselves. We have attempted to explain the mind from the glimpses and pieces we are able to put together as we focus our attention and research on the brain. But we have missed a most fundamental and mysterious aspect of the mind: learning, thought, creativity and intelligence are not processes of the brain alone, but of the whole body. Sensations, movements, emotions and brain integrative functions are grounded in the body. The human qualities we associate with the mind can never exist separate from the body.

Of course we know that our brains are encased in our skulls and are in ceaseless communication with the rest of our bodies. But in practice — when we think about thinking, when we try to encourage it, to mold conditions favorable to learning and creative thought — we tend to regard it as a kind of disembodied process, as if the body's role in that process were to carry the brain from place to place so it can do the important work of thinking.

The notion that intellectual activity can somehow exist apart from our bodies is deeply rooted in our culture. It is related to the attitude that the things we do with our bodies, and the bodily functions, sensations, and emotions that sustain life, are lower, less distinctly human. This idea is also the basis of a lot of educational theory and practice that make learning harder and less successful than it could be.

Thinking and learning are not all in our head. On the contrary, the body plays an integral part in all our intellectual processes from our earliest moments right through to old age. It is our body's senses that feed the brain environmental information with which to form an understanding of the world and from which to draw when creating new possibilities. And it is our movements that express knowledge and facilitate greater cognitive function as they increase in complexity. This is the conclusion which neuroscientific research supports in ever richer detail. Although there is a tremendous amount that we don't know about the brain, there is a great deal we have learned in recent years. And I believe that knowledge will have a powerful effect on the way we raise and teach children, and the ways we see ourselves and learn throughout our lives.

We need to become more aware of the body's role in learning as it is being dramatically clarified by scientific research. This book attempts to incorporate these new insights into a more valid and dynamic view of learning. In particular it seeks to illuminate the many ways that movement initiates and supports mental processes.

WHAT YOU WILL FIND IN THIS BOOK

Part One, *Ways of Knowing*, focuses on brain and physical development — the growth of the body/mind capacities with which we learn. Intelligence, which is too often considered to be merely a matter of analytical ability — measured and valued in I.Q. points — depends on more of the brain and the body than we generally realize. Physical movement, from earliest infancy and throughout our lives, plays an important role in the creation of nerve cell networks which are actually the essence of learning.

We will explore three distinct but interconnected kinds of body/mind processing: sensation, emotion, and thought. Sensations received through our eyes, ears, nose, tongue, skin, and proprioceptors are the foundation of knowledge. The body is the medium of this learning as it gathers all the sensations which inform us about the world and about ourselves.

Next we will examine the deep ties that bind body, emotion and thought together. Our view of the role of emotional processing is being transformed by recent neuroscientific research. What is emerging is a new picture of emotions — as a body/mind system that provides important information to reasoning processes.

Then we will turn our attention to thinking, and the need for movement to anchor thought and build the skills with which we express our knowledge as lifelong learners. No matter how abstract our thinking may appear to be, it can only be manifested through the use of the muscles in our bodies — speaking, writing, making music, computing, and so on. Our bodies do the talking, focus our eyes on the page, hold the pencil, play the music.

In Part Two, *Smart Moves*, we will zero in on the importance of movement and introduce Brain Gym, a coordinated set of integrative movements that enhance learning for everyone.

Finally in Part Three, *Nurturing and Protecting Our Learning Systems*, we will consider the need to manage stress, as well as nutrition and other physical requirements of learning. As we shall see, stress, in addition to its already well publicized effects on health, is extremely damaging to learning potential. Stress is a root cause of many of the learning problems that we see in people labeled hyperactive, ADD, ADHD, and emotionally handicapped. You will learn things you can do to reduce the affects of stress in your life. The most important of these is to include more movement in your life, particularly integrative movements requiring balance and coordination that assist nervous system development and functioning.

WHERE THIS STORY BEGAN

My fascination with the role of movement in the learning process came out of the miracles I witnessed with children labeled "learning disabled." When working with these children I found that they were more easily able to learn when we began their learning sessions with simple, whole body integrative movements. My fascination continued as I myself experienced measurably greater ease in thinking, communicating, and learning anything I undertook — from writing a book to downhill skiing — as I did the movements with them.

It had never been easy for me to learn. Indeed, if I were a child in school today I would be labeled "learning disabled" or "Attention Deficit Hyperactive Disorder" due to my inability to learn to read before the age of ten and my need to move in order to learn. My daughter had some of the same difficulties when she went to school. These realities gave me a personal stake in understanding why movement assisted learning so dramatically.

The changes brought about in "learning disabled" children by such simple physical activities intrigued me so much that I had to know why they worked. So the search for understanding began, and has led me to the recognition that movement activates the neural wiring throughout the body, making the whole body the instrument of learning. What a step away from the idea that learning occurs just in the brain.

Though modern science is helping us to appreciate the role of the body and the need for movement in learning, modern life may be making it harder than ever before to benefit from this insight. Children tend to spend large amounts of time with the TV, computers or video games, and — like their elders — develop lifestyles that preempt regular exercise. When we do move, it tends to be competitive or compulsive, risking early injuries. Our daily existence is highly stressful, and as a society we are plagued with a fear of personal violence which is amplified by the media. Too often, the available and recommended alternative to all this stress and hyperactivity is drugs of one sort or another. All these factors, and many more, markedly decrease the ability to learn, and with it our ability to be creative and reach our full potential as human beings.

The first step in countering these harmful trends is, I believe, to understand the mind/body system's enormous innate capacity to learn and the role of movement in activating that capacity. For me, this unfolding scientific story is endlessly fascinating — and immensely significant for our future as individuals and as a global civilization. It can have, and has had, an immediate impact on people who discover that movement profoundly improves not only learning but creativity, stress management and health; on business people who need to deal with stress and yet remain productive; on the elderly in their quest to maintain clear thought, memory and vitality; on educators, teachers and parents concerned with the success of all our children; and on the children and adults whom we have offhandedly labeled as "learning disabled," "Attention Deficit Hyperactive Disorder," or "emotionally handicapped," as if these were true pathologies. These people will find effective, non-drug options for taking charge of their own lives, enhancing their abilities to learn and create, and to lead enriched, joyful lives.

So to begin this journey of understanding, I'd like to start with a miracle — the amazing neural plasticity of the human mind/body system I observed in the transformation of a little girl named Amy.

AMY'S TRANSFORMATION

Amy was a beautiful ten year old with long golden curls and a brilliant smile. She was the right height for a fifth grader, but she walked with a noticeably bad limp as she dragged one leg behind her. And she spoke with an erratic, monosyllabic speech pattern that made very little sense. Amy had suffered brain damage from physical abuse at six weeks of age. With a very supportive mother and step-father, she had grown to be a loving, enthusiastic child.

Since Amy could neither read, write nor communicate, the school placed her in a separate classroom with five "emotionally handicapped" children. Working as an elementary school counselor, I offered to take three of the children from this group during recess each day just to give the teachers a break. Amy was one of the children. The other two children were eight year old boys. One boy was labeled mentally retarded (both parents were also considered to be mentally retarded). The other boy was labeled emotionally handicapped due to his violent outbursts.

It was a cozy group in my office, the size of a large closet, and for me it was a highly memorable experience. During the first week I repatterned each child using Dennison Laterality Repatterning. Each day thereafter, we did five minutes of Brain Gym activities. These are simple, physical movements (described later in Chapter 7) which activate whole brain functioning, especially areas of the frontal lobes. We also drank lots of water.

After these activities, we would go outside and kick a soccer ball around for ten minutes. The boys loved this and Amy would run after the ball, squealing and giggling with laughter. On rainy days, we spent the time talking, doing art and singing. There was always much laughter. Sometimes I read the children stories. Other times we made up stories together with all sorts of funny voices and dialects, often including drawing.

If a fight occurred, I had a two minute rule that everyone get into a Brain Gym sitting position called Hook-Ups. After quieting and integrating themselves in this way, the children were able to responsibly express their frustration or needs. This process encouraged more temperate emotional expression and released their tensions. Sitting in Hook-Ups became a valuable interpersonal tool that cultivated honesty without fear or violence.

The children and I became buddies, and our daily activities became routine. Two months after I began working with Amy, her mother called with extremely gratifying news. The family's pediatrician was amazed at Amy's sudden ability to speak in sentences. Because I was so close to Amy, I simply hadn't noticed the shift.

As the months proceeded, Amy was able to connect with the ball and actually kick it, so that the boys now enjoyed her in the game. With her limp much diminished, Amy could now kick the soccer ball "straight as an arrow." Amy loved horses, but the horse she had drawn for me our first day together resembled a horse only in color. The horse she drew for me at the end of the school year was an identifiable *horse*.

After five months Amy was reading at second grade level and loved to write. At seven months she had told a convincing lie demonstrating her ability to access creative, higher level reasoning. By the end of the school year, she was reading at close to grade level, wrote highly imaginative stories and could communicate effectively.

Amy had been in school for five years and had made only small progress under excellent resource teachers. Her sudden leap in ability coincided with the addition of movement to her daily experience — movement in the form of Brain Gym, soccer, art and music. The two boys also showed remarkable progress in their academic work during that year. Their ability to remain calm and collected in emotionally challenging situations also improved.

This experience greatly reinforced my conviction that movement was somehow essential to learning. My growing realization that the body was just as important as the brain when it came to learning led to the questioning and study which resulted in this book. I had witnessed significant academic accomplishments in children and adults after Brain Gym movements, but Amy's experience demonstrated increased ability in everything she did.

It was fascinating and baffling all at the same time. We have spent years and resources struggling to teach people to learn, and yet the standardized achievement test scores go down and illiteracy rises. Could it be that one of the key elements we've been missing is simply movement? My curiosity led me to a closer examination of the labyrinth of neurophysiology which I had been teaching at the university for years. My quest expanded to the exponentially growing information base about mind/body function and the essential link of movement, the senses and emotion to effective learning. It's time to take a serious look at our own misconceptions about our bodies. In so doing we can free the mind/body system to reclaim its infinite potential for learning, thought and creativity.

2.≈

Neural Networks
Superhighways to Development

*The growth of the human mind is still high adven-
ture, in many ways the highest adventure on earth.*
— *Norman Cousins*

Amy's dramatic progress was miraculous to all of us involved
in her life. She provided us, first of all, with a vision of undaunted
spirit. At the same time, her transformation gave me a profound and
hopeful insight into the enormous plasticity and healability of the
human body/mind system.

Human nature itself is highly adaptive and flexible. As a
species we have adapted to and succeeded in a wide variety of
environments from equatorial rainforest to arctic tundra. It is the
plasticity of our body/mind system that enables us to adapt, to build
tree houses and igloos.

Neural plasticity is an intrinsic, beneficial characteristic of the
nervous system which gives us both the ability to learn, and the
ability to adapt in response to damage — to relearn. From shortly
after conception and throughout a lifetime, the nervous system is a
dynamically changing, self-organizing system. It follows no single
master plan and is never static. We develop our neural wiring in
direct response to our life experiences. Ability and increased potential grow hand in hand. As we grow, as we move, as we learn, the
cells of our nervous systems connect in highly complex patterns of
neural pathways. These patterns are organized and reorganized
throughout life, allowing us greater ability to receive outside stimuli
and perform the myriad jobs of a human life.

This plasticity gives the nervous system enormous potential
for change and growth. In the case of damage to neurons, as with

Amy, other neurons can "kick in" and take over the lost function. We also see this dramatically with stroke patients who are able to reorganize their neural apparatus to reestablish lost functions, like speech.

All of this neural organization takes place in response to stimulation and activity, i.e., use of the neural pathways. Movement and practice establish and elaborate these pathways.

HOW WE LEARN

In essence, the story of neural healing is also the story of learning. We are born with almost our full complement of nerve cells or neurons. Typically, a newborn's brain is only slightly organized, responding to sounds and to gravity, and ready to take in and react to the material world. Though we vary genetically, we all have basically the same immense potential. Given the proper amounts of nutrients, oxygen, stimulation and freedom to move, we all design and redesign complex nervous systems — and think nothing of it. The inherent plasticity and capacity of our minds is awesome — and many people believe that as human beings we haven't even begun to tap into the full mental potential available to us.

Learning proceeds as we interact with the world. In the brain and body, this learning takes the form of communication among neurons. As we receive sensory stimuli and initiate movements, our neurons form extensions called dendrites to other neurons. Dendritic extensions bring the nerve cell into communication with other nerve cells. Neuronal groups form patterns of communication that become pathways and, with use, superhighways, through which we easily access and act upon our world.

The process of nerve cells connecting and networking is, in reality, learning and thought. As associations are made and information is synthesized, pathways become complex networks. These networks can be altered as the system continues to self-organize in ever more complex ways.

NEURONS

To proceed any further in the story of learning, we need to take a closer look at the leading characters — our neurons. Neurons (nerve cells) are specialized cells, adapted specifically for transmission of electrical messages throughout the body. The human nervous system is thought to consist of 10^{11} neurons, about the same number as stars in the Milky Way galaxy. No two neurons are identical, yet their functional forms fall into a few broad categories.[1]

There are three main types of neurons: sensory, intermediate, and motor. The sensory neurons bring sensory information to the Central Nervous System (the brain and spinal cord) from all over the body: from the skin, the eyes, the ears, the tongue, the nose and the proprioceptors. Proprioceptors are sense organs that relay information about muscle position or tension or activity of joints and equilibrium. The proprioceptors are located throughout muscles, tendons, joints and mechanisms of the inner ear.

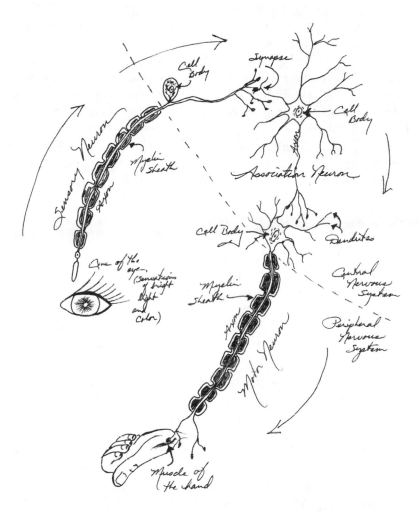

Figure 2.1: Types of Neurons

Intermediate neurons have a networking function. In the spinal cord and brain, intermediate (association) neurons relay information via their dendrites to networks of other intermediate neurons all over the brain.[2] The great intermediate net of association neurons accounts for 99.98% of the neurons in the Central Nervous System (CNS). They bring all the information together, process it and then animate the body, the muscles and glands, to respond by way of motor neurons.[3] The great intermediate net can be considered *command central*, having instantaneous access to the brain's complete information network.

Once the information is processed, the great intermediate net initiates action by sending messages on to appropriate motor neurons that originate in the brain. Motor neurons carry the messages away from the CNS to muscles and glands to activate their function. Every action requires motor neuron activation. For gross motor movements, as in swinging your right arm back and forth, a single motor neuron may stimulate or cause the simultaneous contraction of 150 to 2,000 muscle fibers. For more precise movements, fewer than ten muscle fibers are stimulated by one neuron. This more focused distribution enables more exact control for the muscular actions of high level skills like those of concert pianists or brain surgeons.[4]

Bundles of neurons form nerves, like the sciatic nerve that is a conduit of millions of both sensory and motor neurons, supplying innervation to and from the leg.

All of the structures in a neuron are involved in guiding and programming an organism's behavior.[5] The cell bodies contain the nucleus and other important organelles of the cell. The cell bodies are usually housed in the bony protection of the spinal column and skull because they contain the genetic and regenerative hardware for the whole cell.

Dendrites are the highly branched, thick extensions of the cell body that gather information and conduct impulses toward the cell body. The axon is usually a long, thin fiber that conducts nerve impulses away from the cell body to another neuron, a muscle or a gland. As neurons are used, over and over, they lay down over the axon a multilayered, white, phospholipid, segmented covering called myelin. Myelin increases the speed of nerve impulse transmission and insulates, protects and assists axon regeneration if the nerve is damaged.

When we first learn something, it is slow going, like beating a path through untraveled terrain. But as the neurons are activated repeatedly, more myelin is laid down. The more myelin, the faster the transmission. In highly myelinated neurons, impulses travel at 100 meters per second. Therefore, the more practice, the more myelin, and the faster the processing — until it becomes easy and familiar, like driving fast on a superhighway. Myelin is responsible for the color of the white matter in the brain and spinal cord. Unmyelinated nerve fibers look gray and, along with cell bodies, constitute the gray matter in the brain and spinal cord.

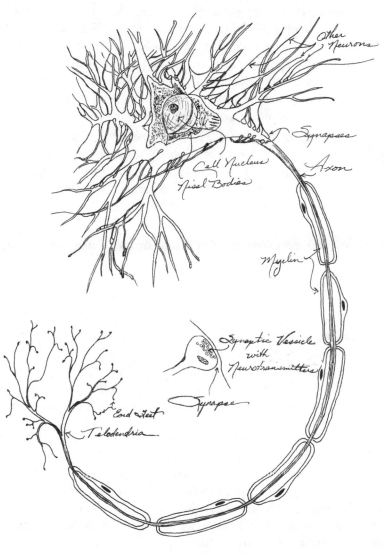

Figure 2.2: Motor Neuron

Multiple sclerosis and Tay-Sachs disease are related to destruction of myelin sheaths.[6] The recent movie *Lorenzo's Oil*, based on a true story, dealt with a rare disease that destroyed myelin on the neurons. Two dedicated parents, determined not to believe in the terminal diagnosis of this disease, studied myelin composition and were able to arrest the disease. Then, with the use of specific fatty acids (oils), were able to assist the reformation of the lost myelin. This again, is an example of the remarkable healability of the human nervous system.

At the ends of the axons are telodendria (telephone trees) with end feet. In these end feet are synaptic vesicles containing specific chemicals, called neurotransmitters. Upon activation, neurotransmitters cross the gap (synapse) between the neuron and the cell membrane of the target neuron, muscle or gland to stimulate or inhibit activation of that membrane. Information is transferred from one cell to another at these specialized points of contact.

Some neurotransmitters are excitatory, increasing message transmission by lowering the membrane potential, or ionic polarity across the membrane. Others are inhibitory, decreasing message transmission by raising the membrane potential. Membrane potential and specific neurotransmitters will be discussed later.

Synapses are the sites of action for most drugs that affect the nervous system, and many psychiatric disorders result from disruption of synaptic communication.[7]

Transmission of nerve impulses occurs in only one direction, from the cell body, through axons to the end feet of the telodendria. Messages are transmitted chemically across synapses and electrically down the nerve fiber. To give you a better picture of the process, here is an outline of events that occur when you accidentally place your foot on something sharp. Dendrites in the pain receptors in the sole of your foot take in the stimulus. Messages from dendrites are transmitted across the cell body and along the axon to the telodendria and end feet. From synaptic vesicles, neurotransmitters are released across the synapse which activate receptor sites on the next neuron, usually an intermediate neuron in the spinal cord. This neuron then connects, via synapse, with a motor neuron whose axon carries the message to muscles in the foot so they don't step down hard on the rock. Simultaneously the intermediate neuron connects with another intermediate neuron taking the impulse to the sensory cortex of the brain where the whole idea of a sharp rock under your foot is realized.

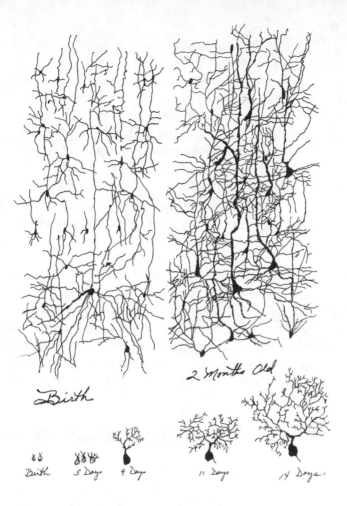

Figure 2.3: Nerve Nets (Newborn and 2 Months Old)

This is the body's way of communicating between the external and internal environment. This constant molecular communication can be restructured, depending on usage, undergoing coherent, synchronized change as learning occurs. The wondrous flexibility of our nervous system accommodates a large diversity of skills. We may develop nerve nets to support the fine muscular control and musical sense of the pianist or the spatial acuity of the painter. It is largely up to us. In a sense, we custom design our own nervous systems to meet the choice and challenges of our interests and livelihoods.

NERVE NETS

During the processes of thinking, remembering and being

mentally and physically active, new dendrites are grown from proteins synthesized in the Nissl Bodies in the cell body of the neuron.
These new dendrites vary from less than twelve to more than a
thousand per nerve cell. They act as contact points and open new
channels of communication with other neurons as learning occurs.[8]
Their role is absolutely essential because, as Solomon Snyder observes, "communication between cells or groups of cells is crucial for
the survival of every multicellular organism."[9] Nerve net development is seen graphically in the following diagram.

Dendrites create increasingly complex interconnecting networks of neural pathways, through which reactions and thoughts
travel in the form of electrochemical impulses. These ever branching
pathways are in a continual state of becoming. As long as stimulation continues, more dendritic branching occurs. If the stimuli stop,
the branching stops. These pathways alter from moment to moment
throughout our lives.[10] Ultimately they form only a few permanent
connections at the synapses with particular target cells. Experience
can further modify these synapses as well. Many synaptic connections are made as new learning occurs. Later, these linkages are
pared down in a specific way that increases efficiency of thought.[11]
Neurons may have anywhere from 1,000 to 10,000 synapses and may
receive information from 1,000 other neurons.[12]

THE GREAT INTERMEDIATE NET

With our current understanding of the great intermediate net,
we might liken it to an unstructured, free-form information network
using simultaneous, parallel processors. While electrical impulses
travel through computer circuits a million times faster than electro-
physiological pulses travel in neurons, the computer is currently
limited to a single processor. A single processor, no matter how fast
it is, is eventually overwhelmed by information and bottlenecks
occur. Even attempts to circumvent these bottlenecks using high-
capacity parallel processors run eventually into information management problems. It is very difficult to design programs that can
avoid the bottleneck effect, i.e., causing some bottlenecks to be too
busy and others idle.

The great intermediate net has no such limitation. Through
the complex interconnection of neurons, even with slow moving
impulses, a true free-form information network is created, making
all information within the brain available at any time from any point.
The comparison and manipulation of information is truly simultaneous with no naturally occurring bottlenecks.

A more typical information database, a mailing list for instance, collects all applicable data (a "subset" of the total available information), compiles it into a single collection and stores it on a library shelf alongside other databases. The only way pieces of information can be shared among databases on the shelf is to compile them separately into all other pertinent databases. As long as the information inside the various databases remains accurate, there is no management problem. When a database becomes outdated, however, new data must be manually collected and re-compiled with the existing collection to create a new database. This would have to be repeated for all other pertinent databases, and so the process of collecting and compiling continues unabated in the face of incoming information.

The great intermediate net, however, is a true, free-form information network. All information, not just one or more subsets, is instantly updated and made available for manipulation, learning and growth. Take the simple example of meeting someone new at a dance. All of the available information — name, appearance, content of conversation, body movement during dancing, environment, emotional context, etc. — is stored throughout the great intermediate net in free-form association with already existing information. Meeting the same person later immediately updates the network with new information. The great intermediate net is so immensely flexible that it really doesn't resemble a computer at all. The programming of the brain is so agile and adaptive that there are normally many alternate pathways for processing information.

Looking more closely at the neurons within this great information processing system, we see how much more flexible the brain is than even the most advanced computers. Within a computer the smallest possible memory location is either a 1 or a 0 (on or off). In the brain however, the smallest possible memory location (neuron) represents a computer in and of itself because so much information comes into that single point. And, the neuron is not only a computer, it is an adaptive computer that is constantly changing with new input.

The nervous system is very complex, both because of the number of connections within it and because some synapses inhibit while others excite the target neuron. The specific balance of forces and information determine how this exquisitely organized society of neurons operates. With an estimated one quadrillion nerve connections within the brain, at any one time the possible combination of messages jumping across the synapses exceeds the number of atoms in the known universe.[13]

If we compare nerve networks to a network of people, specialization results from the specific connections (*who* your contacts are) and the type of synaptic interactions (*what* your contacts tell you and what you let your next in line know about what you have been told).[14] The brain is a system of systems. Neurons organize into local networks, which are integrated into regions and structures in the brain, which in turn work together as systems.

BUILDING BASE PATTERNS

To graphically illustrate how we form base patterns of neurons and build on these all of our lives, let's examine how artistic skill develops. We start by becoming sensorially aware of nature, laying down neural patterns in the brain which represent this awareness. These patterns elaborate as we take in our world through touch, sound, smell, taste and finally sight. The areas of the brain that receive sensory input from touch begin to connect, through association areas, with those areas that receive sound and sight. These contacts allow us to cross-reference our experiences, giving us our familiar, base understanding of nature and our unique, subjective reality.

As we develop our motor skills, our sensory reality can now be translated into a movement of the whole body or a specific movement of the hand. From our internal images and direct sensory input, we begin to draw what we experience.

Our first drawings may be blotches of color that represent our sensory awareness and emotions. Simultaneously, through hand/eye coordination, our hand guides our eyes in a dance which embodies our tactile, kinesthetic understanding of the world. Later we explore line and draw the people and things in our environment, always referring back to our base understanding of size and space. This understanding comes from base patterns established though our experience of gravity and our tactile and proprioceptive senses, integrated finally with vision.

Our knowledge expands as we overlay our understanding of a three-dimensional world with learned techniques that allow us to represent perspective. It is elaborated further as we develop more nerve endings into our hands and gain fine motor coordination. The eye now becomes the trusted window to understand our world as the base patterns becomes more integrated. The eye then guides the hand through eye/hand coordination as we draw what we see, referring to our acquired reality instead of to our hand.

The ultimate artistry comes when we can incorporate all the base patterning from our knowledge of the world with our senses, emotions, movement and technical skill — to create something beyond and different from our reality. It is from this place of play, where the integrated brain, rich with base patterns, looks for novel possibilities, that the artistic within us reaches its pinnacle.

As nerve networks continue to build upon and change our base patterning throughout life, our proficiency and complexity increases. Yet even as great artists, in our later years we continue to refer back to the base patterns we developed as young children, through which we take in and understand our world.

The development of a skill, like all learning, starts with the establishment of our basal understanding of the world, through our senses, emotions and movement. Upon these basal patterns, we continuously add new learning in the form of more and more complex nerve networks. The base patterns provide a framework of information from which new nerve networks elaborate to increase our understanding and abilities throughout life.

REMODELING THE BRAIN

Most neural pathways develop through stimulation and experience gained from interaction with the environment. This is especially true for people open to experiencing new and novel ideas and situations throughout their lives. As Michael Merzenich observes, "whenever we engage in new behavior, the brain remodels itself."[15] The brain retains this capacity even into old age. "In a healthy brain," Deepak Chopra writes, "senility is not physically normal."[16] The more active learning people do, the less likely they are to show symptoms of Alzheimer's disease.

Intellectual activity develops surplus brain tissue that compensates for damage. The harder you use the brain, the more it will grow. In a stroke, even where the neurons in the affected part of the brain are permanently damaged, PET scans show that the victim may recover.[17] According to Stanley Rapoport, chief of the Neurosciences Lab at the National Institute on Aging, older brains actually rewire themselves to compensate for losses. They can shift responsibility for a given task from one region of the brain to another.[18]

The plasticity and exquisite organization of the nervous system gives us a window on the potential for life-long learning and healing. As Amy began actively and consistently using all of her senses and integrated movement, she was able to reorganize her neural networks in more complex and efficient ways. What looked to be a person with major physical and learning disabilities, became a person with only specific learning difficulties. As she overcame each challenge, the complexity and efficiency of her nervous system grew. She has not only the neural hardware, but also the integrative tools to facilitate continued growth and reorganization throughout her life. Amy reminds me that everyone is in the process of becoming. So why limit anyone with labels like "learning disabled," "emotionally handicapped" or even "mentally retarded"?

3. ≈

Sensory Experience

Learning is experience. Everything else is just information.

— *Albert Einstein*

It may be a long time, if ever, before we are able to unravel the wondrous mysteries of the human mind, mysteries of thought, emotion, learning, imagination, creativity, and the many marvelous capabilities that every person possesses. But there are many things we do understand thanks to the cascade of neuroscientific observation and research in recent years. These new insights help point the way to the fullest development of our capacities.

One area of research that is yielding particularly far-reaching discoveries has been the investigation of the brain's development and its total interdependence with the rest of the body. Our knowledge of this development has been illuminated by our ability to observe it, even before birth, in ever finer detail. The story of the brain's development is intriguing in itself, but even more fascinating for what it tells us about the evolution of the capacities of the human mind.

What we know, feel, learn, and think is shaped by how we know, feel, learn, and think. How we do these things is in turn dependent on the sensory-motor systems through which all our experience of the world and of ourselves is mediated. These sensory-motor systems shape our experience, and are shaped by it. So the story of how these systems unfold is a vital key to understanding learning.

SENSATION AS INFORMATION

Thought, creativity and learning arise from experience. As we experience, we bring in information and build the neural networks that allow us to use that information so we may better understand the world and how to thrive in it. A major component of experience is sensory input from our environment via our eyes, ears, taste buds, nose and skin; and from our bodies via nerve receptors on each muscle and organ.

Our whole body is designed as a fine tuned sensory receptor for collecting information. The sensory organs (eyes, ears and nose) that pick up distant signals, are perched high atop the trunk of our body which serves as a stable bipod. The receptor systems sit on the bipod, meeting the environment straight on. The parabolic ears reflect sound into the ear canals, the eyes take in the periphery as well as the broad forward expanse, and the nose detects minute chemical messengers in our air. Augmenting these are the taste buds which monitor dissolved chemicals at the gateway to the gullet, and a vast array of touch receptors.

Every square inch of skin has receptors for touch, pressure, heat, cold and pain, with more on the lips, hands and face. Through these receptors, our spacesuit skin can gain an accurate reading of our external environment while protecting us from water loss. And internally, every movement sends a wild array of impulses speeding toward the brain to keep it informed of all changes in position and of where the body is in space. All of these sensations give us images of ourselves and our world and provide the essential raw material from which knowledge, thought and creativity can emerge.

SENSORY EXPERIENCES BUILD NEURAL NETWORKS

Our sensory apparatus is so vital to learning that it begins developing within a couple of months after conception, in utero. We first learn about gravity through our vestibular system, even before birth. Hearing, smell, taste and touch build on our gravitational sense to give us our first images of the world. Only later are we able to put these increasingly complex sensory images together to accommodate sight.

Nerve networks grow out of our unique sensory experiences, laying down intricate patterns that govern all our higher level brain development. Experience determines the shape and intricacy of these patterns. They are laid down in accordance with the activities we experience and all of our environmental circumstances.[1] The richer our sensory environment and the greater our freedom to explore it, the more intricate will be the patterns for learning, thought and creativity.

Images derived from our sensory experience are the stuff of

thought and creativity. Images — in the form of shapes, colors, movements, feelings, tones, spoken or unspoken words — arise from our acquired patterns throughout all areas of the brain: color and shape patterns from the occipital lobe, tones and words from the temporal and frontal lobes, emotional experiences from the limbic system, and movement patterns from the basal ganglion of the limbic system. When we hear the word truck, all our experiences with trucks are instantly available to us as images — a heavier vehicle, noisy, dangerous, big wheels, diesel smell, sense of riding in one, how they feel as they pass us on the road, even the emotions of trucks as extensions of our power. From these images we make sense of new learning, tie remembered images together in different ways and come up with new ideas. Broad-based knowledge depends on these intricately woven, yet separate multi-sensory complexes of images that have been put together and reworked over and over again from our sensory experiences.

Consider, for example, the way we learn and incorporate new words into our vocabulary. Each sound, word, and phrase is supported by an elaborate internal image display. Whenever we read anything, the brain is actively putting the words into known sensory images so we may understand them. Notice that when you can't get an image of something you have read, it is difficult to determine the meaning.

Our sensory experiences, both external and internal, shape our way of imaging and, therefore, our thinking. New learning occurs as new sensory experiences modify, change and make ever more complex our images of our world and our selves. Our bodies are fully involved in this quest.

DEVELOPING OUR SENSES

In order to understand how essential sensory input is to learning, thought and creativity, we must explore how the brain grows and matures, beginning with its earliest structures and functions.

Dr. Paul MacLean, Chief of the Laboratory of Brain Evolution and Behavior at the National Institute of Mental Health in Washington, DC, developed a theory that postulates three distinct areas of the human brain. According to his Triune Brain Theory, the three parts are delineated biologically, electrically and chemically and are based on developmental patterns and evolved functioning. He named these three areas: 1) the reptilian brain, 2) the limbic or early mammalian brain, and 3) the neocortex or neo-mammalian brain.[2]

The reptilian brain or brain stem is the first area to develop. This is the oldest evolutionary part of the brain, developing between conception and fifteen months after birth. The job of this brain is self-preservation. The reptilian brain monitors the outer world through sensory input and then activates the body to physically respond in ways that ensure survival.

Automatic and reflex reactions such as a baby's cry or its quick movement of the leg away from pain, are partially regulated by this area of the brain. It is also the part of the brain which takes over when we encounter danger or stress, because it initiates and regulates the body's fight-or-flight response. The reptilian brain oversees the mind/body's survival imperative, insuring that basic needs are met before other, higher functions can proceed smoothly.

The baby's first job is to satisfy its need for food, warmth and shelter. So it learns to make appropriate responses that signal caretakers to provide for those needs. Eventually the baby learns — through its sensory systems — enough about its world, and about how to work its body, to master its environment and ultimately provide for itself.

The reptilian brain includes the brain stem, medulla oblongata, pons and cerebellum. All sensations go first through the brain stem and then are sent on from the switch-board (the pons) to the thalamus (in the limbic brain) and/or the neocortex for interpretation. Nerve nets must be developed first in the reptilian brain. The rest of the brain can then know what is happening in the outer world and respond to it. When we gate (close down) the reptilian brain, we are in a state of sleep where we neither receive nor react with the outer world.[3]

The reptilian brain forms nerve nets encoded with our sensory-motor base patterns upon which learning, all the rest of our lives, will build. Nerves appear three weeks after the egg is fertilized and immediately begin to link up with other nerves. These forming nerve nets originate from the billions of neurons in the central nervous system.[4] As the reptilian brain forms, prenatally and in those first fifteen months of life, we develop an estimated 100 trillion nerve nets that link all our senses and muscle movements. These give us an understanding of the material world and our safety in it.

THE VESTIBULAR SYSTEM: SENSE OF MOTION AND EQUILIBRIUM

When we think about our senses, most of the time we only consider the five senses that take in information from outside our bodies: seeing, hearing, smelling, tasting and touching. However, just as important to our development and our lives is the integration of sensory input which gives us information about gravity and motion, and about our body's muscular movements and position in space — the vestibular system and proprioception. These play a surprisingly significant role in our awareness of the world and also, as we shall see, in our ability to understand and learn.

The first sensory system to fully develop and myelinate by five months after conception is the vestibular system, which controls the sense of movement and balance. This system maintains both static and dynamic equilibrium. Static equilibrium refers to the orientation of the body, mainly the head, relative to gravity, for example when you are standing still. Dynamic equilibrium maintains body position, mainly the head, in response to sudden movements such as acceleration, deceleration and rotation when you are in motion, as when walking.[5]

There are several small organs involved in vestibular sensation. From them we gather information about the head's position relative to the ground. These are the most sensitive of all the sense organs, lying in the mastoid bone (the lump behind the ear lobe), and part of the inner ear. They include the utricle, saccule, semicircular canals, and vestibular nuclei of the medulla and pons.[6]

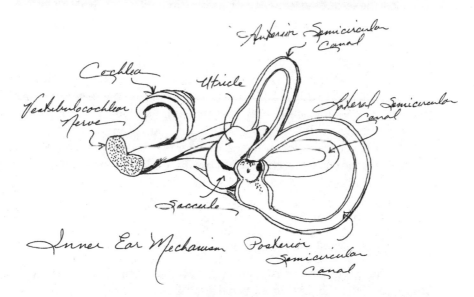

Figure 3.1: Mechanisms of the Inner Ear

The utricle and saccule monitor the static equilibrium of the body. The walls of both the utricle and saccule contain the macula with hair cells, a gelatinous layer and otoliths (calcium carbonate crystals). Each time we move our heads the otoliths move, pulling the gelatinous layer, which pulls on the hair cells and makes them bend. This bending initiates sensory nerve impulses along the vestibular nerve to the brain. These impulses go through nerve tracts to the cerebellum that monitors and makes corrective adjustments in the muscle activities, including eye movements, that originate in the cerebral cortex. This causes the motor system to increase or decrease its impulses to specific muscles, especially the core (torso) and neck muscles, to contract or relax. In this way our muscles adjust instantly so we don't lose our balance or equilibrium.[7]

With information from the utricle and saccule we are able to maintain a stable bodily posture relative to the ground. Travelling by car, air or water, however, can create a sense of disequilibrium which sometimes results in car, air or sea sickness.

Information from the eyes contributes to the sense of equilibrium as well. "About 20 percent of the messages from the eyes, from the retina and extraocular muscles," as Homer Hendrickson points out, "go to areas of the brain concerned with balance mechanisms. Each of these subsystems must match and check with the other subsystems to produce consistent static and dynamic balance against gravity."[8]

Consider what happens when you read in a car. You are holding your eyes static as you read but the rest of your body is moving, especially the head. The system is having to work very hard to keep the eyes level and static in a moving head. At the same time it is attempting to balance the rest of the body with the constant change of gravity, acceleration and deceleration. When no resolution to the confusion occurs, the body vomits, which may be its way of getting our attention to release the eyes. A similar thing occurs in IMAX theaters where the eyes are having to move a lot, the body is static, and the communication between the two is confusing.

DYNAMIC EQUILIBRIUM

The three bony semicircular canals lie at approximately right angles to each other and maintain dynamic equilibrium by detecting imbalance in three planes. When the head moves due to rotation of the body, the endolymph fluid in the semicircular ducts flows over hair cells and bends them. Impulses from the bending hair cells follow the same pathways as those involved in static equilibrium.

According to Eugene Schwartz, even the slightest alteration of fluid and otoliths within the semicircular canals leads to changes in the muscles of the neck, trunk, limbs and musculature of the eye.[9] The vestibular system is already visible in a two month old embryo.[10] There is much activation of the head as the fetus moves in the amniotic fluid, then as the child goes from early movements and crawling to walking and running. The stimulation from these movements is crucial to brain processing.

The vestibular nuclei, a plexus of neurons lying in the medulla oblongata and pons, carries impulses from the semicircular canals and cerebellum to the Reticular Activating System (RAS) in the brain stem. The RAS is a nerve reticulum that carries impulses from the medulla oblongata and pons to the neocortex. Beginning in utero, the RAS "wakes up" the neocortex, increasing excitability and responsiveness to incoming sensory stimuli from the environment. This "wake up" by the RAS gets us ready to take in and respond to our environment, and to learn.[11-12] This connection between the vestibular system and neocortex as well as the eyes and core muscles is highly important to the learning process. When we don't move and activate the vestibular system, we are not taking in information from the environment.

Children love to spin or ride for hours on hand-pushed merry-go-rounds, activating the vestibular system. But have you noticed that as an adult you would prefer to just watch? There is a reason for this. As we go through puberty, the endolymph fluid in the semicircular canals thickens in response to reproductive hormones. This thickening causes the hair cells to be bent for a longer time, thus causing the whole system to take a longer time to return to a comfortable equilibrium.

Amusement parks and flight simulators that are designed to be sensory events have really capitalized on our vestibular systems. When they activate the vestibular system, the RAS wakes up the rest of the brain to the incoming stimuli. The rides then put the whole vestibular system off balance and out of equilibrium, causing not only a full body experience but also an adrenalin "high." Adrenalin, our survival drug, allows for even more sensory input to the system in our attempt to perceive any danger in our environment. It gives the body a real, but not necessarily healthy, workout.

From conception to the first fifteen months after birth, the vestibular system is very active as the child gains a sense of gravity and knowledge of the physical environment through movement. Every movement of the child stimulates the vestibular system, which stimulates the brain for new learning. From this sensory "wake up" and basal understanding of gravity a child is able to perform the most remarkable feats of balance. Beginning with only reflexive movement at birth, the child learns to stand, walk and even run in a gravitational field by approximately one year of age. This initial learning allows us to walk on logs across streams, walk up stairs, ride bicycles, skate and millions of other things that require a strong sense of balance.

THE SENSE OF HEARING

By twelve weeks, the fetus moves spontaneously. Nerves, lungs and diaphragm begin to synchronize, exercising the lungs for the first breath after birth. The fetus is surrounded by the first patterns of sounds that will be absorbed by the nervous system. These include the mother's heartbeat, her breathing, digestion and voice. At five months the fetus responds to phonemes of language (varying vibrations of sound such as the vowel sounds) that it hears through the amniotic fluid, spoken by the mother.

Using fiber optic cameras, Dr. Alfred Tomatis discovered that the fetus will move a specific muscle, in the arm or leg for example, when it hears a specific phoneme. The particular muscle moved varies in each fetus studied, but each time the same phoneme is sounded, the same muscle will move. This early connection of a muscle response to sound suggests the significance of anchoring sensory input with action for learning to occur. There are approximately fifty phonemes in language world wide. This sensory-motor response to phonemes allows the fetus to begin the process of learning language in utero.[13-14]

By twenty-four weeks the fetus displays rapid eye movements during its sleeping time. The fetus responds to music by blinking its eyes and moving as though dancing to a beat. By the seventh month, the fetus is thought to exhibit purposeful movements that are more than just reflexive.[15]

Once the amniotic fluid has dried out of the eustachian tubes and outer ear canals, the sense of hearing becomes one of the most accurate and important to the newborn. For most of us, the sense of hearing is perfect at birth and goes downhill from there. The cochlea in our inner ear is made up of an elaborate mechanism of hair cells,

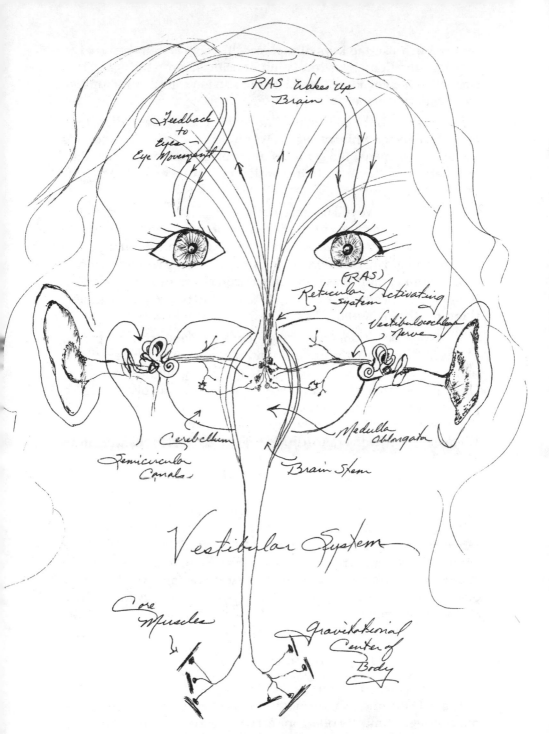

Figure 3.2: The Vestibular System

set up much like the keys of a piano. These hair cells respond to specific vibrations by stimulating specific nerve endings. This elegant "inner keyboard" is able to pick up ten sound vibrations for every one on a piano.

Hearing is the baby's first line of defense. Babies will instinctively turn their dominant ear out when sleeping, to pick up sounds in the environment. If a sound is unfamiliar, loud or sudden, they will startle and then scream in an attempt to scare away the danger and to elicit help.

As adults, we still use this mechanism. If I am in an unfamiliar place, I will instinctively turn my dominant ear up while sleeping to alert myself to any danger. At home, where I feel safe, I usually sleep with my dominant ear down to block out incoming sounds. Since it is one of our earliest senses, hearing becomes important for alerting the brain to incoming learning, whether for protection or understanding, throughout our life.

Noise pollution (loud and/or constant sounds over a period of time) especially in the upper sound range, destroys these delicate hair cells of our "inner keyboard", thus reducing our hearing acuity. Dr. Tomatis discovered that these upper vibrations of sound also play an important part in maintaining alertness and energy within the system. He noticed, for example, some surprising consequences when monasteries in France dropped their Gregorian chanting in an attempt to modernize in the 1960's. These chants provided the upper register vibration and harmonics (overtones) that maintained alertness. As a result, the men in these monasteries needed more sleep, were less productive, and tended to get ill more often. Tomatis equated this to the experience of factory workers who had also lost the upper range of hearing because of constant factory noise, and similarly became listless and non-productive.[16] Overly loud music or exposure to constant sounds at the same vibration can cause damage.[17] Protecting our wonderful hearing mechanism is important, not only for survival and active listening, but to provide the alertness that comes with the higher vibrations — all of which assist learning.

THE SMELLS OF LIFE

Smell is also quite acute at birth. There are billions of tiny hair cells inside the bridge of the nose right under the frontal lobe of the brain. These stimulate olfactory nerve nets for every smell (chemicals in the air) known to man. Infants can distinguish the scent of their mother's breast from that of a strange mother's by the age of six weeks.[18] Smell is strongly linked to memory and plays an important role in the baby's early learning and throughout life. Think of situations where you smelled something and the sensation brought back a flood of memories. A developmental expert in Germany claims that memory can be greatly assisted by rubbing the nose prior to learning something you really want to remember.[19]

Smell is also used to alert us to danger. When people or animals are afraid, they secrete pheromones that can be easily picked up by certain animals (dogs, for example) that will react to that fear. Like a dog, the baby or child may be able to pick up the sense of danger and fear felt within its immediate environment, and act to protect itself.

Our sense of smell also becomes important during puberty, as sexual scents increase. These are strong stimulants to the reptilian brain for display behaviors (grooming and preening), mating, and elimination of outsiders (protecting one's territory). Though our society does its best to override these natural urges, they still show up beautifully in our teenagers![20]

THE SENSE OF TOUCH

The skin is the largest organ of the body and is replete with nerve sensors for light touch, heavy touch, pressure, heat, cold, pain and proprioception. Proprioception is the sensation from muscles, tendons and the vestibular system that enables the brain to determine movement and the position of the body and its parts in space. All these sensations go through the brain stem to the thalamus and then to the somatosensory cortex of the cerebrum (parietal lobe).[21] With all these sensors, the skin becomes one of the primary organs for early environmental learning.

Just the act of being touched increases production of a specific hormone within the brain, Nerve Growth Factor (NGF), which activates greater nervous system and, specifically, nerve net development. Sensory neurons are stimulated by NGF during embryonic development. Later on, and into adulthood, NGF stimulates sympathetic neurons, which monitor sensory impulses for the autonomic nervous system — the instigator of fight or flight responses. In the brain, NGF stimulates axon growth and neuron hypertrophy (nerve net development), helps maintain neuronal function and increases synthesis of acetylcholine.[22] When touch is lacking, children (and possibly adults) exhibit depressed motor and mental functioning. There may in fact be a connection between lack of touch and lowered acetylcholine levels found in Alzheimer's patients.[23-24]

Jean Ayers also discovered a link between touch-sensitivity (inability to tolerate touch) and learning disorders in children.[25] Her highly successful program for learning disorders deals with waking up the sensory system by appropriately activating all the touch receptors. She uses light touch, pressure, fine brushes and balls rolled across the skin surface, especially on the arms, legs and back, all integrated with movement.

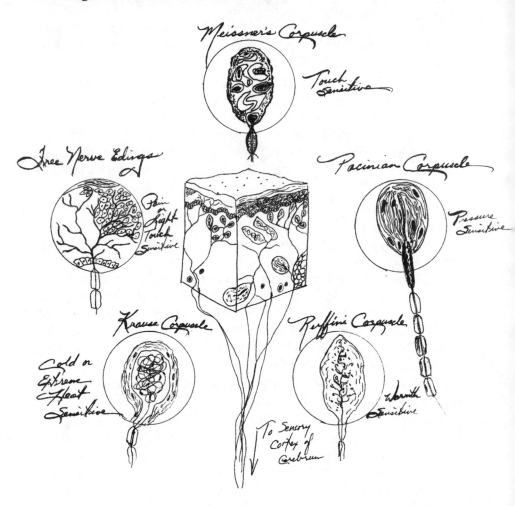

Figure 3.3: Sensory Areas of the Skin

Touch right after birth stimulates growth of the body's sensory nerve endings involved in motor movements, spatial orientation and visual perception (as well as touch). If these nerve endings are not activated, the RAS that awakens the neocortex will not operate fully. This leads to impaired muscular movements, curtailed sensory intake, and a variety of emotional disturbances and learning defects.[26]

The absence of touch may so slow nerve development that essential bodily function development may not occur, and death ensues. In a study done in orphanages in France during World War II, orphans that were not touched exhibited high premature death rates. Even negative touch (spanking or beating) resulted in a much reduced death rate. Joseph Chilton Pearce talks of a program ("Project Kangaroo") where premature babies were carried around in a pouch on the front of the nurse or mother, next to the skin. This constant touch has greatly decreased the mortality rate in these preemies. Touch alone stimulates sensory-motor growth, nerve net development and gives the baby a fighting chance at life.[27]

TOUCH AND LEARNING

There is a greater array of receptors for touch around the mouth and hands than in any other area of the body. This is shown in Penfield and Jasper's original mapping of the sensory and motor cortices of the cerebrum. (See Figure 3.4).[28] Touch is an integral, natural part of life. Babies love to put things up to their mouths—not to eat them, though that may happen inadvertently, but to touch and fully sense them with the mouth and hands.

Throughout our lives, using "hands-on" experiences or manipulatives during the learning process greatly increases learning efficiency. My college students have commented that just having clay available to manipulate during a lecture allowed them to more easily take in information. Whenever touch is combined with the other senses, much more of the brain is activated, thus building more complex nerve networks and tapping into more learning potential.

Touch is a strong anchor in behavior and learning. If children are gently touched on the shoulder while they are reading, the brain connects the encouraging touch with the reading and helps to anchor the positive experience. A Canadian elementary school teacher recently told me of an experiment with touch in the classroom that bears this out. The teachers focused on students that acted up in class and did not do or turn in their homework. Five times a day the teacher would catch these students "being good" and touch them on the shoulder while saying (in an accepting way), "I appreciate your doing your work." When they were acting up, the teachers ignored them. In all cases, within the first two weeks, all the students were behaving in class and handing in their homework.

I realize there is a fear of inappropriate touching in our society, which has led us to avoid touching at a time when children (and adults) need it more than ever. It's time to relearn appropriate supportive touch and value it for its function in development and learning.

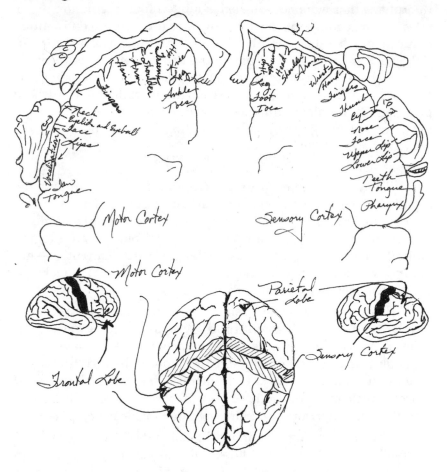

Figure 3.4: Mapping of the Sensory and Motor Cortices of the Cerebrum (After Penfield and Jasper)

PROPRIOCEPTION

Proprioception, the body's sense of itself in space, is one of our most important ways of knowing. Charles Sherrington beautifully described it as "our secret sense, our sixth sense." As Oliver Sacks points out, proprioception is so much taken for granted that it wasn't until Sherrington "discovered" it in the 1890's, that we began to appreciate its distinctive role in our sense of ourselves.[29]

All of our muscles have proprioceptive receptors which sense the degree of stretch in the muscle. These stretch receptors let us constantly know everything about our physical position and provide the feedback necessary for us to move and maintain our balance. As exquisite learning tools, proprioceptors allow us to explore our environment, understanding it through our muscle sense.

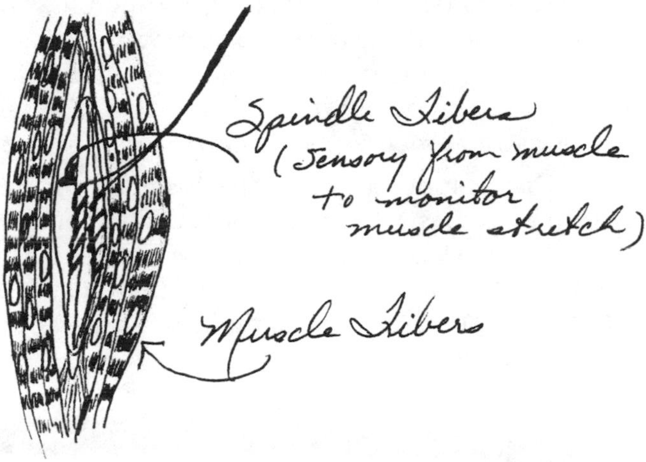

Figure 3.5: Proprioceptors

Developmentally, the proprioceptive system is intimately tied to the vestibular system which allows the balance necessary to move from an inert position. Babies begin moving from the core muscles, the inner muscles of the trunk. There is constant feedback from the proprioceptors to the motor cortex of the brain that allows more and more complexity of movement. So babies go from the belly wiggle, to rolling over, to sitting up, to standing up and finally walking.

Successful movement requires secure balance, which depends on a sophisticated proprioceptive system constantly aligning every part of the body. Proprioception gives the feedback necessary to maintain optimal muscle contraction and relaxation for balance in our environment. Thus the popular phrase "being centered" invokes the importance of the proprioceptive sense when doing yoga or the martial arts. These skills place emphasis on the core postural muscles where we first learn about balance and gravity through proprioception. When the feedback system between proprioceptors and muscles is well developed through use, balance is constantly maintained.[30] When stress interferes with the balanced activation of this system, then we become "uncentered" and lose our balance and our physical sense of ourselves in space. This is when accidents like scratches, bruises or broken limbs occur, because our proprioceptive awareness is concentrated on running from danger, rather than maintaining balance.

Parents and teachers often notice periods of physical awkwardness and lack of coordination in children who are in the midst of, or recently emerged from, growth spurts. What they are seeing is actually a lag between the body's growth and its proprioceptive sense of itself in space. When the proprioceptive sense adapts to the new sizes and proportions, the gawkiness disappears.

Our proprioceptive sense constantly sends feedback to the brain that readjusts the balance of our shoulder and neck muscles in order for the eyes to remain level while reading. It monitors our ability to sit in a chair, listen to information and take notes. It also lets us know what muscle choreography is necessary to walk on uneven ground without falling.

MIMICRY, MODELING AND REHEARSALS

Besides monitoring bodily balance, the sensitivity of the proprioceptive system also allows us to learn about our environment. If you have gone for a walk with a small child, you have probably noticed that when they come to something new and intriguing, they actually move their body to mimic the configuration of the object. Children are great imitators, acutely aware of and then modeling adult movements in their walking, talking, hand gestures, and other physical activities. This modeling on the body allows them to sense the world around them from within to understand it.

Children are great observers, spending hours watching and role-playing. Rich imaginations allow them to rehearse complicated movements like running, swimming, and even flying. This rehearsal requires more and more sophistication of the nerve pathways and builds the nerve networks necessary to master complex skills.

Adults do the same thing when learning a new skill. Beginning skiers, as they watch other skiers, will actually make small modeling movements to entrain the sense of skiing upon their own muscles. Researchers have found support for the theory held by many sports trainers that athletes who mentally imagine and "rehearse" movements in advance will be more successful in accomplishing them.

Learning a motor skill by observing and mentally practicing it through visualization allows the brain to rehearse the neural pathways that control the muscles involved. These rehearsals involve minute muscle fluctuations that send a wave of sensory information from the muscle to the brain and strengthen the networks.[31]

SEEING TAKES MORE THAN OUR EYES

Touch and proprioception are important organizers of the visual aspects of learning. Vision is a very complex phenomenon, with only a small percentage (less than 10%) of the process occurring in the eyes. The other more than 90% of vision takes place in the brain from association with touch and proprioception. As babies touch their environment, they learn dimension, texture, line and even color. A complete visual picture emerges at about eight months after birth. Touch is very important to vision. Listen closely to a child who is seeing something new. The child immediately reaches out to touch the object while saying, "Let me see that!" Touch is the major contributor to full understanding in vision.

Images coming in through the eyes are turned upside down and backwards as they enter the optic nerve and cross the optic chiasma. They are then funnelled through the thalamus to the occipital lobe where primary vision is processed. For full vision to occur, information from all the cerebral lobes must be accessed. Information from the sensory and motor cortices associates the image with learned sensory and movement functioning. Gravitational and vibrational information from the temporal lobes relates the image to where we are in space. And, as noted earlier, approximately 20% of the messages from the eyes, retina and extraocular muscles, go to areas of the brain concerned with balance mechanisms. All the information together allows us to right the image and bring it into full context in the visual association areas.[32]

An experiment in which scientists fitted themselves with special pairs of glasses shows how our vision is educated to comprehend the world. These glasses had mirrors that turned the view of the world upside down and back to front. At first, the disoriented experimenters could barely move without bumping into something, but after a few days they adjusted and the reversed world came to look "right way up." Touch and the proprioceptive sense that guides vision had adjusted the new visual input to this new physical orientation. The fully intact vestibular system "knew" that the world had not gone topsy-turvy. This, together with touch and proprioception, provided feedback which allowed their eyes to adjust. The scientists could walk around without problems and saw the world just fine — until they took the glasses off at the end of the experiment. Then they had to go through a relearning process all over again, with several days of hitting and falling over things.[33-34] This experiment demonstrates graphically that the brain has to assemble our visual world from learned pieces through our other senses, especially touch and proprioception.[35]

It's easy to forget, or ignore, how much of vision is learned. We have to train ourselves, through books, movies and art to see three dimensions in a two-dimensional space. We could call this visual literacy. Tribal people I have encountered in Africa and Australia who have never experienced books, simply cannot see a mountain scene in a picture on a two-dimensional page. They experience color and line, but no texture or perspective, because in actuality, there is none.

Linear perspective, which is so convincing that it seems natural, is actually an artistic invention that goes back only to the 1400's, a technique developed to bring more three-dimensional reality to art. Artist M.C. Escher used the eye's inaccuracy and dependence on inner brain images to master illusion in his art.[36] In the 1960's, Dr. Bella Julesz also explored the ambiguity of the eye, using the first computer-generated 3-D images of randomly placed dots to study depth perception in human beings. From that work, Dan Dyckman and Mike Bielinski went steps further in using advanced computer technology for 3-D art so popularly seen in the *Magic Eye* books.[37]

THE EYES IN MOTION

Our eyes are designed to move and accommodate for light, to give us as much sensory detail about our world as possible. The eyes must be actively moving for learning to occur. Many of the cranial nerves (coming from the medulla oblongata) connect to the eye, including the trigeminal, facial, abducens, oculomotor, and trochlear. These activate movement of the eyeball in all directions, contract or relax the muscles of the pupil to regulate light hitting the retina, and change the shape of the lens to accommodate for near or far vision. They also monitor proprioceptive stretch and touch sensations on and around the eye.

In a three-dimensional environment, such as outdoors, the eye is in constant motion gathering sensory information to build intricate image packages necessary for learning. The brain integrates these image packages with other sensory information like touch and proprioception to build a visual perception system. The eyes are equipped with different kinds of visual focus, of which three-dimensional focus is vital for learning, yet we emphasize two-dimensional focus in learning situations.

The retina, the sensory nerve layer of the eye, contains light-receptor cells of which approximately 95% are rods (so called because of their shape) and 5% cones. The rods are distributed around the periphery of the retina and are stimulated best under dim light conditions. The cones are grouped in a small area of the retina called the fovea centralis and require bright light for stimulation. Major concentration on the fovea for reading in a two-dimensional field is

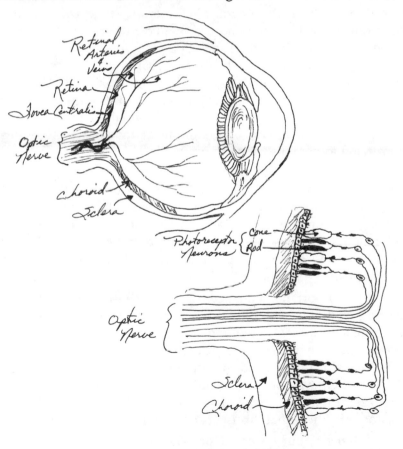

Figure 3.6: The Eye and Light-Receptor Cells

called foveal focus. The combination of rods and cones allows for three-dimensional as well as two-dimensional focus and peripheral as well as foveal focus.[38]

Considering the ratio of cones to rods, it strikes me that we were not designed to sit for long hours engaged exclusively in foveal focus activities, like reading, and watching TV or computer screens. The eyes need to actively experience the world as a whole for vision to develop fully. Active sensory and motor functioning of the eyes helps to entrain the body on shapes and movement of natural forms and to develop the spatial awareness necessary for clear perceptions and thought.

THE IMPORTANCE OF SENSORY LEARNING

Experiences and sensations *are* learning. Sensations form the base understanding from which concepts and thinking develop. Sensory enriched environments are imperative to learning, as neuroanatomist Marian Diamond discovered in her work with rats. These enriched environments included playgroups of ten to twelve rats in large multi-level cages filled with a variety of bridges, ladders, swings and slides, assorted toys, and changing stimuli. Diamond discovered that compared with rats whose mobility and stimuli were restricted, rats in enriched environments actually developed structural changes in their brains, and exhibited behavior which could be interpreted as demonstrating improved intelligence.[39]

In the New York Longitudinal Study, 133 subjects were followed from infancy into adulthood. It was discovered that competency in adulthood stemmed from three major factors in the early learning environment: 1) rich sensory environments, both outdoors and indoors, 2) freedom to explore the environment with few restrictions, and 3) available parents that acted as consultants when the child asked questions.[40-41]

The importance and need for rich sensory and hands-on learning continues throughout our lives. However, many of our educational practices derive from the unexamined assumption that people will learn best if given lots of information in either lecture or two-dimensional written form. And in order to learn they must sit still, keep their eyes forward and take notes. We have only to look at the glazed eyes and vacant stares of students in a lecture hall or classroom to know that this is a belief that needs to be abandoned.

In general, our system of formal education relies too much on language as the medium of instruction. What's wrong with that? To answer that question I would like to refer back to Einstein's maxim, "Learning is experience. Everything else is just information." Words, though important, are only bits of information. They are not experiential and only poorly substitute for the directness and freshness of hands-on learning.

Words can only be understood when they provoke some kind of image in the mind of the learner. If students cannot access the underlying images, the words are not comprehensible. A lot of confusion is introduced when students miss the meaning of the teacher's words. Experiences, on the other hand, are direct and real. They involve senses, emotions and movements, and engage the learner fully. Real things happen when we experience with our senses, and in the experiencing we observe, relate to past experiences and notice patterns. Words are useful in this process, they help us to organize our thoughts about the sensations. But they are no substitute for the force and vividness of actual experience.

Learning occurred most easily for my college Biology students when we took field trips into nature, and then discussed scientific concepts as they were experienced. The next best thing was making sure every lab session was filled with rich sensory experiences and that lectures were short and became sensory-oriented discussions and hands-on activities.

Learning first comes in through our senses. As we explore and experience our material world, initial sensory patterns are laid down on elaborate nerve networks. These initial sensory patterns become the core of our free-form information system that is updated and becomes more elegant with each new, novel experience. These initial sensory patterns become our reference points and give us the context for all learning, thought and creativity. From this sensory base we will add emotions and movement in our life-long learning dance.

4. ≈

The Role Of Emotions

My research has persuaded me that emotion is integral to the process of reasoning. I even suspect that humanity is not suffering from a defect in logical competence but rather from a defect in the emotions that inform the deployment of logic.

— *Antonio R. Damasio*[1]

It's not surprising that many of us believe emotion is somehow antagonistic to thinking. The notion that the best thinking occurs in the cool clear light of reason, high above the distraction and messiness of emotion, has a long history going back to Plato, Kant and Descartes. It has profoundly influenced our culture, particularly in the area of education.

People make distinctions between thought and emotion in the same way they make distinctions between the mind and body. However, despite our deeply ingrained assumptions, these distinctions don't actually exist. Body, thought and emotion are intimately bound together through intricate nerve networks, and function as a whole unit to enrich our knowing. And research in the neurosciences is helping to explain how and why rich emotional development is essential for understanding relationships, rational thought, imagination, creativity and even the health of the body.

Even computer scientists seeking to simulate human thinking recognize that artificial intelligence is limited and incomplete because it lacks emotion. Computer scientist David Gelernter makes this point emphatically: "Emotions are not a form of thought, not an additional way to think, not a special cognitive bonus, but are fundamental to thought." If we subtract emotion from thought, what remains is merely one end of a continuous spectrum — linear/logical thought — and to identify this narrow high-focus band with thought in general is entirely inaccurate.[2]

Gelernter goes on to assert that emotions, which are insepa-rable from thought, are also "inextricably tied up with bodily states. The bodily state is part of the emotion, feeds it and helps define it. This means that ultimately you don't think just with your brain; you think with your brain and body *both*."[3]

DEMONSTRATING THE LINKS BETWEEN
REASON, EMOTION, AND THE BODY

Gelernter's insights are borne out by the growing cascade of brain research concerning the interconnection of emotion and thought. In a highly ingenious series of experiments, Antonio Damasio and his colleagues have demonstrated that when the emotions and the body were dissociated from cognition, rational behavior and learn-ing were absent.[4] The significance of this finding to our understand-ing of learning, and to educational theory and practice, cannot be overstated.

The subjects of Damasio's experiments were patients who had damage to the frontal lobe of the brain, particularly the area that connects directly with the substantia nigra of the limbic system, which processes emotions. Though the damage did not impair the patients' intellect or memory in any detectable way, it left them changed in two extraordinary and profound respects. First, they were unable to make reasonable decisions in personal and social matters — decisions which had been made as a matter of course before the damage to their frontal lobes. Instead they made foolish, imprudent, and irrational choices. Second, they were left with drastically reduced emotional reactivity. This sudden and momen-tous change was acknowledged by the patients themselves, when they recognized that they no longer reacted emotionally to things they "knew" would have affected them before the injuries to their brains.

Damasio and his colleagues set out to explore the underlying linkages between these two symptoms — irrationality and lack of emotion — caused by the damage to their patients' frontal lobes. In a series of experiments, known as the Gambling Experiments, sub-jects played a card game in which the cards were rigged so that a normal person could gradually learn to accumulate winnings. Ra-tional choices, learned from the results of drawing the cards, were rewarded; irrational choices which ignored what could be learned from the game, were punished with losses. Frontal lobe damaged patients, even when they professed to be cautious, failed to learn from their losses. Normal subjects, even those who considered themselves high-risk gamblers, learned the low-risk successful strategy to win the game.

WATCHING THE BODY LEARN

The researchers then added an intriguing twist. They hooked up the players to a polygraph machine, which allowed them to continuously track the players' choices with their skin conductance responses. At first normal and brain-damaged players responded the same way to their wins and losses, the polygraph registering similar reactions following their turns of the cards. But after a few turns, the polygraphs of the normal players began to exhibit a striking new pattern. *Before* making a risky move, they showed a response on the polygraph. And as the game went on, each time they were about to make a risky decision, that anticipatory response grew larger. "In other words, the brains of the normal subjects were gradually learning to predict a bad outcome, and were signalling the relative badness of the particular [choice] before the actual cardturning."[5]

This learning curve, corresponding step by step with an emotional response expressed in and through the body, eloquently demonstrates the interrelatedness of knowing and feeling, and of both with the body. The critical element for learning — which is precisely what is missing in the patients whose emotions do not connect with their thinking — is this bodily alarm. When the emotions and bodily sense are dissociated from thinking, real learning does not occur.

EMOTIONS AND SURVIVAL

From these experiments, Damasio developed his theory that emotions provide the essential criteria on which we base rational decision-making for our lives. He believes emotions inform the thinking process about the right direction to go based on survival or social risk. Emotions are felt as bodily states and are the means through which the mind knows about how the body feels as a touchstone for cognitive survival.[6]

When planning, strategizing, and reasoning, we rely on the stored knowledge that we have accumulated in our lifetime. For instance, suppose you have to decide whether or not to quit your job. A whole flood of past experiences and future projections will spring to mind. These experiences carry with them an emotional content. Memories of success or frustration in finding new jobs elicit the associated gut feelings that these memories produce.[7]

According to Damasio, this marking of experience with emotional value assures that we first and foremost promote our bodily survival. Qualities that are good or bad for us, as registered by the body, can be recalled and become the basis for predicting outcomes. This insures that our reasoning strategies advance our survival.[8]

Our capacity to emotionally mark and remember experiences is also important for the survival of our society. Emotions add the element of pleasure or pain to the learning of social behavior. This insures that each individual learns rules and values that advance the purposes of society and enable it to function. Without healthy emotional development of individuals, humans could not adequately become socialized and the values, rules and wisdom of the society would be lost.

How, then, do emotions develop, and what conditions promote healthy emotional growth?

THE LIMBIC SYSTEM

Emotions meet at the intersection of body and mind. This is almost literally true since most emotional processing occurs in the limbic system, the area that lies between the reptilian brain and the cerebral cortex. The limbic system has links with the neocortex allowing for emotional/cognitive processing. It also works in concert with the body to elicit the physical signs of emotions like the flush of embarrassment, and the smile of joy. Limbic system emotions also determine the release of neurotransmitters that either strengthen or weaken our immune system.

The limbic system consists of five major structures in the brain: the thalamus, hypothalamus, basal ganglia, amygdala and hippocampus.[9]

The thalamus acts as a relay station for all incoming senses, except smell. It also relays motor impulses from the cerebral cortex through the brain stem and out to the muscles. In addition, the thalamus interprets pain, temperature, light touch and pressure sensations, and it functions in emotions and memory.

The hypothalamus controls the pituitary gland and normal body temperature, food intake, thirst and the waking and sleeping states. It is also the center for mind-over-body phenomena, allowing enormous feats of strength and endurance during emergencies. In addition, the hypothalamus is involved in rage, aggression, pain and pleasure.

The amygdala has links to brain areas involved in cognitive and sensory processing, as well as those involved in bodily states related to a combination of emotions. It is involved with the recognition of facial expressions and body language. It allows us to assess a situation by coordinating bodily reactions that serve as internal warnings so we respond appropriately with fear and anxiety.[10] It also formulates memories related to fear and anxiety.

The hippocampus uses sensory input coming through the thalamus and emotions in the hypothalamus to form short term memory. Short term memory, with nerve net activation in the hippocampus, can then enter permanent storage as long term memory throughout the brain.

The basal ganglion connects and orchestrates impulses between the cerebellum and frontal lobe, thus helping to control body movements. It facilitates the fine motor control in our facial and eye muscles necessary to communicate our emotional states to others and in learned, motor based memory like learning to play the piano.[11] The basal ganglion is one of the areas connected with the frontal lobe through the substantia nigra that coordinates thought involved in planning the order and timing of future behaviors.[12] (See Figure 5.7.) This ties into Damasio's findings that emotion, body and reason are physiologically inseparable.

The intricate wiring of the limbic system shows that in order to learn and remember something, there must be sensory input, a personal emotional connection and movement. As we experience the world, the collage of images and our responding actions are all run through an emotional filter in the limbic system that determines the value, meaning and survival potential of the experience in light of past experience. Socially, everything we do stems from our need to be accepted within our group so we may survive. Emotions interpret our experience and help us to organize our view of the world and our place in it.

All of our emotional/cognitive processing appears to be biochemical. How we feel about a situation triggers specific neurotransmitters. Objectively speaking, to the mind/body every experience is simply an event. The way we choose to perceive that event, colored by our emotions, determines our response to it and our potential for learning from it.

If we perceive the event as a disaster, the neurotransmitter adrenalin is released and the mind/body responds with a series of survival-oriented reactions. With increased adrenalin we also produce the neurotransmitter cortisol which decreases our ability to learn and remember.[13] If instead we choose to perceive the event as a learning experience, an adventure, other neurotransmitters like GABA, acetylcholine, interferon and interleukins are released.[14] These increase our ability to establish or reorganize neural networks so we may effectively think and remember. We will be returning to the subject of neurotransmitters in a later chapter. The point here is that emotions, and the release of neurotransmitters that they elicit, are intimately intertwined with cognitive function.

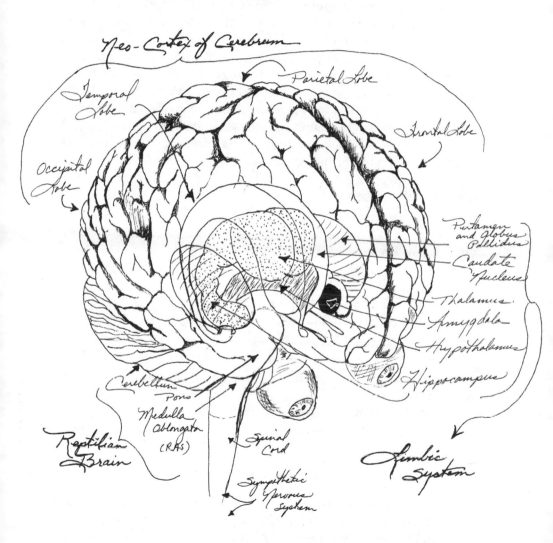

Figure 4.1: The Limbic System

WHAT DOES THIS MEAN FOR EDUCATION?

The implications of these insights are enormous, especially in the realm of education. Elizabeth deBeauport brings this home succinctly when she writes: "What's missing from all our educational efforts? The feeling brain. Affection was the first characteristic of mammalian growth. When we began to care, we agreed not to be like reptiles and simply slink away."[15]

Our mind/body system learns through experiencing life in context, in relationship to everything else, and it is our emotions, our feelings that mediate that context. In order to learn, think or create, learners must have an emotional commitment. Otherwise, education becomes just an intellectual exercise. Yet schools by and large deliver knowledge in piecemeal, segregated subject areas, in an unemotional, unsocial environment. The connection to the student's own personal concerns or future survival is usually remote. Most school lessons expect students to settle down to serious, intellectual business, devoid of social or emotional content. And teachers complain of having to be disciplinarians, instead of educators, in their efforts to put a lid on the social, emotional interactions among members of the class.

Students who are highly motivated to learn, already possessing an emotional commitment, will learn because they love to learn. Others will do well because they have come to understand the personal survival importance of education to societal success and therefore approach learning with some emotional/survival commitment. But those who lack emotional commitment to the current educational curriculum and who cannot appreciate its application for their lives, may fail miserably in school.

Education would be more effective if homes and classrooms became learning societies, actively engaging emotions and social relationships in the service of knowledge acquisition. The Danish school system comes pretty close to this ideal in many respects. (Some of the features of the Danish system are described in Chapters 5 and 15).

DEVELOPING EMOTIONS

Exploration and expression of emotion is necessary stimulation for development of the limbic system and its connections to other brain areas. As with sensory development, we are not born into the world with this capacity fully formed. We must develop the neural networks that support emotional processing through social experience and expression.

By approximately 15 months of age, the limbic system begins the process of adding emotion to the base patterns for sensory input and learned motor functioning. Out of this union, relationships between the individual and its world are discovered and stored first in short, and then in long term memory.

If you put two one-year-olds in a room together, they will hardly notice each other as they go about their sensory-motor job of understanding the material world. But at about 15 months of age, they pay attention to each other for the first time and interaction begins. With this interaction comes the awareness of the child's place in the world as a unique, separate individual who is connected to others by common lineage, emotional bonds, language and specific cultural paradigms. Between ages 2 and 3, children realize they are separate from their mother and the concept of "I" develops. From this new-found point of separation a child recognizes that this is "my mommy, my daddy, my toy". Through this recognition the child bonds with its parents, siblings, and caretakers. The social and family sense of concern or protection through bonding that assures societal survival is anchored in the emotional development of the limbic system.

LEARNING BY IMITATION

In these early developmental years, exploration takes on a whole new dimension. Children begin to imitate the people in their world, gaining a physical and emotional understanding of significant persons and social relationships.

What we call "terrible two's" behavior is simply the child's exaggeration of our movements and emotions to gain a full sensory-motor understanding of them. The child is intrigued by the physical sensations of these new-found emotions, and great theatrics often occur. We may label these outbursts as temper tantrums, when they are simply emotional, physical, multisensory learning activities. Expression through movement is very important to the learning of emotions. At this age, the child has no cognitive or manipulative thought directing the emotion. They simply become the emotion! If parents understand this, they can be entertained by a wild and wonderful performance/mirror of themselves instead of seeing the two's as terrible. The amount and frequency of "terrible two's" behavior will diminish when the child's caretakers become aware of the importance of the modeling they are presenting to the child.

This physical/emotional link continues throughout our lives as our bodies continue to be the primary vehicle for expression of feeling. Notice the "goose bumps" you have when you experience a deeply moving scene in a play or great music that speaks to the soul. Notice the movement of choir members who are emotionally absorbed in their singing. Notice your own movements as you express a deep emotion. It is literally impossible to express emotion without motion. The major sensory areas of the face and hands are usually very active in the process. Hand and facial expression of emotion stimulates large areas of the brain for more sophisticated connections between emotion and thought.

Between ages 15 months and 4 years the child explores the emotional richness of its world. The initial exploration involves emotions generated by the hypothalamus and amygdala which include states of rage, fright and aggression. These are linked directly to the reptilian brain for their expression and so become raw reaction without any cognitive control or understanding. As the nerve networks develop and link into the cortical centers in the temporal lobes for thought and higher cognitive functions, emotions such as anger, sadness, happiness and frustration emerge. This neural link-up with cognitive areas allows these gross emotions to reach conscious awareness and for stories, historical events, media presentations and observations to affect us emotionally.[16]

WHY WE NEED TO EXPRESS EMOTIONS

The exploration and expression of these gross emotions is essential to the later development of the refined emotions of love, altruism, compassion and joy, as nerve networks link into the frontal lobes of the cerebrum. Our emotions then provide us with the passion and action to live fully.

When emotions are connected directly to survival and fear, their expression may become an explosive reaction centered in the sympathetic nervous system and the brain stem. This reactive kind of emotion, though natural for a 2 year old, has long been feared in adults because it often leads to violence. Given this fear of violence, children are often restrained from any expression of strong emotions, even when they are just discovering them.

When we encourage people to express emotions, even anger and sadness, we show respect for their feelings. Because the person feels valued, the emotional response is usually linked to reason.

Children who are allowed to naturally and responsibly express emotions are better able to constructively or creatively use them throughout life. Talking about feelings is of particular benefit as we engage thought and reasoning processes to comprehend and verbalize the emotional experience. This helps to strengthen the important emotion-cognition link.

On the other hand, when people are given no outlet for emotional expression, they may start to doubt their personal value. The suppressed emotions lose their links with conscious awareness and this state of denial becomes linked with the survival centers. As a result, the emotion is then connected to fear and self-doubt. When the emotions are finally expressed, they can often emerge in a violent, explosive outburst. If they remain suppressed, denied, they precipitate a chronic release of adrenalin and depress learning, memory and immunity.

While visiting and teaching in a variety of other cultures over the past five years, I have often been deeply impressed by enlightened societal attitudes towards the expression of emotion. Among the native people of Botswana and Lesotho, I have experienced great joy and passion. People from these cultures are not afraid to express emotion from their whole being, whether it be healthy anger at injustice, sadness or joy. Joy was their main expression, coming from their whole body and mind. It would manifest in song, in a brilliant smile that went on forever, or in a deep embrace. They readily expressed joy in the simple act of meeting me, or enjoying a harvest, or watching a child, or waking to a new day.

In our culture, the expression of anger is more common than the expression of joy, and often does not even appear odd. On the other hand, a person expressing joy on the street may actually be considered *mad*. Why is it that in our culture we are much more attuned to and respectful of — and perhaps skillful at — expressions of anger than of joy? Could it be that fear of expression of one has made us wary of the other, and led us to discount and intellectualize away anything that might be construed as "emotional"? However, as science itself now affirms, our emotions, motives and thoughts are inextricably linked.[17] Emotions are part of thought. Once found they are always there. When we respect this inseparability and affirm a productive place for emotions in all educational environments we cultivate fertile ground for lifelong learning, thought and creativity.

I felt such fulfilling emotions among the all-embracing relationships of African communities in South Africa. These sojourns of the past few years have confirmed my belief in the importance of emotion to the health and well-being of any society. Passion, meaningful relationships with others are a large part of what we are missing and looking for in our own society. Encouragement and acceptance of rich emotional development are essential to our lives as individuals and as a society.

EARLY ALTRUISM

In the early years, the developing limbic system enables the child to form relationships and social bonds. This is the perfect opportunity to teach children about behavior toward other people and how to take care of other children, pets, objects and the environment. Signs of the development of altruism and empathy appear around three years of age. These qualities are ultimately important for the survival of the species.[18]

The development of altruistic behavior begins with showing concern and awareness for another child's or adult's needs. The child moves from the possessive relationship to the idea of caring for the possession: "this is mine and I must take care of it." Taking the extra time to tend to a pet when your three year old discovers the pet needs food, even if you are already ten minutes late, honors altruistic learning and will last a lifetime.

Being willing to show concern and search for a lost toy rather than saying "we'll buy a new one," instills a sense of value in the child. Altruistic learning is crucial in our society where concepts of "restore, reuse and recycle," are having a painful time germinating. It may be that our land-fills, hospitals and mental institutions are overflowing because the early seeds of altruism weren't germinated during limbic development.[19]

Learning to control our emotions is also an appropriate task for this relationship brain. In order to avoid conflict we often give children what they want, when they want it. This deprives them of the opportunity to learn about delayed gratification. A painless way to assist this important learning process might be to play a time game. When a child asks for a snack, say "Sure, and I will give it to you in three minutes." Then set an egg timer and ask the child to let you know when it's time. Then give the child the snack. The time period can be lengthened with the learning. When children know their needs will be met, they easily develop a sense of time and learn delayed gratification. This lesson will serve them well the rest of their lives.[20]

EMOTION AND MEMORY

What is the connection between sensory physical awareness and emotion that gives us our memories? If you ask people to recall their earliest memory, they will usually go back to a time after the limbic system starts to mature. As the limbic system gears up, nerve networks connect the sensory and motor base patterns to emotion and memory is established.

Take a moment to recall an early memory. What were the colors, the sounds, the smells, the tastes, the emotions? What do you remember about your physical movements, who else was there and what did you feel about them? Memory is usually rich with bodily sensations of sight, sound, smell, taste, emotions and movements. The neural relatedness of these gives us our remembered pictures.

My first memory was of my mother swinging me on a small back yard swing strung between the house and a tree. I distinctly remember it was cool, probably Autumn, with clear, bright colors in the air and on the trees. The smells were crisp and pungent Autumn smells. I remember feeling secure watching my mother's face with her blue scarf as she talked and laughed at my giggling. The feel of my body going back and forth, first very gently, then feeling it in my stomach as the swing went higher. It is a very physical, sensual memory and I see it now as in a movie clip. Imagination, dreams and cognition arise from this intricate interplay within the limbic system.

The limbic system allows us to see things in context for the first time. This new-found awareness is used to understand ownership, our relationship to everything else and our place in society. "It" becomes more than just something that we eat for survival. It is now recognized as "spaghetti," wiggly, the color of my shirt, mine instead of my sisters, and I can make a story with it.

This is also an important time for physical imprinting, the development of body memory. As children encounter new information, they will move to embody it on all their muscles and senses. Allow yourself to be guided on a walk with a three year old child. When they come to something new, they will actually move their bodies to conform with the physical configuration of the new object to better understand it. Movement facilitates the entrainment process in understanding relationships physically.[21]

BASE PATTERNING AND MEMORY

The nature of memory has long been a subject of conjecture

and debate. There is a growing consensus among brain scientists that memory is not stored in a single location in the brain. Instead, memories are constructed from neural pathways that fire together as patterns. These networks are constantly subject to modification and elaboration so we may link ideas and memories in infinite combinations.

The base patterns of memory form as we experience our sensory environment in greater and greater detail. Different sensory areas of the brain realize specific sensations. Patterns develop that allow us to recall those different sensations together as a single memory. These patterns are associated with the specific brain areas where that specialized sensory information is processed, for example, the occipital lobe for visual sensations, the temporal lobe for sound. So that when you recall a memory of your mother on a particular day, the images, sounds, words, smells, movements, emotions arise from different places in the brain but are linked neurally and thus can form a single memory. Which of course may lead you directly to another memory because neural networks are so complexly interwoven.

According to this model, that is how we integrate new learning. Evolving patterns become base reference points to understand new information. As we are presented with new learning, the brain recalls past experience and provides an image display of base patterns from each area of the brain simultaneously. New information can then be integrated into existing base patterns, thus changing and enriching the nerve networks and giving us a more complex world view.

Information starts as short term memory in the limbic system where sensory images are combined with emotional components that add important survival information. If the information is valued and practiced, it becomes the template for reorganization of previous patterning. This reorganization of base patterns becomes long term memory in the free-form information system throughout the brain. We continue to elaborate and modify the patterning throughout our lives. The base patterns, 90% of which are acquired within the first five years of life, give us the template on which to attach all future learning.[22]

PET scans show that a cellular information highway speeds through all parts of the brain to coordinate memories for personally experienced events, called episodic memories. In a study at the University of Toronto, participants showed a stronger memory for words analyzed by meaning, as compared to words perused on a letter-by-letter basis. Episodic memories (or the meanings of words, as this Toronto study shows) have an added emotional component which appears necessary for complex memory development.[23] Image displays and memory in the brain are ubiquitous and appear to be triggered more by episodic experience than just straight line rote processing. The memory function is more than a linear library system. Memory appears to be a free form information system that facilitates information retrieval from all brain areas instantly and simultaneously. Therefore, in order to most efficiently remember something, it is best to connect it to a sensory, emotional, physical episode.

Each person's patterns are specific and unique. The number of possible base patterns is infinite. These base patterns determine the way we process and act upon our learning. As templates, these base patterns can be modified, reorganized and pruned for more efficiency as knowledge increases. They provide the basis of our beliefs, which in turn can be transformed by new information and broader insight. "The somatotropic map in the brain is modified by experience," Eric Kandel observes, "learning can lead to structural alterations in the brain."[24] Limbic brain development, with its rich emotional connections to all brain areas allows us to constantly enlarge our data base. The base sensory, motor and emotional patterns become the template for new learning. Each step makes it easier for the system to learn, process, re-organize information and grow in greater understanding and complexity.

THE LIMBIC JEWEL — IMAGINATION

Imagination is more important than knowledge, for while knowledge points to all there is, imagination points to all there will be.

— *Albert Einstein*

As the limbic connections elaborate, all of the elements come into place for the development of imagination. Imagination will naturally spring from the sensory-motor patterning in relationship with emotion and memory. This is a process you can actually see unfolding if you observe how children respond when you read to them. As they concentrate on listening to you read to them, they are absolutely quiet. In their brains they are elaborating internal pictures and emotions connected to their already acquired understanding. They are actively forming new nerve networks.

When you have finished reading the book, the child immediately says: "read it again," and "again" and "again"! The repetition allows them to elaborate and myelinate the new nerve paths. If you happen to say the wrong word as you are reading, they will let you know. This consistency is important to the integrity of their imaginative pictures. They will then tell you the story to embody it in movement and sensation through speech. Finally, they will play act it. The physical play gives them the sensory understanding of the concepts and anchors all the parts together.[25]

As the child grows older and you are able to read more complex stories, books without pictures or few pictures are more desirable in assisting the imaginative process. Also, it is always good to encourage children to make up and tell you their own stories.

PLAY

In the early formative years, play is almost synony-mous with life. It is second only to being nourished, protected and loved. It is a basic ingredient of physical, intellectual, social and emotional growth.
— Ashley Montague

The value of make-believe cannot be stressed enough. The child can take its world, and through play and familiarity organize it into more and more complex mental and emotional patterns. The time from ages two to five is a crucial stage for children's cognitive development as they learn to process information and expand it into creativity. Interactive communication and play, when children are learning from each other's imagination, accelerates the process.

These marvelous changes unfold naturally, and happily do not require adult supervision and meddling. Unfortunately, however, these days there seems to be less time and opportunity for children to simply play. Even playgroups seem to be organized and structured. There appears to be an assumption that children need to be entertained and their play orchestrated. I see it a lot in organized sports for children. Adults are in charge and competition is the goal. Rarely do you just see children initiate "pick up" games that were routine when I was a child.

Some of my greatest learning occurred while playing with the neighborhood kids in the big vacant field behind our house. It had a tree smack dab in the middle with gullies, rocks, sandy areas and bushes from which to make hideouts or bows and arrows. There was enough room to ride our imaginary white stallions and play cow-boys and Indians. Hours and days slipped by as we concocted one idea after another. We made our own toys from sticks, feathers, stones, chalk, string, glue, big packing boxes, our parents' old clothes — anything. Co-creating toys from spontaneous imagination with a playmate enhances brain development exponentially. Play provides the skills necessary for cooperation, co-creativity, altruism and understanding.

Dr. Paul MacLean ties the process of imaginative development to the development of play that becomes the essence of creativity and high level reasoning. He feels the link between the emotional limbic brain and the frontal lobe of the neocortex allows for the ultimate expression of human creativity and development.[26]

Play represents full mind/body integration, through specific myelinated pathways between the limbic system (thalamocingulate division), and the frontal lobes of the neocortex. When we are able to take in our fill of sensory stimuli, process and integrate it with richly developed base patterns, and express new insights in a creative way,

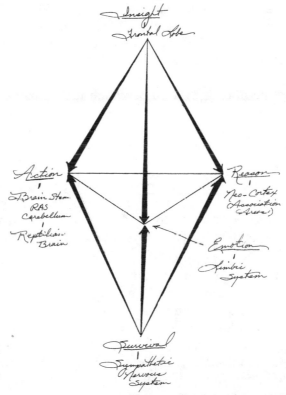

Figure 4.2: Trowbridge Model of Balanced Functioning

we are then truly at play. The human urge to create comes from the play impulse. Play on words, punning, and wit have contributed to creative thought in literature and drama throughout the ages. Composers, choreographers, and artists of all kind express their integration through play. The exhilarating play of modern science spills over into mathematics, paradoxical puzzles and language.[27]

Play at the simplest physical level as well as the furthest reaches of the intellect, depends on a balance of all the elements of our humanity. As Anthony Trowbridge has shown in his elaboration of Paul MacLean's triune brain theory, emotion is one of the key elements of that balance.[28] When the emotions are brought into dynamic equilibrium with reason, insight, action and even survival; learning becomes a rational, creative process. If any part of the brain processing is left out of the learning process, integration of patterning and appropriate action are limited. When dynamic equilibrium is lost, learning and creativity suffer.

TV AND IMAGINATION

Television, computer games or automated toys often occupy time in children's lives that they would use less passively if they had fewer such props to fall back on. If children are given space and encouraged to create, they naturally will entertain themselves without sophisticated equipment or adult intervention. A lot of creativity comes from just being in a place where it is allowed to happen spontaneously. I strongly agree with Joseph Chilton Pearce's stand and Jane Healy's suggestion that TV be banned before the age of eight so that imagination and language skills have a chance to be established.[29-30]

This diagram from the American Heart Association says a lot. TV has preempted physical movement, interactive communication and play. And we could add to this the developmental lack of imagination that demands full sensory, motor and emotional practice.

Daydreaming and imaginative play promote the child's perceptual maturity, emotional growth and creative development. TV inhibits the process, and interferes with kids' learning how to play. Children naturally learn by doing and through interaction with other people. In that sense, learning via TV is unnatural. Learning also requires time for reflection, and for absorbing and processing experience. A study has shown that students who were heavy TV viewers (more than six hours a day) were more likely to have low IQ's than light viewers (two hours or less a day). "TV gives children stunningly complex pieces of information," Kate Moody writes, "but this knowledge is largely unintegrated and lacks sufficient context and meaning."[31]

TV bombards viewers with a constantly changing stream of pictures, words, and movement that are too fast for the young brain to assimilate. The child may be able to repeat what he has heard, but without any depth of understanding. It's that depth of understanding — which comes from the integration of new experience with the child's developing mind/body patterning — that leads to imagination and creative reasoning. The child is left passive without the internal mental, emotional, and physical involvement necessary for cognitive development.

CAUTION:
CHILDREN NOT AT PLAY.

Figure 4.3: (From the American Heart Association)

The child's ability to process is exhausted by overstimulation in an attempt to follow what is happening on the TV screen. This causes the child's eyes to go into ocular lock (staring) and disassociative hearing (no connection between words and pictures). As a defense, the brain goes into lower alpha brain wave activity, where active thought and reasoning can't occur.[32]

It's important to emphasize that the act of watching TV itself, regardless of the content, has a lasting impact on a child's learning. Ages two to five are a crucial time for brain development. The brain is primed to learn how to take in and make relationships out of information. When children watch TV, they are habituating to a learning state that lacks physical, emotional and even some sensory (smell, taste, proprioceptive) involvement. This habituation will affect life long learning patterns. John Rosemond, director of the Center for Affirmative Parenting in Gastonia, North Carolina cites a study that shows preschoolers who watched a lot of Sesame Street tended to do less well in school than children who watched no TV.[33]

I hear over and over again from teachers today that children have no imagination. Though kids can recite verbatim the newest TV commercials, when asked to make up a product and write a commercial for it, they draw a complete blank. Even with guidelines and suggestions, many of them lack the basic neural networks to play with ideas and be creative.

DREAMS

We get a chance to experience our imaginative richness in our dreams. The limbic system is the area of dreams — our inner imaginative expression. The limbic system is dependent on the Reptilian Brain for imaginative expression during wakefulness. But when the Reptilian brain is gated (shut off) in sleep, the limbic system gives us our internal expression in dreams. Most dreams are full sensory experiences with strong emotional overlays.

Dreaming is important for the processing of emotional events and even appears to assist in the release of emotionally stressful situations. This is shown graphically in a recent study, where REM (Rapid Eye Movement — Dream) sleep was associated with a surge of adrenalin which more than doubled during REM sleep.[34-35] The elaborate connections of the limbic system, which forms the bridge between the body and the neocortex, supplies the emotional elements imperative to live and relate at our highest level.

SUGGESTIONS FOR HEALTHY DEVELOPMENT OF
THE LIMBIC SYSTEM IN CHILDREN

A. Encourage spontaneous imaginative play, either alone or with other children. Allow children to create their own toys. Steer clear of non-creative, fully constructed commercial toys.

B. Read to and participate in full attention communication with the child. Encourage creative, imaginative story making.

C. Encourage and allow full emotional expression moving to rational dialogue by the age of 4 years.

D. Encourage lots of movement and interaction with other children to develop playground rules, sharing and the beginnings of altruistic behavior.

E. Honor care of other people, pets and objects.

F. Encourage a sense of time and delayed gratification

G. Discourage any TV or video games

H. Provide a low stress environment and model rich emotional expression and stability. Model JOY.

I. Control caretaker's stress with Brain Gym (Hook-Ups) and encourage integrative movements daily.

5. ≈

Making Connections

*When we try to pick out anything by itself we find
it hitches to everything in the universe.*
— *John Muir*

I had a human brain in a jar when I first began teaching college years ago in Colorado. I always felt a sense of awe and reverence when I took it out of the jar to explore it with students. Here lay the whole universe of this person in my hands — all their genetic and cellular memory, their life story, their pictures and understanding of the world, all their feelings of love and hatred, the way they moved and interacted with the world, their passions and sacred dreams. Here in my hands was the physical record, the neural relationships of a unique individual, a being unlike any other that has ever been or ever will be. I still feel this awe and wonderment when I truly AM with another human being, of whatever age. This unique and unlimited person can be the doorway to worlds I might never otherwise visit.

During the same teaching stint, I teamed up with a geologist to teach field courses in the desert every Spring. Experiencing the desert through the eyes and minds of twenty-eight students turned out to be a great learning adventure. Each individual drew from a unique developmental background, emotional understanding and specific way of processing new information. Each had synthesized their understanding into skills and thought patterns uniquely their own. Each made the desert new and fascinating with their unlimited ways of experiencing and perceiving it for the first time. And each became a rich resource of new insights for me.

The unique set of connections which each of us makes from the very first moment we encounter the world, shapes our understanding of the world and of ourselves. Indeed, these connections **are** our selves, constantly moderating our experience of the world, constantly changing as experience is integrated with connections we have already made. And they are expressed and embodied in the knowledge, competencies and skills which make every human being unique and irreplaceable.

These crucial connections are the special province of the neocortex, which associates the world for us, constantly integrating movement, the senses, and emotions. It is the most plastic area of the brain, the novelty brain that loves fresh input and as much variety as a lifetime can present. Like other parts of the brain, the neocortex is totally interdependent with the body as a whole, but at the same time follows its own timetable in unfolding and developing. Understanding this process gives us a much clearer view not only of our enormous capabilities — particularly in the area of learning — but also of the ways the development of these capabilities can be impeded or helped to flourish.

INTRODUCING COMMAND CENTRAL

The largest structure of the human brain is the cerebrum, where Command Central resides. To get a sense of its size, put your hands together in very loose fists with your two thumbs pointing up in front of you. Covering the cerebrum like a thin peel that covers an orange, is the cortex, or neocortex. The word neocortex refers to its evolutionary advancement over the non-mammalian brain. The neocortex is composed mainly of three types of neurons in a thin layer 2 to 5 mm. thick that covers the surface of all the convolutions of the cerebrum. It contains 10 to 20 billion or more nerve cells, mainly the Great Intermediate Net of association neurons, or what I consider to be Command Central.

Command Central neurons are held together by 80 to 100 billion neuroglia (glial) cells. Glial cells form a supporting meshwork by twining around nerve cells or lining structures in the brain and spinal cord. Some bind nervous tissue to supporting structures and attach the neurons to blood vessels.

If spread out, the neocortex would cover 500 square inches of surface area. It uses 1.5 pints of blood every 60 seconds and burns 400 Calories every day. The neocortex constitutes only one fourth of the brain's total volume, yet it has approximately 85% of the total neurons in the brain.[1]

The neocortex is made up of grey matter, the unmyelinated cell bodies of neurons, which have unlimited ability to form new dendrites and reorganize dendritic patterns from new experiences throughout life. It is estimated that the nerve nets within the neocortex of an adult have over 1 quadrillion (that's a million billions) connections in a normal brain and are able to process 1,000 new bits of information every second. This means that at any one time, the possible combinations of signals jumping across the synapses in the brain exceed the numbers of atoms in the known universe.[2]

The white matter is composed of myelinated axons extending from or going to nerve cell bodies in the neocortex. These axons quickly carry sensory information to the neocortex, and carry its motor commands to the body.

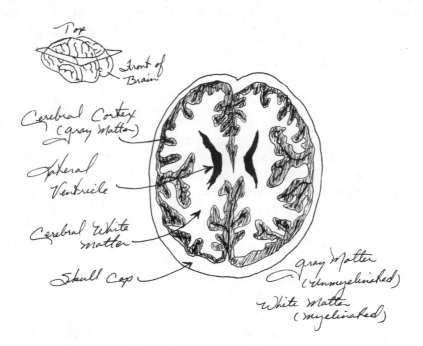

Figure 5.1: White and Grey Matter of the Cerebrum

This very second as you read these words, your brain is monitoring the light, heat, cold, sounds, and smells around you. It monitors the functioning of all your organs, and every touch and pressure on your body. It knows who and what is in the room with you. It knows where every muscle in your body is and which are lengthened, which relaxed, and which contracted. It constantly makes muscle adjustments to keep your body, especially your eyes, aligned to the book. It moves the muscles of the eyes to track across the page, adjust for distance and adjust for light. And it visually takes in the words on the page, integrates them with specific remembered images, sounds, and movements in your life, to understand each word and meaning in your special context so that you may evaluate the relevance of the text, judge its correctness, consider the ways you might implement it — amazing!

At birth the neocortex weighs 350 grams (about 12 ounces), which is 25% of its adult weight. It grows by increasing dendrites and glial cells, at the rate of 1 milligram every minute to 50% of adult weight by six months, 75% by two and a half years and 90% by five years of age. From these figures, we could assume that 90% of base neural patterns form before a child even goes to school. By five years of age the child has mastered gross motor control over gravity, learned a world of information through its senses, put these together into language, music and art, and become socialized enough to interact with family and strangers in culturally acceptable ways. This amazing feat of neural development — taking in sensory experiences and creating mental models — will continue to be refined and augmented constantly throughout a lifetime.

FROM SENSORY EXPERIENCE TO UNDERSTANDING

As sensory experience floods our system, it travels through the brain stem and the reticular activating system and on to the thalamus of the limbic system. All pathways from the sensory nerve endings to the neocortex pass through the thalamus, except for smell. The thalamus not only monitors sensory input and adds emotional context to the information, it has direct connections with all areas of the neocortex. This close association, from the thalamus to the neocortex and then from the neocortex back to the thalamus, is called the thalamocortical system.

These subtle, invisible transactions among sensory/emotional/motor areas of the brain allow us to create meaning from our experience. In the process of developing the base patterns which organize our experience, different lobes of the cerebrum are involved: the occipital lobe for visual understanding, the temporal lobe for hearing and gravitational understanding, and the parietal lobe for touch, pressure, pain, heat and cold sensations and proprioception all over the body.

The linkages among these areas give us the images that comprise our memory. You might, for example, remember a time when you dropped a ball and it bounced with a rubbery sound. You might also remember a glass dropping and shattering. Out of remembered experiences like these, we build concepts like: all things fall, glass things break, rubbery things bounce. Through our base patterning we construct models of the way things work, make predictions, organize physical responses, and come to more complexity of understanding as we assimilate new learning.

MAPPING THE CEREBRUM

Curiosity about how each area of the brain works has probably existed since Aristotle's time. But ever since Wilder Penfield began exploring the brain during surgery, we've been driven in our attempt to specifically map all the areas and functions of the brain. In the 1930's, Dr. Penfield discovered that the brain itself has no pain receptors. This made it possible for him to perform brain surgery using only local anesthesia on a fully awake patient. During the course of an operation, Penfield was able to use an electric probe with a mild current to stimulate the neurons of a live, fully conscious brain and talk with it's owner about what was happening. To each stimulus, the patient would give a physical or verbal response, or have a memory flashback which he could describe as a coherent recollection of an earlier experience.[3]

In this way, Penfield was able to begin identifying the function of different brain areas. Today we can use the PET Scan (Positron Emission Tomography), MRI (Magnetic Resonance Imaging) and SQUID (Superconducting Quantum Interference Device) to assist in our pursuit to understand brain function.[4]

The PET Scan measures the rate at which the brain burns up glucose, its primary fuel. Volunteers receive injections of minute amounts of a radioactively labeled glucose compound that their brain cells absorb. PET scans then chart where more glucose is being used during specific activities.[5]

Each hemisphere of the cerebrum contains four lobes that are shown in Figure 5.2.[6] A very elementary overview of the four cerebral lobes' functions follows:

Occipital Lobe: Primary Visual Area (receives sensory impulses from eyes, interprets shape, color and movement); and Visual Association Area (relates past to present visual experience, recognition and evaluation of what is seen).

Temporal Lobe: Primary Auditory Area (interprets basic characteristics of sound, pitch and rhythm); Auditory Association (Wernicke's Area) interprets speech; Vestibulo Area (sensations from semi-circular canals — gravitational sense, balance and vibrational sense); Primary Olfactory Area (sensations related to smell). These tie directly into the memory centers of the limbic system.

Parietal Lobe: General Sensory Area[7] (touch, pressure, pain, cold, heat and proprioception); Somesthetic Association Area (integrates and interprets sensations — shape and texture without visual input, orientations of objects, relationship to body parts, and past sensory experiences); Gustatory Area (taste: sensation of sweet, salt, sour and bitter).

Frontal Lobe: Primary Motor Area[8] (controls specific muscles all over the body); Premotor Area (concerned with learned motor activities of complex, sequential nature — skilled movements); Frontal Eye Field Area (voluntary scanning movements of eyes); Broca's Area (translates thoughts into speech and development of inner speech as described by Luria).[9]

All of these lobes accept external stimuli and information from the opposite side of the body, via the brain stem and limbic system. This information is then integrated, organized and reorganized with sensory-motor memory in the association and gnostic areas of the neocortex (The Great Intermediate Net), so that new experiences can be understood in light of past experiences.

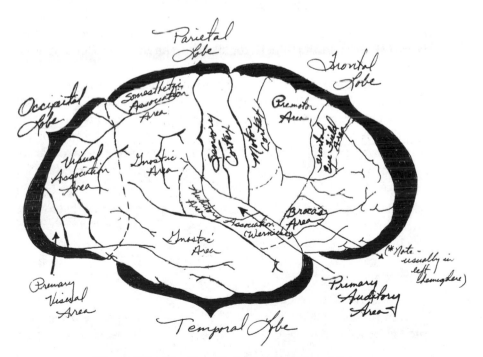

Figure 5.2: The Four Lobes of the Neocortex

The association areas occupy the greatest portion of each lobe and are concerned with memory, emotions, reasoning, will, judgment, personality traits and intelligence. The gnostic area is the common integrative area collecting information from all four lobes. It is located among the somesthetic, visual and auditory association areas. This area also receives impulses of taste and smell, sensory information from the thalamus and impulses from the lower portions of the brain stem. It integrates sensory interpretations from the association areas and impulses from other areas so that a common thought can be formed from the various sensory inputs. An example of the integrative image that emerges might be: "this cold red apple is soft, but it smells fresh and sure tastes good." It then transmits signals to other parts of the brain to cause the appropriate physical response to occur, again via the limbic system and brain stem.[10] This response might be "bringing the apple to the mouth, opening the mouth and biting into the apple again."

The occipital, temporal and parietal areas partially develop along with the brain stem and limbic systems, but exhibit a major growth spurt at approximately age four. It is not until approximately age eight that we get a major growth spurt in the frontal lobes.

PUTTING IT ALL TOGETHER

To get a snapshot of the complex functioning that occurs when we put all the building blocks together, we have only to look at what happens during the act of seeing the first violets bloom in the Spring. In order to see the violets, the body and eyes must move into position and focus. This act requires gross motor integration in the brain stem, orchestration through the basal ganglion in the limbic system and fine motor coordination in the frontal lobe of the neocortex. Further movement occurs as the iris muscles contract to accommodate for light, and the ciliary muscles on the lens accommodate for distance.

Light reflected from the violets registers on the photosensitive cones and rods of the retinas of both eyes. The cones and rods send specific neurological messages via sensory neurons to the primary visual area of the occipital lobe of the cerebrum. This allows us to "see" the violets.

The frontal eye field coordinates eye teaming, allowing us to track our eyes over the violets. The lines and shape are integrated into structure and three-dimensionality through associative images with the proprioceptive areas of the sensory cortex of the parietal lobe. From there, the impulses diffuse out across nerve net pathways, pulling together information from associative areas in the parietal and temporal lobes.

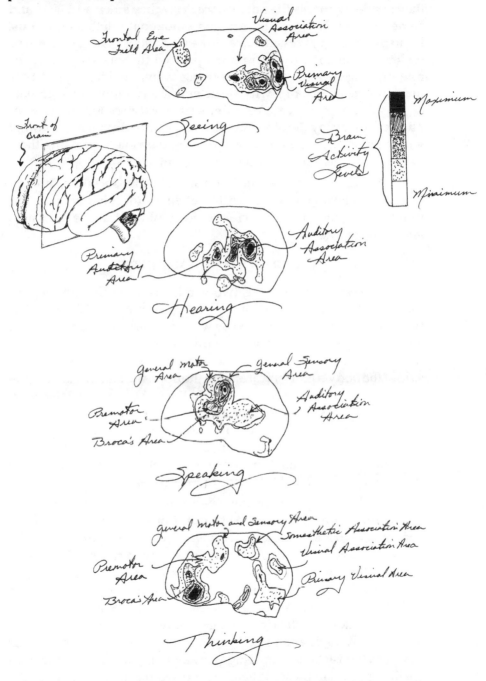

Figure 5.3: Schematic Diagrams of PET Scans of Lobes & Function[11]

The combined images from throughout the brain give us a concept of violets including their name, function, where and what they are doing in this time and space, how they smell and taste and some memory of their physical and emotional relationship to us. From this memory we can make new associations, like gathering the violets and making cards from the pressed flowers, extracting the dye, putting them in a salad, drawing them, or figuring out how many are in an area of lawn. These new associations can stimulate us to solve a puzzle, make a decision, create something new or physically employ the object in our lives. The brain can then prompt various muscular responses, like picking the violets, pressing them in a book, eating them, jumping over them, etc.[12]

The activation of all the brain areas in an associative, integrative dance allows us to play with the violets (or any object) in our minds, thus generating new, creative ideas of what can be done with and to the object.

THE BRAIN'S TWO HEMISPHERES

The cerebrum contains two hemispheres, each with the four lobes described above: occipital, parietal, temporal and frontal. The two hemispheres are connected by white matter — connective motor and sensory axons — in a structure called the corpus callosum. Interestingly, the cerebrum has a crossover pattern such that each side of the body communicates with the opposite hemisphere. Information coming into the left ear goes to the right temporal lobe of the cerebral cortex, while the right hand is controlled by the left motor cortex of the cerebrum. All sensory-motor functions on the right side of the body are either realized or controlled by the left hemisphere. And all sensory-motor functions on the left side of the body are realized and controlled by the right hemisphere.

Each hemisphere of the cerebrum develops and processes information in a specific way. To put it in simple terms, the logic hemisphere (usually the left) deals with details, the parts and processes of language, and linear patterns. By contrast, the gestalt (usually the right hemisphere) — meaning whole processing or global as compared to linear — deals with images, rhythm, emotion and intuition.[13] Because some people are transposed and process the logical functions on the right and gestalt functions on the left, I will use the terms logic and gestalt instead of right and left. The corpus callosum then acts as a superhighway allowing quick access to both the linear detail in the logic hemisphere and the overall image in the gestalt hemisphere for integrated thought.

Following is a very simplified summary of the basic differences between these two hemispheres:[14-15-16]

LOGIC	GESTALT
Starts with the pieces first	Sees whole picture first
Parts of language	Language comprehension
Syntax, semantics	Image, emotion, meaning
Letters, sentences	Rhythm, flow, dialect
Numbers	Image, intuition
Analysis — linear	Intuition — estimates
Looks at differences	Looks at similarities
Controls feelings	Free with feelings
Planned — structured	Spontaneous — fluid
Sequential thinking	Simultaneous thinking
Language oriented	Feelings/experience oriented
Future-oriented	Now-oriented
Technique	Flow and movement
Sports (hand/eye/foot placement)	Sports (flow and rhythm)
Art (media, tool use, how to)	Art (image, emotion, flow)
Music (notes, beat, tempo)	Music (passion, rhythm, image)

Figure 5.4: Summary of Differences between the Brain's Hemispheres

Both hemispheres contain all functions until specialization starts to occur. This specialization develops at a different rate in each individual. However, on average the gestalt hemisphere exhibits a growth spurt of dendrites between ages four and seven and the logic hemisphere between seven and nine years. Under normal circumstances, complete hemispheric specialization is in place between nine and twelve years of age. The more that both hemispheres and all lobes are activated by use, the more dendritic connections form and extend across the corpus callosum and myelinate. The more myelination, the faster the processing between both hemispheres and the rest of the brain.

When fully developed, the corpus callosum carries four billion messages per second across the 200 million or more mostly myelinated nerve fibers connecting the two hemispheres of the brain. This integration and quick access leads to full operational thinking so that ideas and concepts can be manipulated, resulting in formal reasoning.[17-18-19]

Recent research shows that two regions at the front of the corpus callosum in ADHD (Attention Deficit Hyperactive Disorder) are markedly smaller than those of non-ADHD people.[20] It has also been found that females have 10% more fibers across the corpus callosum than men.[21]

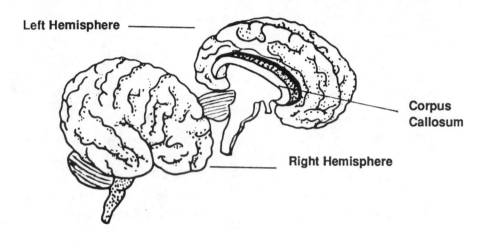

Figure 5.5: Hemispheres and Corpus Callosum

These differences may not be genetic. I believe that the experiences necessary to develop full sensory-motor-emotional patterns have been more limited both for those labeled "learning disabled" and for men in our society. These people may have missed interactive relationships that include rich dialogue and emotions. My guess is that with more activation of both frontal lobes and acceptance of emotional experience and expression, this corpus callosum discrepancy would vanish.

CONNECTING THE HEMISPHERES

The differing functions of the two cerebral hemispheres has by now become such a familiar part of popular lore about the brain, that it's not uncommon to hear people described as left- or right-brained. In fact all of us do have a certain degree of hemispheric dominance.

People may exhibit a preference for either analytic or global processing, particularly in times of stress.

But the more we access both hemispheres, the more intelligently we are able to function. Actually, it is necessary to use both hemispheres of the brain to be maximally proficient at anything.

Creativity, for example, is not exclusively a gestalt hemisphere function. It is a whole brain process that requires technique and detail from the logic hemisphere and image, flow and emotion from the gestalt hemisphere. Similarly, ease with language requires the words and proper sentence structure from the left and the image, emotion and dialect from the right. This integration allows ease of reading and writing as well as comprehension and creative access.

Cross lateral movements, like a baby's crawling (and, as we shall see in Chapter 7, Brain Gym movements), activate both hemispheres in a balanced way.[22] These activities work both sides of the body evenly and involve coordinated movements of both eyes, both ears, both hands and both feet as well as balanced core muscles. When both eyes, both ears, both hands and feet are being used equally, the corpus callosum orchestrating these processes between the two hemispheres becomes more fully developed. Because both hemispheres and all four lobes are activated, cognitive function is heightened and ease of learning increases.

When learners, and teachers, take advantage of this simple way of increasing the brain's efficiency, learning is bound to be more engaging and successful. I've been delighted to see math, for example, being taught in new ways that utilize both hemispheres of the brain. Times tables were deadly for me — endless hours of memorization. Teachers are now setting up cooperative learning groups in their classrooms that are responsible for coming up with a rap that they then teach to the rest of the class. The numbers from the logic side and the rhythm and image from the gestalt side provide a winning combination for ease of learning.

WHAT CAN THE BRAIN DO — AND WHEN CAN IT DO IT?

In describing the functions and anatomy of the neocortex, I've mentioned several developmental turning points. These are very important landmarks for anyone who wants to know what we are capable of doing, and, equally important, when we become capable of doing it. Failure to recognize these landmarks, and thus to accommodate each individual's specific learning pace is a root cause of many problems in education today.

Development of the cerebral cortex starts in the womb and continues until we die. Certain areas of the brain are feeding into the cerebrum at various times as natural development occurs. This is very much a continuous process but we can delineate a few landmarks. The following chart gives a "ballpark" rather than exact developmental picture. We all naturally develop at our own pace in our perfect time.

Age (approximate) Development

Conception - 15 months   **Reptilian Brain**
Basic survival needs — food, shelter, security and safety
Sensory development starting with vestibular system, then hearing, tactile, smell, taste and finally seeing — rich sensory activation
Motor development moving from reflexes to core muscle activation, neck muscles, arms and legs leading to rolling over, sitting, crawling and walking — motor exploration

15 months - 4 $\frac{1}{2}$ years   **Limbic System / Relationship**
Understanding of self/others, self/emotions, self/language
Emotional exploration; Language exploration/communication; Imagination; Gross motor proficiency; Memory development; Social development

4 $\frac{1}{2}$ - 7 years   **Gestalt Hemisphere Elaboration**
Whole picture processing/cognition,
Image/movement/rhythm/emotion/intuition
Outer speech/integrative thought

7 - 9 years   **Logic Hemisphere Elaboration**
Detail and linear processing/cognition
Refinement of elements of language
Reading and writing skills development
Technique development — music, art, sports, dance, manual training
Linear math processing

8 years   **Frontal Lobe Elaboration**
Fine motor development — skills refinement
Inner speech — control of social behavior
Fine motor eye teaming for tracking and foveal focus (2-dimensional focus)

9 - 12 years   **Increased Corpus Callosum Elaboration & Myelination**
Whole brain processing

12 - 16 years   **Hormonal Emphasis**
Learning about body, self, others, community, and meaningful living through social consciousness

16 - 21 years   Refining Cognitive Skills

Whole mind/body processing, social interaction, future planning and play with new ideas and possibilities

21 +   Elaboration and Refinement of the Frontal Lobes

Global / systems thinking

High level formal reasoning

Refinement of emotions — altruism, love, compassion

Insight

Refinement of fine motor skills

Figure 5.6: Landmarks of Cerebral Neocortex Development

We must get away from the notion that we simply experience the world until we go to school at the age of five and **then** we learn. Learning is a progressive, constantly changing process that serves to enrich and expand our understanding throughout life. The neo-cortex is always growing neural networks linked to the brain stem and limbic system, developing the neural connections that enable it to become the integrator of knowledge.

Even at the age of about twenty-one, there is a growth spurt of nerve net development in the frontal lobes. It's the time when people realize their parents are smarter than they thought, as emotional refinement allows for insight leading to altruism and love.

There is also another spurt of growth at approximately age thirty with further refinement of muscle movement, especially of the hands and face. Increased fine motor coordination leads to greater achievements for musicians like pianists and violinists who can move their fingers with more agility. We also see it in vocalists who are now able to command a greater range with their vocal cords (muscles). And we see it dramatically in character actors who can now control their facial muscles with such subtlety that they express any emotion with just their faces.[73]

READING AND WRITING — WHAT'S APPROPRIATE?

In the usual course of development, children are accessing gestalt function at the time they traditionally begin attending school, at about five years of age. The gestalt hemisphere begins development and enlargement between the ages of four and seven, while the logic hemisphere doesn't enlarge until ages seven to nine.[24] The most natural way, then, for children to learn when first in school at age five and six is through image, emotion and spontaneous movement.

Under normal circumstances children at the age when they first enter kindergarten already have wonderful imaginations and a very large vocabulary. The British curriculum of education, from which ours is derived, however, begins alphabet and number recognition immediately, with reading following in quick order. This might not be a problem if we involved image, emotion, and movement, and built on the student's imagination and vocabulary. Strangely, we do just the opposite. We teach children to "sit still," learn letters and numbers in a linear fashion (that includes printing, a very linear, logic hemisphere process), and read books with simplistic vocabulary, no emotion and few images.

By age four or five children naturally love to "write" stories — very elaborate stories. They usually write in a pretend cursive style, because they are mimicking grown-up writing, and because they enjoy the natural rhythm and flow of it. This process is anchoring learning in a holistic way and could be an excellent point of departure for new learning.

HOW THE DANES MAKE LEARNING TO READ EASIER

The Danish school system, respecting natural brain developmental patterns, does not start children in school until six or seven years of age. They teach writing and reading from a holistic, gestalt processing format and then move to the details later, around age eight, when the logic hemisphere is ready to handle it. Reading is not taught until age eight — and Denmark boasts 100% literacy.[25-26]

Children in Denmark are given the freedom and encouragement to write stories. Though the teacher cannot decode them, the child can, so the children read their stories. The stories are rich in elaborate, image-based vocabulary. As the child reads his or her story, the teacher notices which images are emotionally important to the writer. The teacher makes use of this information, for example by saying: "It sounds like `dinosaur' is one of your favorite words. Would you like to see how I write that?" The children almost always want to know how adults write words. So after the teacher writes out the word "dinosaur" in cursive, the next story the child writes will have the usual undecipherable scrawl with the word "dinosaur" interspersed. The child has learned the whole word without effort.

For reading, the teacher asks for a favorite song which she writes in cursive and then has the children follow the words as they sing. This establishes an emotional-relational connection, so important to the memory process, since memory is closely linked to emotion in the relational limbic system. There is a lot of movement and rhythm play in each learning process.

I can vouch for the effectiveness of this approach by recalling my own experience of learning the alphabet. It took singing the alphabet song and also physically making the letters with my body to help me finally learn my ABCs. I still find myself singing it when I have to file papers in alphabetical order.

In contrast to the Danish system, I remember my first reading book having a lot of words like "the," "and," "yes," "can." Just recently a child brought me a book she was working on in kindergarten. The name of the book was: *YES I CAN*. Now, what kind of image do words like these elicit? To learn something new it is imperative that we tie it into something familiar and — at this young age — something with a concrete image. Teachers give students three letter words because they appear simple, but in reality they are far more difficult than "dinosaur" because they hold no internal image or emotion.

BLOCK LETTERS AND WRITING BLOCKS

Another unnatural challenge has to do with learning to print block letters as the first step in writing. Printing is a highly linear process that takes us away from the more continuous rhythmic flow of language, both as it is experienced in the mind and as it is expressed through the hand — as in cursive script. In many European schools they never teach printing, and find children have no difficulty going from writing in cursive to reading block printed text, usually at the age of eight. I am surprised there hasn't been more research done on the comparative effects of the ways writing is introduced in different school systems worldwide. Educators in Germany have told me they are finding that students are now having more difficulties with language since they have switched over to teaching block printing as the first step to language.

In the American school system we follow the British lead. At age five we teach a child to print which, in my estimation from my work with children, is the origin of many writing blocks in people today. At this early age, children have to work very hard at printing since it defies the natural development of brain functions. After age seven, when the brain is developed enough to accommodate the discrete and linear operations necessary for printing, we then teach them cursive. It is a crazy game that only serves to maintain high stress levels in the child and leads to "learned helplessness." This learned helplessness occurs when the person decides that whatever they do will be wrong. So they quit, make only a marginal effort, or just give up.[27]

This is not the only example of learned helplessness resulting from a pedagogical strategy that sacrifices long term gains for short term, illusory results. The excessive use of low level skills tests, usually of rote memory, and usually timed — as often as two or three times a week right up through college is a graphic example. Rote memory is a straight line process requiring none of the depth of understanding that comes from whole brain activation. In short, rote memory does not require thinking. These tests induce learned helplessness by promoting situations and habits where students only study for the tests, and students with test anxiety end up in a state of perpetual stress.

Under these circumstances there is no time or space to develop deep understanding of concepts, test out new ideas through verbal and written action, or develop deductive reasoning skills. The long-term educational effects are as predictable as they are unfortunate. The National Science Foundation analyzed not only the six most widely used national standardized tests, but also the tests designed to accompany the four most commonly used science and math textbooks in fourth and eighth grade and high-school classes. These tests were found to focus on lower-level skills (primarily rote memo-rization and application of routine formulas), instead of problem solving and reasoning which curriculum experts say should receive the greater emphasis. The study also noted that since states judge schools and determine teacher assignments based on students' test scores, these tests inadvertently set the agendas of many teachers.[28]

Research done by Herman Epstein shows that formal reason-ing has not been a natural outcome of our current educational process. He discovered that at age eleven, only 5% of the population is at a formal reasoning level. Only one quarter have reached this level by age fourteen, and in adults he found only half are fully functional formal thinkers.[29]

FROM KNOWLEDGE TO MEANING

The final goal of any learning experience should be the crea-tion of meaning. Real knowledge occurs as we take in our rich sensory environment and piece it together in our own unique way to give us a picture of our world. This becomes our reality. Each new experience refers to it, each new experience reorders and expands it.

From this reality, we are able to make decisions and take actions that explore, test and anchor our beliefs and our understanding. The process by which we integrate our experience into a growing understanding of the world should be the prime concern of the educational system. Demonstrating that understanding, through work assignments that require thinking, should be an indispensable part of any learning experience.

Skills manifest as conscious physical responses demonstrating knowledge acquisition. Thinking itself is actually a skill dependent upon the whole, integrated mind/body system. The whole system must be active in order to take in information, select what is important about that information, integrate it with existing patterns and finally, to anchor it with movement. Thinking and learning is anchored by movement.[30-31] Actions such as doodling, eye movements, speaking aloud to oneself or to others, writing things down, are familiar movements that occur during thinking. Without movement of some kind, you don't get conscious thought. The final outcome of this process is meaning.

USE YOUR HEAD — AND YOUR BODY

Real learning — the kind of learning that establishes meaningful connections for the learner — is not complete until there is some output, some physical, personal expression of thought. Much of learning involves the establishment of skills that enable us to express our knowledge. Speaking, writing, computing, drawing, art, playing music, singing, moving gracefully in dance and sports: the development of our knowledge goes hand in hand with the development of the skills that support and express that knowledge.

As we build these skills we use the muscles of our bodies, establishing neuromuscular routes as well as their ties to cognitive routes. Learning is not all in your head. The active, muscular expression of learning is an important ingredient of that learning. This point may seem obvious when you think about it, but not many people are used to thinking about muscles in this way. We tend to relegate muscles to the domain of the body, not the mind. But it is through expression that we advance and solidify our understanding.

Usually this expression takes the form of speech (or sign language in the case of deaf people) or writing, which of course use a great deal of very highly coordinated muscular actions. Language is an indispensable and distinctly human capacity that serves to integrate knowledge and facilitate thought. Humans have other means of expression and integration as well: pictorial, symbolic, musical, gestural, to name a few. And of course there are mediums that blend all or several skills into a unified expression of meaning. Drama, for instance, integrates words, visual elements, bodily demonstration and very often music. Artistic expressions — in drama, music, dance, visual art, literature — represent highly skilled use and integration of body, thought and emotion. Artistic expression is immensely valuable to overall personal development and cognitive understanding.

The same could be said for sports. Athletic activities integrate many different kinds of knowledge with skilled muscular coordination — knowledge about space and time and human dynamics like teamwork, motivation, goal seeking. Educators should not lose sight of their value. Arts and athletics are not frills. They constitute powerful ways of thinking and skilled ways of communicating with the world. They deserve a greater, not lesser portion of school time and budgets.

I am happy to see that with the widespread interest in Howard Gardner's Theory of Multiple Intelligences, schools are including more varied skills and activities in the classroom. According to Gardner's theory, we have seven kinds of intelligence: logical/mathematical, linguistic, visual/spatial, bodily kinesthetic, musical, interpersonal, and intrapersonal.[32] Schools have always emphasized the linguistic and the logical/mathematical intelligences, but often they have neglected the other important ways that we know and learn. Inclusion of the other intelligences in the school curriculum is a positive step toward creation of higher level skills and greater integration of knowledge.

HOW LANGUAGE INTEGRATES BODY, MIND, AND EMOTIONS

> *Language ... is the source of thought. When the child masters language he gains the potentiality to organize anew his perception, his memory; he masters more complex forms of reflection of objects in the external world; he gains the capacity to draw conclusions from his observations, to make deductions, the potentiality of thinking.*
>
> — *Alexander Luria*[33]

Language is perhaps the most spectacular example of integrative processing that engages body, mind and emotion. Through language we powerfully orchestrate and develop our capacity to think. As with other human capacities, understanding how language develops can also help us to understand both how it can be undermined and how it can be encouraged to flourish.

The sensory and motor networks that enable language begin to form very early in life. The natural progression of language occurs as the child moves from a sense of vibration and rhythm in utero to tone and hearing as a toddler. The intricate combination of all these elements leads to speech. The child mimics the intonation and cadence of her models and delights us with the ability to intone first and then to speak. As the child plays with sounds, she develops nerve nets and myelinates nerve fibers to the muscles of the voice box (larynx). She is able to synchronize the tonal vibrations she is hearing with the sounds she makes by learning to contract or relax the muscles of the larynx. Higher tones are produced by more contracted vocal fold muscles, while the long wavelength lower tones depend on lengthened or relaxed muscles. Playing with sounds, even crying, is essential for this motor development.

Movement, through the motor cortex, is very much a part of verbal expression. In Figure 3.4 you will note that almost half of the motor cortex deals directly with vocalization. The motor cortex stimulates muscular movements of the larynx, tongue, mouth, jaw, facial muscles and eyes that form and give expression to the words. Muscular memory of how to form the words appears to be housed in the basal ganglion of the limbic system. Within the basal ganglion is a specialized area called the substantia nigra, which connects the basal ganglion with the frontal lobe — significantly, with those areas that control vocalization and thought. The basal ganglion, especially the substantia nigra (see Figure 5.7), is actively involved in movement, thought and speech. It orchestrates gross motor movements from the cerebellum and fine motor movements from the motor cortex of the frontal lobe to accommodate movement based on thought, including speech.

The neural connections between the motor cortex and the formal reasoning area of the frontal lobe underscore the importance of movement to thought processing. Most people need to discuss, write or draw a picture of new ideas they get. These skills tie directly into the skill of thinking.

Language acquisition entails several essential steps. The ability to discriminate rhythm and tone along with the new-found ability to form words, allows the child a greater sensitivity to dialect or accent. This heightened awareness makes learning a second language easier for children than adults. In order to learn to speak accurately, we must be able to hear the full tone, including the higher harmonics that occur in normal speech.

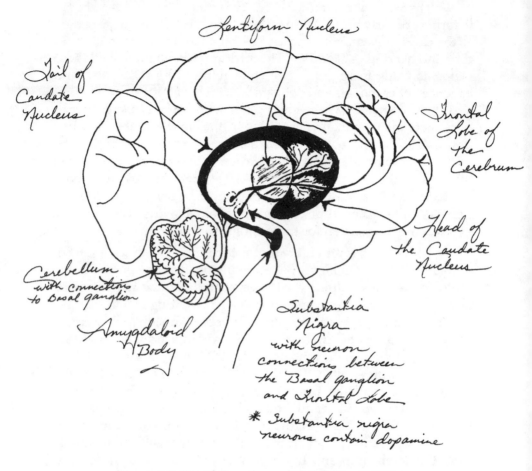

Figure 5.7 Basal Ganglion with Substantia Nigra
Connections to the Frontal Lobe

When these capabilities are impaired, language acquisition suffers. Some observers believe this is actually a widespread problem in our society. According to Jane Healy, "Children are not speaking properly because they're not hearing words pronounced slowly. TV is too fast."[34] Children with recurring ear infections in the first years of life may miss these complex tones, and therefore be more at risk for later specific hearing and speech difficulties.[35]

Children between ages fifteen months and four years gain a

functional sense of objects and people and then categorize and name them. The language-modeling of the caretakers plays a vital part in the learning for the child, and movement facilitates the expression of that learning. Words become playthings to label the world with. The child and its significant others engage in a game of vocabulary building that puts a name to each object. If we go beyond just the name to the object's function, the child can broaden its understanding even more. An example would be: "I can put this on to keep warm," rather than "This is a shirt." Understanding the function of an object rather than just its name, creates a far broader context of the child's relationship with the object. This relational approach accommodates optimal development of the limbic brain that searches out relationships. Since speech and language help us to define our world and our thinking, more open-ended speech may strongly facilitate greater creative thought processing.[36]

Parents should be aware that prior to age four, even though language is progressing, the child is taking most of its behavioral cues from what it sees, not from spoken commands. The parent may have told the child not to do something, but the physical stimulation is so compelling that the sensory fascination overrides the verbal command. The child may even be able to tell the parent what it was told not to do, but without full comprehension of the meaning. My daughter's fascination with the cat, for example, overrode my constant warnings about the cat's justifiable retaliation. Many warnings and scratches later, she finally understood the connection.

Broca's area of the left neocortex of the brain enlarges after age four, insuring the ability to produce clear speech. Wernicke's area also enlarges in the left neocortex, assisting language comprehension that is connected to higher reasoning. This development helps enable children to override motor enticement that would have them do an action even if they were told not to. At approximately four years of age is when parent/child talks begin to become meaningful and effective.

OUTER, STREAM OF CONSCIOUSNESS SPEECH

Once speech is in place, the child will process thought through outer speech until about age seven. I distinctly remember ages four, five, and six as being very verbal times for my daughter. I got to a point where I would cringe every time I heard "Mommy, what ...?" or "Mommy, how ...?" or "Mommy, why ...?" and I found myself looking for a moment of quiet so I could think. The child may talk continuously as she discusses her world and all the new relational insights she is gaining.

Stream of consciousness speech is the problem-solving tool of the four to six year old, and "Why" becomes the generator of that process. This stream of consciousness speech, in varying degrees, is essential to language and thought development. Inner speech development doesn't normally occur until around age seven, so children literally think out loud. I'm sure children of this age wonder if adults ever think because we are so quiet.

So insistent is the need for outer speech, to hear one's own voice and thoughts, that silent reading is ineffective before the age of seven. A whole classroom of children can be focused on reading aloud to themselves or sharing their stories with another person without bothering other classmates.[37]

WHY CHILDREN NEED TO SPEAK

The translation of thought into speech or into the written word is a very complex task. It involves sensory areas, primary auditory, auditory association, primary visual, visual association, motor speech and gnostic areas of the neocortex.[38] Movement becomes a vital part of language as integrated thought patterns are transmitted to the vocalization areas of the motor cortex and basal ganglion of the limbic system to bring thought into the formation of words, first in speech and later in writing.[39] The neocortex is the novelty brain that loves challenges, and language can become a great adventure as it unfolds from age four on.

In Figure 3.4 mapping the functions related to the sensory and motor cortices of the parietal and frontal lobes, you will note the large area of the brain dedicated to sensations and motor function of speech and vocalization. There are more nerve endings going across the temporal-mandibular joint (TMJ) — from sensory neurons or to motor neurons activating muscles of the face — than at any other place in the body. These muscles give us facial expressions that amplify our words and the meaning behind them. They give our eyes expression and they move the tongue, mouth and jaw for enunciation.[40] The concentration in this area of muscles and nerves related to verbalization and expression suggest that it is a prime site for exercises that can enhance communication.[41]

Talking (or signing in the case of deaf children) is essential to language development and to thinking. In most African cultures, children are encouraged to tell stories and repeat myths of the clan as well as to communicate their ideas in the family circle. In our culture, particularly with the advent of TV and video games, children have even less opportunity to interact verbally in a meaningful way.

The Paul Rankin study done in 1928 set daily communication times as 45% listening, 30% speaking, 16% reading and 9% writing.[42] In 1975 Elyse K. Werner did a similar study showing that listening had increased to 54.93%, speaking decreased to 23.19%, reading to 13.27% and writing to 8.61%.[43] In the 1993 American's Use of Time Project, TV takes up 38% of our free time while reading a book, newspaper, or magazine accounts for less than 10% or fewer than 3 hours per week.[44] While the percentage of speaking time was not addressed in this study, my guess is that it accounts for no more than 10%.

We have become a listening society where conversation is becoming a lost art. The importance of talking to a child in full sentences is paramount. This activity allows the child to hear and then mimic full ideas. Books also lay out ideas in complete sentences, thus assisting full thought development. Monosyllabic, incomplete speech patterns, as exhibited in the sitcoms on TV, model and foster incomplete speech patterns even in adults. We begin to think in incomplete sentences which carries over to incomplete idea development. We can hear it in the typical teenage communication of "You know?" "It's like ... you know?" etc. This incomplete language development shows up graphically in students' inability to think and write. "The culprit," Jane Healy maintains, "is diminished and degraded exposure to the forms of good meaningful language that enable us to converse with others, with the written word, and with our own minds."[45]

Parents, teachers, and caregivers who wish to ensure the proper development of all their children's communication skills, need to engage them in full, conscious dialogue. This assists them in developing and trusting their ability to communicate valuable information, creative thoughts and intimate feelings. One of the best gifts a person can give to another person is conscious listening and communication. It becomes reciprocal as both parties learn.

When new ideas are presented, if students are able to verbalize and "flesh out" the ideas with other students, or work together on group projects, the thought becomes anchored in understanding and memory. And yet, how much opportunity do students have to develop and express full ideas in the classroom?

Unfortunately, activities which permit children to talk through their ideas are often seen by teachers and administrators as merely disorderly. However, pedagogical exercises that require quiet, orderly classrooms may actually be inefficient and inappropriate ways of eliciting thinking and understanding. Typical classroom activities that are supposed to promote quiet thinking such as silent reading, filling out worksheets, drills on low level skills and the like, often seem designed more for the purposes of crowd control than education. And sometimes this is the message the children get. As one child recently told me, the activity that teachers in her school call "SSR," (for sustained, silent reading) is universally interpreted by the students to mean "sit down, shut up, and read!"

INNER SPEECH

The final lobe to develop and elaborate, at about age eight, is the frontal lobe. Broca's area of the frontal lobe is the area for development of inner speech. Inner speech naturally occurs and allows a person to process information internally at a much faster rate than verbalization would allow.

As a young child says a word, the movement of that word becomes memory in the basal ganglion and a language pattern is developed. Language elaborates as more and more such patterns are developed. These language patterns correspond to inner images and gestures related to specific sounds. So that when a child hears the word (sound) "NO," it gets an inner image that allows it to stop a certain action. The child starts to use these sounds in outer speech to control its own movements and behavior.

When this language patterning has strengthened, the child can begin to connect the image with a non-verbal sound inside and use inner speech for the control of movement and behavior. These tools are closely linked and necessary to develop reasoning skills.[46]

One out of every three boys in the U.S. is in a remedial reading program by grade 3 (eight years old). Stress — which I will discuss later in greater detail — may be one of the factors that has kept these children functioning in the brain stem and sympathetic nervous system. Their lack of movement has inhibited important pattern development necessary for inner speech and formal reasoning.[47]

Inner speech developed in the same area of the brain that controls skillful movements of the hand. As we evolved into problem solving, tool using animals, the frontal lobe became the center for fine motor coordination, pattern recognition, simultaneous processing of information, high level planning and global thought.[48]

Inner speech also controls social behavior by allowing a person to think of all the consequences of an action before acting. Historically, as people began to band together, increasing complexity and specialization of culture led to self-awareness and monitoring of one's behavior with respect to social norms. We police our minds for antisocial or disruptive impulses through the self-talk we do with inner speech.[49]

In Chapter 4 we discussed the important contribution that emotions make to reasoning and thinking. The frontal lobe is able to synthesize thought with emotion through the thalamocingulate ganglion of the limbic system to give us compassion, reverence for life, unconditional love and all-important play. The link-up of the frontal lobe with the limbic system and social behavior affect the development of a sense of altruism and empathy. Because of its connections with the medial dorsal nucleus of the limbic system (that connects to the stomach), the prefontal cortex receives a strong impulse from the great visceral nerve coming from the stomach area.[50] This feeling in the gut is presumably necessary for an individual's identification with the feelings of others. And this may be necessary for the "insight" to feel a concern for the future of others as well as the self.

It is the full activation and balance of all parts of our mind/body system that allow us to become effective, productive thinkers. With the full development of the neocortex and its integration with the rest of the brain's structures, we are able to creatively play with ideas, use fine motor skills to present them to others, and reach out as human beings to the world at large.

6. ≈

Movement

Movement is the door to learning
— *Paul E. Dennison*

The more closely we consider the elaborate interplay of brain and body, the more clearly one compelling theme emerges: movement is essential to learning. Movement awakens and activates many of our mental capacities. Movement integrates and anchors new information and experience into our neural networks. And movement is vital to all the actions by which we embody and express our learning, our understanding and our selves. So in this chapter, I will focus on movement, particularly on the part it plays in learning. Is what we now know about this subject reflected in the ways we raise our children and the ways they are taught in school? What happens when it isn't?

Movement within the womb gives us our first sense of the world and the beginning knowledge and experience of the laws of gravity. We build on that movement to shape our vision, to explore the shape and form of our environment, and to interact with the people and forces around us.

Every movement is a sensory-motor event, linked to the intimate understanding of our physical world, the world from which all new learning derives. Movement of our head aligns our sensory organs (eyes, ears, nose and tongue) to environmental input. Subtle movements of the eyes enable us to see at a distance, experience three dimensions, sense our periphery and focus on small letters on a page. Refined movements of our hands allow us to touch and manipulate our world in infinitely complex ways. Movement aligns us to pick up smells that will key our memory to events, or sounds that will form internal images for protection and/or understanding. Movement allows us to experience the wind upon our face, just for the learning of it.

Imprinted on the muscular/memory structure of our bodies is not only the knowing of how to sit, stand, walk and run, but where we are in space and how to move with grace and reason — and even to create something beautiful and exquisite in the process. Movement gives our faces the ability to express joy, sadness, anger and love in our very human quest to be understood.

Every number and letter has movement to it. It has a shape felt and imprinted on the musculature so it can be repeated and elaborated through the movement of writing. Through years of learning (movement integrated with sensory input) we are able to play with, reassociate and create new understanding. Through movement we can put thoughts and emotions into words and actions and enrich the world with our creative ideas.

Every time we move in an organized, graceful manner, full brain activation and integration occurs, and the door to learning opens naturally. Howard Gardner, Jean Ayres, Rudolph Steiner, Maria Montessori, Moshe Feldenkreis, Glenn Dolman, Neil Kephardt and many other outstanding innovators in the field of learning espouse the importance of movement to the learning process.

ASSUMPTIONS ABOUT WHAT'S "MENTAL" AND WHAT'S "PHYSICAL"

Part of my purpose in this chapter is also to question a societal prejudice that tends to downgrade physical achievement and minimizes its importance in "serious" endeavors like work and school. Like other deeply held assumptions about the brain which we discussed in earlier chapters, beliefs about the distinctiveness and superiority of human reason have long colored attitudes towards the physical basis of thinking.

The very idea that areas of the brain responsible for movement could be located in the cerebral cortex, presumed to be the province of higher thought, was troubling even to scientists when it was first proposed. The German physicians Eduard Hitzig and Gustav Fritsch first made this discovery in 1864, confirming it by stimulating the cortical surface on living dogs and observing muscular contractions on the opposite sides of the body. When the English neurologist John Hughlings Jackson suggested the existence of a motor cortex within the cerebral hemispheres, he definitely touched a different sort of nerve. "There seems to be an insuperable objection to the notion that the cerebral hemispheres are for movement," he wrote in 1870. "The reason, I suppose, is that the convolutions of the cortex are considered to be *not* for *movement* but for ideas."[1]

This objection still persists today, and in fact is addressed by Howard Gardner in his delineation of the Bodily-Kinesthetic Intelligence:

> A description of use of the body as a form of intelligence may at first jar. There has been a radical disjunction in our recent cultural tradition between the activities of reasoning, on the one hand, and the activities of the manifestly physical part of our nature, as epitomized by our bodies, on the other. This divorce between the "mental" and the "physical" has not infrequently been coupled with a notion that what we do with our bodies is somehow less privileged, less special, than those problem-solving routines carried out chiefly through the use of language, logic, or some other relatively abstract symbolic system.[2]

In addition to many other pertinent observations, Gardner points out that rather than considering motor activity as subservient to "pure" thought, we might follow neuroscientist Roger Sperry in reversing our perspective and consider thinking as an instrument directed to the end of executing actions. "Rather than motor activity as a subsidiary form designed to satisfy the demands of the higher centers, one should instead conceptualize cerebration as a means of bringing `into motor behavior additional refinement, increased direction toward distant, future goals and greater overall adaptiveness and survival value.'"[3]

Learning involves the building of skills, and skills of every manner are built through the movement of muscles — not just the physical skills of athletes, dancers and artisans, but also the intellectual skills used in classrooms and workplaces. Storytellers entertain, teachers teach, politicians lead through the complex muscular expressions of language, speech and gesture. Medicine, art, music, science: competence in these and other professions develops through an intricate internal networking among thought, muscles, and emotions. Skills are all of a piece, muscles are no less important to skill development than any other component.

MOVEMENT ANCHORS THOUGHT

To "pin down" a thought, there must be movement. A person may sit quietly to think, but to remember a thought an action must be used to anchor it. We must materialize it with words. When I write, I'm making connections with thought by moving my hand. I may never need to read what I wrote, but the movement is necessary to gain the thought — build the nerve networks.

Most people find that talking anchors their thinking. Talking is very much a sensory-motor skill, requiring fine motor coordination of millions of facial, tongue, vocal fold and eye muscles, as well as all the proprioceptors in the face. Talking allows us to organize and elaborate our thoughts. When we talk about what we've learned, the physical movements internalize and solidify it in nerve networks. That is why, after presenting new material to a class, I ask them to grab someone and share verbally how the information relates to them personally. Acetylcholine, a neurotransmitter, is released across synapses of activated neurons to stimulate muscle function during talking. Increased and consistent release of acetylcholine at these nerve endings stimulates and attracts dendritic growth in the area, thus increasing nerve networks.

Many of us have a distinct tendency to think better and more freely while engaged in a repetitive, low concentration physical task. I've heard people say they think best when they are swimming laps in a pool, taking a walk, or while shaving. An older woman student in one of my classes spent a whole semester knitting through my lectures, never so much as lifting a pencil to take a note, and finished the course with an A as well as nine sweaters. I myself like to chew, especially crunchy things like carrots, when I'm deep in thought. I realize that movement is actually helping my thinking.

Neuroscientists have sought for some time to find an actual neural link between areas in the brain involved with movement and those involved with cognitive activity. If found, it would explain, for example, why some people with Parkinson's Disease show signs of mental deterioration along with physical degeneration. Only recently, research has shown that two areas of the brain that were associated solely with control of muscle movement, the basal ganglia and the cerebellum, are also important in coordinating thought. These areas are connected to the frontal lobe area where planning the order and timing of future behaviors occurs.[4]

HOW MOVEMENT LEADS TO LEARNING

To understand the basis of this movement-thought link, we must return to our earliest brain development. The baby undergoes a miraculous feat of strength and coordination as it goes from inert lying to walking in its first year. That feat is matched only by the massive elaboration of nerve networks established and learned though practice of each new movement.

As a baby's repertoire of movements grows, each development places the sensory apparatus, especially the ears, mouth, hands, nose and eyes in an increasingly advantageous place for environmental input. The vestibular system is tied to the core muscles of the abdomen and back and it is these muscles that first work to lift the head — a very liberating accomplishment. As the neck muscles strengthen, the child is able to lift the head to hear the world with two ears and start to see it with two eyes. Being held upright on the mother's back or front, as well as lying on the ground, allows the baby to actively work and strengthen its neck muscles.

Incidentally, this leads me to question the wisdom of excessive use of the popular baby carrying seats that double as car seats. These seats keep the baby at a 45 degree angle that inhibits active muscular movements either of the neck or core muscles. Even though the baby's eyes are forward, because movement is inhibited the baby is not as actively developing vision.

The baby explores feet and hands with its mouth bringing the appendage muscles into play. The eyes assist baby's first attempts to roll over as it follows an object with its eyes and uses the core muscles to move the whole body. The core muscles then come into play as the baby strengthens the shoulder girdle area, by lifting the shoulders as well as the head, in response to sensory stimuli.

As the nerve nets to the core muscles elaborate and myelinate from use, the baby is able to hold itself up to sit against gravity and to creep. With practice, first with one end of the body and then the other, the baby goes from scooching to finally being able to crawl. Again, this is highly dependent on core muscle activation so the shoulders and pelvis work together.[5]

We have known for years that children who miss the vitally important crawling stage may exhibit learning difficulties later on. Crawling, a cross-lateral movement, activates development of the corpus callosum (the nerve pathways between the two hemispheres of the cerebrum). This gets both sides of the body working together, including the arms, legs, eyes (binocular vision) and the ears (binaural hearing). With equal stimulation, the senses more fully access the environment and both sides of the body can move in a more integrated way for more efficient action.

A special education teacher told me of her concern as her son went from creeping to walking. She had read all the literature on the importance of crawling to eye teaming development for reading, and definitely didn't want him to miss this stage. So she would crawl over him, not letting him stand up for a good two months. I've occasionally wondered if she didn't replace dyslexia with claustrophobia!

When my daughter came along, I still hadn't read the literature on the importance of crawling. At seven months old she was given a nifty bright green walker with a round bumper bottom that allowed her to run all over the house and afforded my husband and me a great deal of entertainment. Unfortunately, our fun preempted her crawling for longer than a few weeks. When she began having difficulties learning to read in first grade, which demands cross-lateral hand eye coordination, we felt it might have been linked to her lack of crawling.

Ultimately, with all this motor development, the child stands against gravity and learns to balance enough to walk, and very shortly run. It is a mammoth undertaking. The beautifully coordinated and graceful children of rural Africa as they run for long distances or balance nimbly on a rock ledge, provide a magnificent glimpse of the inherent intelligence and beauty of movement.

MOVE MORE, LEARN MORE

It is essential to the learning process to allow children to explore every aspect of movement and balance in their environment, whether walking on a curb, climbing a tree, or jumping on the furniture. A Navajo teacher and mother told me that when she was a child, she and the other children would explore the mesa from early morning until after sunset. Neither she nor any of the other children were ever seriously hurt in this adventure, and she felt it was essential to her total learning process. Yet with current perceptions that the world is a dangerous place for children, she has never allowed her children to go up on the mesa. Without the mesa to explore, the children had made TV their favorite pastime. She admitted her children had movement and balance difficulties. She thought these might also relate to the learning difficulties, especially reading and writing, that they were experiencing in school.

In a study of more than 500 Canadian children, students who spent an extra hour each day in gym class performed notably better on exams than less active children. Similarly, men and women in their 50's and 60's put on a four month aerobic training program of regular brisk walking, increased their performance on mental tests by 10%. And in a close look at thirteen different studies on the exercise/brainpower link, exercise was found to stimulate the growth of developing brains and prevent the deterioration of older brains.[6]

Recent research is helping to explain how movement directly benefits the nervous system. Muscular activities, particularly coordinated movements, appear to stimulate the production of neurotrophins, natural substances that stimulate the growth of nerve cells and increase the number of neural connections in the brain. Animal studies are confirming this link. In a study at the University of California, Carl Cotman found that rats who ran in their exercise wheels had more neurotrophins than sedentary rats.

In another experiment by William Greenough at the University of Illinois, rats who became proficient at the precise, coordinated movements needed to nimbly run across ropes and thin metal bridges had a greater number of connections among the neurons in their brains than rats who were sedentary or rats who merely ran in automated wheels.[7]

MOVEMENT AND VISION

Vision is very much a bodily function. When a child is outside exploring its environment, the eyes and eye muscles are in constant motion. Our visual sense functions most effectively when our eyes are actively moving, taking in sensory information from the environment. When our eyes stop moving, they no longer take in sensory information, and processing is occurring only inside the brain. Notice that when you stare, you miss what is happening in your environment. In an active learning situation, the external eye muscles are constantly moving the eyes up and down, side to side, and all around. The internal eye muscles constrict or dilate the pupil for proper lighting and the ciliary muscles on the lens either lengthen or broaden the lens for far and near vision.

When the body and head move, the vestibular system is activated, and the eye muscles strengthen as they move in response. The more the eyes move, the more the muscles of both eyes work together. Efficient eye teaming enables the student to focus, track and concentrate when reading. As the eye muscles strengthen and move more in concert with each other, more connections to the brain are developed and available.[8] This occurs because 80% of the nerve endings in the muscles are connected directly, via proprioception and the vestibular system, with motor nerves to and from the eyes.[9]

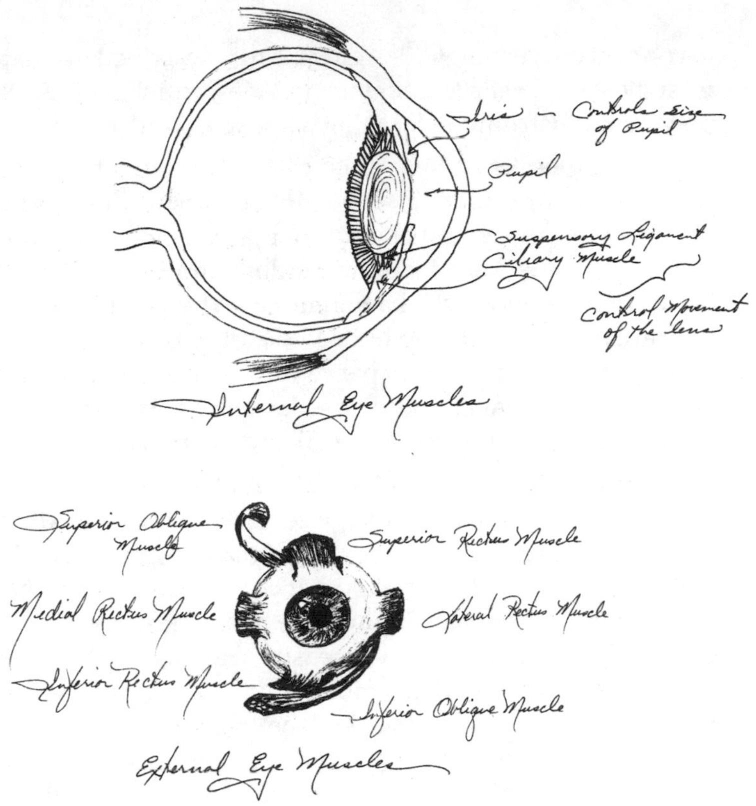

Figure 6.1: Internal and External Muscles of the Eye

I often find that children with learning difficulties experience distress when I ask them to focus on my thumb as I move it through their entire visual field. Their eyes jump, they complain that it hurts, and they have difficulty maintaining their focus. This visual stress, when the eyes don't focus effectively or track together efficiently, is due to inadequate muscular development in the eyes, often caused by lack of movement.

Babies start out following the movements of their hands or feet with their eyes. In time, specific nerve networks elaborate and hand-eye coordination develops. The baby is able to bring the objects of the world to the eye for scrutiny and learning. Hand/eye, foot/eye coordination then allows the infant to accurately move in response to objects in its environment. With practice and maturation of the networks, a shift occurs and eye-hand coordination develops. The eye now leads the hand movements, so that the vast array of internal knowledge becomes the template for movement. We can now learn to connect movement with sight as Amy, described in Chapter 1, did with the soccer ball. This connection is essential in writing, drawing, playing an instrument, learning a sport or dancing.

The muscles of the eye also play an important part in classroom learning. Before entering school, three-dimensional and peripheral vision allow the greatest environmental learning. They integrate the visual with the kinesthetic to understand shapes, movement of natural forms and spatial awareness. When children enter school, they are often expected to quickly develop their foveal focus for up close, two-dimensional paper work. At school, foveal focus is necessary to see small, static, two-dimensional letters on a page. The transition from three-dimensional and peripheral to foveal focus is very abrupt and in many cases unnatural.

Before approximately age seven, the ciliary bodies (muscles that shape the lens of the eye) are short, causing the lens to be thin and elongate. With the lens in this shape, the incoming image is spread out across the retina, bringing into play maximum rod and cone stimulation. This lens shape easily accommodates three-dimensional, peripheral and distance vision. At about age seven, these muscles lengthen, allowing the lens to round out and more easily focus the image only on the fovea centralis of the retina for natural foveal focus.[10] Children who have looked at books in the home may have already acquired some foveal focus if the process was their choice and free of stress and pressure to perform.

A TALE OF TWO CULTURES

As with many cultural expectations in the area of learning and child development, the norms of other societies can throw ours into stark relief and raise important questions about things we take for granted. A few years ago, I encountered a fascinating and tragic example of what can happen in this area when two different cultures intersect.

In South Africa, rural African children without available books absorb a rich oral tradition, and have excellent three-dimensional and peripheral vision. Traditionally they can speak three different languages, though they are usually not conversant in English. At the age of five when they first enter school, they have been found by occupational therapists in Kuazulu to be "far superior" to the white children on all but three of the pre-school tests.[11] At this point, they attend the British Standard Schools where they are expected to read the alphabet within the first two weeks, and read English within the first year. However, because their eyes have not yet developed the lens flexibility for foveal focus, they perceive only a blur when looking at a written page. The curriculum is not set up to allow time for foveal focus development. Though these children are highly motivated to learn and have strong family support, they experience humiliation and failure and 25.4% drop out in that first year of school.[12] Due to unnatural expectations, stress and lack of adequate time to develop foveal focus, South Africa has lost, and will continue to lose, a valuable resource in these children.

HOW ARE OUR SCHOOLS DOING?

It's easy to see, when it's pointed out, where the South African schools go wrong. But how well do our schools accommodate the natural evolution of children's movement skills and needs? And how well are our expectations and understanding of their development synchronized with the expectations and tasks we impose on them?

From the earliest grades, school children are taught not to move their bodies during class. They are also taught not to move their eyes beyond a blackboard or their desk. But these restrictions ignore the fact that seeing and "lens resiliency" are intimately connected with movement. The eye ball is not completely shaped with collagen fibers until approximately age nine.[13] Therefore, long periods of reading without relaxing the focus into the distance could possibly cause inflammation and the enlargement of the eyeball leading to myopia or near-sightedness.

Much eyestrain comes from foveal focus overdependence, staring and lack of blinking. Blinking is important because it serves to keep the eye moist and healthy as well as to relax the focus. So it should be encouraged and breaks taken every 7-10 minutes where the eyes can reestablish three-dimensional and peripheral vision in a relaxed, natural way.[14]

Regarding myopia there are three areas of agreement among researchers: 1) significant amounts of myopia occur at an earlier age today than in the past, 2) myopia shows an increase in incidence and amounts as a child progresses from second grade through high school, and 3) today's incidence of myopia is higher than even 20 years ago.[15] F.A. Young demonstrated a significant development of myopia in monkeys by restricting their visual space.[16] Myopia has also been related to high anxiety in the learning environment.[17]

A double-blind study with 538 sixth grade students was

conducted in the Cheshire, Texas, Public School System in 1974. The experimental students performed a half-hour of daily activities, oriented to motor learning and motor-sensory development while the control students did not. The experimental subjects were also allowed more freedom to vary their activity, thereby not having to maintain near focus for the usual long periods of time. The experimental group exhibited a statistically significant lower incidence of myopia, lower test anxiety, and a higher level of academic success.[18]

WHEN ARE THE EYES READY FOR READING?

By age seven or eight, as the frontal lobes of the cerebrum mature, fine motor coordination of muscles throughout the body naturally develops. Before then, we have good peripheral and depth vision, but it is only when the frontal eye field of the frontal lobes matures that accurate enough eye teaming is possible for two-dimensional focus. Eye teaming occurs when the dominant eye tracks across a page of writing and the non-dominant eye follows the movements exactly and blends the information, giving optimal binocular vision. Because we have a nose between our two eyes, we will never have true binocular vision. Therefore, one eye takes the lead, as the dominant eye, to guide the movements of both eyes.

This laterality can be demonstrated by focusing both eyes on a vertical pen held at arm's length and aligned to a vertical structure in the room. Then alternate closing eyes, noticing which eye holds the image of the pen. That is the dominant tracking eye. These fine motor movements ensure ease of information gathering and point to another physiological reason for not starting the reading process until age seven or, preferably, age eight.

VISION AND STRESS

In emotionally stressful situations, an interesting phenomenon occurs that makes it virtually impossible to track across a page of writing. As a reflex response to the sensation of danger, the eyes move peripherally so they can take in as much of the environment as possible. This makes it extremely difficult for the eyes to team and track across a page of writing. Try reading something right after you've seen a scary movie or been in a traumatic situation. I think you will find if very difficult.

When people live with continually stressful circumstances, their outer eye muscles may tend to strengthen, lengthening the inner eye muscles and making foveal focus and tracking even more difficult. Sexually abused or traumatized children exhibit what is called "wall eye" with both eyes in a sustained peripheral focus. When I work with children in special education classes, I find the eyes are always a factor. Just the act of having to track my finger back and forth causes their eyes to hurt and be jumpy. No wonder these children have problems reading and don't want to read. Their muscles hurt and must be retrained before they can comfortably read! As we shall see in the next chapter, Brain Gym provides a simple way to easily activate all the muscles of the eyes. The exercises reduce the stress reaction and assist with ease of reading and comprehension.

Movement is an indispensable part of learning and thinking. Each movement becomes a vital link to learning and thought processing. Just as with our sensory systems, all of us must develop our own elaborate nerve networks of movement patterns, an "action encyclopedia." Thinking is a response to our physical world. In studying the brain, we can only understand it in the context of a physical reality, an action reality. Movement is an integral part of all mental processing, from the atomic movement that fires the molecular movement that orchestrates the cellular (electrical) movement, to the thought made manifest in action.

7. ≈

Brain Gym

In 1986 I was asked to become part of a Hawaiian intermediate school as a Comprehensive Student Alienation Program (CSAP) counselor and tutor. The students I would work with had learning or emotional difficulties and therefore were considered alienated from the school program. It was an experiment for me. Here I was, a trained neurobiologist and professor of biology at the University of Hawaii, having taught college biology for over twenty years, with no psychology or counseling background, asked to work with alienated, pubertal, intermediate kids. All this because I had successfully used accelerated learning techniques with my college classes, and I was just gutsy and curious enough to say "YES."

I had never worked with this age group before, so I spent three weeks during the summer of 1986 on the staff of Supercamp, an accelerated learning program for kids ages 13-17, to gain understanding about students of this age and background. Some of these kids had been adjudicated from New York City on scholarships from the New York City Police Department. It was great training for me in being accepting, open, non-judgmental and capable of seeing the potential in every person. My daughter, who had just turned 12, also consented to give me pointers. And so by the beginning of the new school year the stage was set for this strange experiment in my life.

MY INTRODUCTION TO BRAIN GYM

Having an open and accepting attitude was not, however, the same as having an actual program for helping the troubled children I would face back in Hawaii. At this point, a Nurse Practitioner friend suggested I use Brain Gym with these kids. It had been life-transforming for her son Todd, and I was open to anything that might work.

Todd, though bright and loveable, had been certified learning disabled. As a sophomore in high school he still could not read though the family had spent thousands of dollars on learning programs.

At age 16, Todd was 6 feet, 2 inches tall and the basketball team had recruited him to give them some height. But alas he was clumsy, tripping over the ball as he attempted to dribble down the floor.

In that year his mother attended a Touch For Health conference in California where Dr. Paul Dennison first spoke of his work with learning disabilities and the Brain Gym program. She returned home very excited announcing, "Todd, we're going to Cross Crawl." To get Todd to participate, the whole family Cross Crawled every morning before Todd went to school and every evening before bed. Within six weeks Todd was reading at grade level. He became an important addition to the basketball team soon after.

All the pieces of learning had been there for over ten years but Todd had been unable to integrate them. It took the Brain Gym activities to finally fit the pieces together. A highly successful student, Todd has now completed a college degree in biology.

I figured if something so simple as Brain Gym worked for Todd, it was worth a try. At first I simply followed directions on how to do specific activities that were supposed to activate full mind/body function. I had no preconceived notions as to what would happen with these CSAP kids, but they seemed to enjoy the Brain Gym, and it fit in with my experiment.

Not knowing the protocol, I chose to work with these students without looking at their charts or past histories. What happened next surprised them, and me, and their teachers. They were finally succeeding and in charge of their own lives, emotionally, physically and mentally.

The principal was so impressed he had me make an inservice presentation to teachers, even though my training in the work was minimal. He also signed me up to make a four hour presentation to all the principals on the island. In an attempt to understand the shifts I was seeing in the students I took the Brain Gym In-Depth training a little while later in November, 1986. Thus began my eight year — and continuing — search to understand the molecular, cellular, physical and neurological aspects of this profound work.

MICRO-INTERVENTIONS LEAD TO MAJOR CHANGES

We are all natural learners, born with a remarkable mind/body system equipped with all the elements necessary for learning. Various stressors, however, can introduce blocks that inhibit the learning process. (We will be discussing stress and its impact on learning in the third part of this book.) Frequent ear infection, for instance, is a kind of stressor that may impact learning success. The system is not seriously damaged by the infections and is still theoretically taking in all the information necessary to learn, but learning may be stalled. The learner has difficulty assimilating and integrating new information.

Brain Gym appears to contribute the minor adjustments necessary to enable the system to proceed with the learning process. Dr. Dee Coulter, a cognitive specialist and neuroscience educator who has worked extensively with learning difficulties, refers to these minor adjustments as micro-interventions. She explains that these bring about major change because they supply the necessary integration and also reverse the expectation of failure.[1]

I have seen many such micro-interventions take place after using Brain Gym. Once I worked with an eleven year old Down's Syndrome boy whose teacher had worked daily with him for three months in an attempt to have him learn his numbers 1-10. He had a chart that had the numerals in order on the top line, the numbers written out as words on the middle line, and pictures of objects on the bottom line (e.g., one apple, two shirts, three trees, etc.). His job was to take a laminated card and match it with the appropriate numeral, written number or figure on the chart.

As hard as he tried, he could not "get it." He would pick up a 3, say "seven", and place it on the 10. When reminded it was a 3, he would say "three," but then lay it down on a 5. After using every technique she knew, both the teacher and the student had become extremely frustrated with the project.

I asked him if he would be willing to do a Dennison Laterality Repatterning (discussed below), which he was pleased and excited to do. This series of activities took about fifteen minutes, after which he said he was ready to do his numbers again. He sat back down at the chart, picked up a 3, said "three" and placed it on the 3 in the chart. He immediately picked up a 7, said "seven" and put it on the 7, continuing until the whole chart was filled correctly. I felt the back of my chair shudder a bit and turned to see the teacher with big tears running down her cheeks.

The next day he drank water, did two minutes of Cross Crawl, Brain Buttons and Hook-Ups and then sat down and correctly filled in the chart again. He was given another chart he had never seen, which had the numbers mixed up. He easily and correctly placed all the laminated chips on it. Somehow he had been taking in the information, but it took a "micro-intervention," Dennison Laterality

Repatterning, to link the information up and make it useful.

These micro-interventions are seen on a regular basis by people who use this work for themselves and with others. The examples are simple but profound. Here is a graphic example of one first grade boy's immediate, demonstrable improvement in writing after a few minutes of doing some Brain Gym exercises.

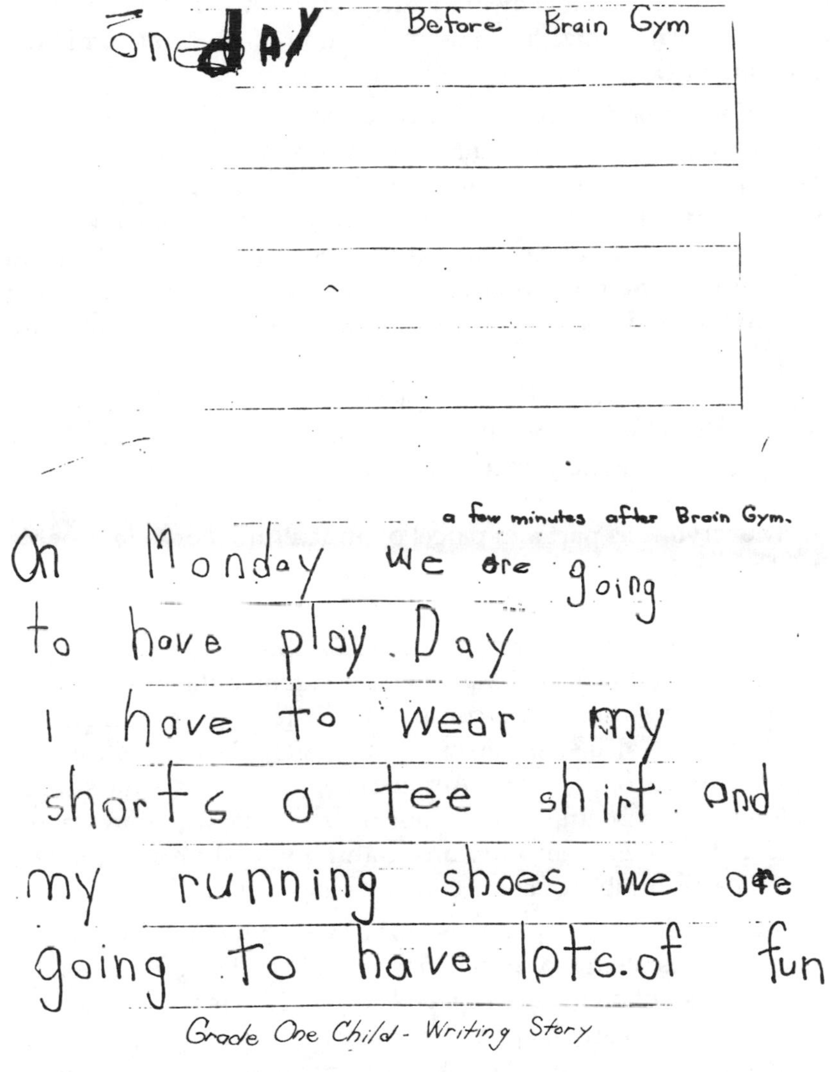

One day   Before   Brain Gym

a few minutes after Brain Gym.

On Monday we are going to have play. Day
I have to wear my shorts a tee shirt and my running shoes we are going to have lots. of fun

Grade One Child - Writing Story

Figure 7.1: First Grade Boy's Improvement in Writing after Brain Gym

EVEN THOUGH IT'S SIMPLE AND EASY, IT DOES WORK

Our society today needs something simple and elegant to initiate and accomplish these micro-interventions. Every learning situation deals basically with the same steps: sensory input, integration and assimilation, and action. Brain Gym facilitates each step of the process by waking up the mind/body system, and bringing it to learning readiness. It activates full mind/body function through simple integrative movements which focus on specific aspects of sensory activation and facilitate integration of function across the body mid line.

The importance of movement in the learning process should be clear from the preceding chapters. As teachers in many cultures have intuitively recognized, numbers, letters and writing can all be taught effectively with lots of movement. Rudolph Steiner, to mention only one noteworthy example believed in helping children to learn through the process of eurhythmia, which anchors learning with rhythm and specific coordinated movements similar to Brain Gym.[2]

The greatest obstacle to full, widespread use of Brain Gym is the strongly held misconception in our society that mind and body are separate — that movement has nothing to do with intellect. Like the air we breathe, this particular misinformation is taken in by nearly everyone as part and parcel of our cultural heritage. People simply find it hard to believe that physical activities can help you think.

And yet many of America's foremost brain researchers gathered in Chicago the first of May, 1995, to examine the link between movement and learning. Exercise, besides shaping up bones, muscles, heart and lungs also strengthens the basal ganglia, cerebellum and corpus callosum of the brain. Aerobic exercise increases the supply of blood to the brain. But a coordinated series of movements produces increased neurotrophins (natural neural growth factors) and a greater number of connections among neurons.[3]

It also doesn't help the case for Brain Gym that these coordinated exercises seem too simple to work. Most of us put more faith in complex solutions to problems. If a program is not hard, time-consuming and costly it appears to have less value. But, as we are able to step past our limited thinking, we are finding out that simple common-sense solutions often produce the most profound results.

SOME BACKGROUND ON BRAIN GYM

I am greatly indebted to Dr. Paul Dennison, who, in his struggle to find a way through his own dyslexia and visual difficulties, put together the Brain Gym program. His integrity, depth of understanding, and love for children and for learning shine through in his elegant work. Paul Dennison developed Brain Gym in the 1970's at the Valley Remedial Group Learning Center in California, where he had been helping children and adults for nineteen years. As an educator all his professional life, his discoveries were based on an understanding of the interdependence of physical development, language acquisition, and academic achievement. Brain Gym grew out of his background in curriculum development and experimental psychology at the University of Southern California, where his research focused particularly on beginning reading achievement and its relationship to covert speech skills.

For more than seventy years, pioneers in sensory-motor training, applied kinesiology and developmental optometry had provided statistical research relating the effects of movement to learning. Dennison began his synthesis of this work in 1969. Over the years, he incorporated Dr. Constance Amsden's Malabar Reading Project, the breakthroughs of Drs. Doman and Delacato,[4] the work of Dr. Louis Jacque and Dr. Samuel Herr, O.D. (leading pioneers in vision training), the work of optometrist Dr. G.N. Getman, Doctor of Chiropractic Richard Tyler and sports kinesiologist Bud Gibbs. Dennison adapted this research, particularly as it related to children with specific language disabilities, into quick, simple, task-specific movements that benefit any learner.

Since establishment of the Educational Kinesiology Foundation in 1987, research projects using Brain Gym have sprung up worldwide with remarkable results. My first attempt to quantify the effects of Brain Gym occurred in 1989 with nineteen fifth grade Special Education students. Their teacher used the Brigance Inventory of Basic Skills test to pre- and post-test these students at the beginning and end of a one year school period. Each student was repatterned and used approximately 5 to 10 minutes of Brain Gym daily. As you will note from the graphs in Figure 7.2 on the next page, the results showed a one to two year average gain for all students on the reading and reading comprehension test and an average gain of at least a year for more than 50% of the students on math. These results, especially in reading, were highly unusual for a whole class of special education students. The most surprising results were the remarkable improvements in self-esteem and in their ability to focus on task.

Brigance Inventory of Basic Skills
Reading & Comprehension

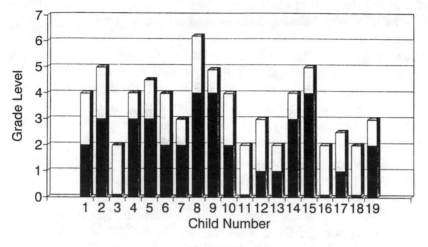

Math Scores

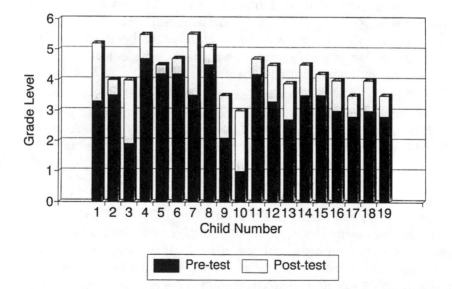

Figure 7.2: Changes in Brigance Inventory of Basic Skills Test Scores of Fifth Grade Special Education Students after A Year of Brain Gym

In 1988 I was part of a guest delegation of twelve educators to the Soviet Union with the Association of Humanistic Psychologists (AHP) Soviet Project. Our job was to work with Soviet educators and introduce effective teaching technologies. I introduced Brain Gym and left fifty Brain Gym manuals with the Institutes of Pedagogical Sciences, in Moscow and St. Petersburg (then Leningrad). One of these books made its way into the hands of Svetlana Masgutova, head of the Accent Institute of Psychology in Orechovo-Zoueva, Russia. In 1991, she asked me to come and meet with some psychologists and medical doctors that she had introduced to Brain Gym. At this time she told me of her extraordinary experiences with this body of work.

In 1989 there had been a serious train explosion an hour and a half from Moscow. Dr. Masgutova had been put in charge of working with the severely traumatized, surviving children. She used every professional tool she had with these badly burned children including art therapy. The pictures they drew were of charred, one-eyed monsters and burning horses depicted in dark tones. After three months, over half of the children had died. The rest were symptomatically depressed, continuing to draw horrifying pictures in their art therapy sessions.

At that time Dr. Masgutova discovered the basic Brain Gym manual on a visit to the Moscow Institute of Pedagogical Science. She immediately started using the activities with the children and within several weeks the pictures they were drawing changed. Bright colors emerged along with rainbows, butterflies and children running through meadows. All of the children exhibited positive perspectives and were healing. This so surprised her, the medical doctors and the children's parents that at the end of six months she compiled her carefully kept records and wrote a professional paper.[5] Experts throughout Russia were interested and invited her to give talks.

When I arrived to teach in 1991, she had assembled fifty psychologists and medical doctors from the Moscow/St. Petersburg area and also from an institute in Tomsk, Siberia, that had been using Brain Gym. They shared with me their remarkable successes with people of all ages, with every problem imaginable. Currently, fifteen major cities in Russia are using the Brain Gym work, with great success.

In 1991 in Botswana, I was invited to work with trainees of the Botswana Insurance Company that were preparing for their Insurance exams. Though people had taken the exam each year, the pass rate had hovered at less than 30%. After my six hour session with these people in February, they committed themselves to continue using Brain Gym when they studied. Every single one of them passed the exam in May. One man named, Walks Tall, had worried the examiner by spending the first 30 minutes of the timed test doing Brain Gym. He was the first person in Southern Africa to receive 100% on the Insurance Exam.

Brain Gym is even playing a part in the emergence of a new South Africa. In late 1993, the Town Council of Verwoerdburg, Pretoria was developing a process to empower their semi- and illiterate trainees and decided to use Brain Gym in a pilot study. An experimental group and control group of eight semi- and illiterate trainees were chosen by the Town Council. The experimental group was exposed to Brain Gym activities over a three day period by Andre Vermeulen, a Brain Gym instructor with Destinatum Ltd. Two weeks after the experimental group had been exposed to Brain Gym, trainers from the Affirmative Vision organization presented the same Life Skills course (Basic Orientation to Modern Society) to the experimental and control group in an identical manner in the same language, Northern Sotho (the mother tongue of the trainees). All variants including time spans, breaks, presenters, translator, content, tests, and workshops were kept the same.

Upon testing the content of the five day course, the evaluators found that the experimental group tested 27.7% better than the control group. They also found that the experimental group was much more confident, creative, attentive, relaxed during training, at ease during testing and involved in the workshops. They had more insights and also more positive attitudes, expressing their desire to learn. Because of this pilot study, banks and mining companies in South Africa are incorporating Brain Gym into their training programs.

BRAIN GYM ENHANCES PERFORMANCE TOO

Brain Gym is also highly effective with sports, music, art and dance of every kind. In order to perform well in any of these, a person must be able to master technique and integrate that mastery with rhythm, flow, emotion and image in a spontaneous way. I have taught Brain Gym to technically good musicians who found they could finally feel and express the passion in the music they played. Visual artists I have taught were stunned by the depth of expression they could achieve in their work. Brain Gym is used in a course called Switched-On Golf that many golfers now consider their secret weapon.

In Hawaii, I was invited to work with a soccer team of boys ages 14 - 16 who wanted to win the state championship. They were good players but all too often, they lost their "cool" during games, got penalties and lost. I did one Brain Gym session with these boys as they focused on this goal: "we are calm, cool and collected and win the state championship." Until the tournament the boys voluntarily carried and drank lots of water and did Cross Crawls, Brain Buttons and Hook-ups (the PACE program discussed below) before and in the middle of each practice and game. Their whole game improved and they qualified for the state championship play-off in Honolulu. There, they easily won the first two playoff games and advanced to the final championship game. The tension during this make or break game was very high and the boys began to lose their cool. During a time out, the boys spontaneously lay on the field and did Hook-Ups as the coach, parents and everyone else looked on in amazement. Then they stood up and won the state championship.

The tremendous contribution and appeal of Brain Gym is its ease and utility. People can do the exercises at any time to enhance anything they do. It is simply movement, free and easy.

A BRAIN GYM SAMPLER

I will go over a few of the Brain Gym movements discussed in the book and their function in maintaining balanced mind/body learning,[6] beginning with a readiness routine we call PACE. PACE stands for *Positive, Active, Clear and Energetic* learning. It is a learning readiness sequence that is usually done at the beginning of the school day, after recess and after lunch to effectively prepare the student for learning. I do it prior to any activity I want to be totally integrated for. It includes drinking **water** for energetic learning and then doing Brain Buttons, Cross Crawls and Hook-Ups.

BRAIN BUTTONS

Brain Buttons are done by placing one hand over the navel while the other hand stimulates points between the ribs. The hand over the navel brings attention to the gravitational center of the body. Here lie the core muscles, important contributors to bodily balance. This action alerts the vestibular system, which stimulates RAS activation to wake up the brain for incoming sensory input. If a person is staring (in ocular lock), this vestibular activation will get the eyes moving again so the brain has access to external visual information.[7]

Figure 7.3: Brain Buttons

The other hand gently rubs the indentations between the first and second ribs directly under the collar bone (clavicle), to the right and left of the sternum. This is thought to stimulate blood flow through the carotid arteries to the brain. The carotid arteries are the first arteries out the heart. Their job is to carry freshly oxygenated blood to the brain. The Brain Buttons lie just above where the two carotid arteries branch. Baroreceptors (pressoreceptors) in the walls of the carotid arteries may account for the effects noticed when rubbing these points. Baroreceptor nerve cells are capable of responding to changes in blood pressure and (through the carotid sinus reflex) maintain normal blood pressure to the brain.[8]

I first realized the value of Brain Buttons when I was teaching an evening course at the University of Hawaii after working at the elementary school all day. The 25 minute drive home after class was deadly. I would find myself falling asleep at the wheel. My students had been doing Brain Buttons as part of PACE at the beginning of the class and I remembered their comments that it really woke them up and got them ready to learn even after their long work day. So I pulled the car over and did my Brain Buttons. It was as if a fog had lifted and I was able to stay alert for the rest of the drive. Many of my students have commented that it brings them back to focus when they are taking a test.

CROSS CRAWL

The Cross Crawl is simply a cross-lateral walking in place. By touching the right elbow to the left knee and then the left elbow to the right knee, large areas of both brain hemispheres are being activated simultaneously. Cross Crawling is like consciously walking, which facilitates balanced nerve activation across the corpus callosum. When done on a regular basis, more nerve networks form and myelinate in the corpus callosum, thus making communication between the two hemispheres faster and more integrated for high level reasoning.

The Cross Crawl movements should be performed very slowly. When the exercise is done slowly, it requires more fine motor involvement and balance, consciously activating the vestibular system and the frontal lobes. The more fine muscle involvement, the more frontal lobe involvement in conjunction with the basal ganglion of the limbic brain and the cerebellum of the brain stem.

Figure 7.4: Cross Crawl

This simple movement is elegant in activating full brain function and major diffusion into the frontal lobes. Whenever I get stuck, as with writer's block, I Cross Crawl or take a walk, and the ideas begin to flow again. Robert Dustman, director of neuropsychology research at the Veterans Affairs Medical Center in Salt Lake City, Utah, found walking to improve mental performance in 50 to 60 year old men and women. He first administered mental and physical tests to a group of relatively inactive men and women in their 50's and 60's. He put the subjects on a four month program of regular brisk walking. At the end of the four months, their performance on the same series of mental tests jumped by 10%.[9]

Cross Crawl is excellent for activating full mind/body function before physical activities like sports, or dance. There are many variations on the Cross Crawl that can be found in the Brain Gym manuals.[10]

HOOK-UPS

Hook-Ups are done by first crossing one ankle over the other, whichever feels most comfortable. The hands are then crossed, clasped and inverted. To do this, stretch your arms out in front of you, with the back of the hands together and the thumbs pointing down. Now lift one hand over the other, palms facing and interlock the fingers. Then roll the locked hands straight down and in toward the body so they eventually rest on the chest with the elbows down. This complex crossover action has a similar integrative effect in the brain as the Cross Crawl. In a balanced way, it consciously activates the sensory and motor cortices of each hemisphere of the cerebrum.

While in this position, rest your tongue on the roof of your mouth behind the teeth (hard palette). This action brings attention to the mid-brain which lies right above the hard palette, and also helps to release a tongue thrust caused by postural imbalance. This configuration connects emotions in the limbic system with reason in the frontal lobes of the cerebrum, thus giving an integrative perspective from which to learn and respond more effectively.[11]

As a counselor, I had a two minute rule. When students (ages 5-15) were sent to me for being disruptive in the classroom, or following a playground fight, they had to sit in Hook-Ups for two minutes before we talked. This consciously brought attention to the motor cortex of both frontal hemispheres and away from the survival centers in the reptilian brain, thus decreasing adrenalin production. Following the two minutes they were able to see both their own and each others' points of view more clearly. None of these students wanted to "get in trouble," and they were grateful to have a tool they could personally use, at any time, to control their own behavior.

Figure 7.5: Hook-Ups

This is my most frequently used Brain Gym exercise. Teachers often use it for themselves when their stress levels rise, and also to quiet and refocus students after changes like recess or lunch.

I invite you to do an experiment. Concentrate on a stressful or extremely challenging situation in your life. Notice where you tense up, where you feel muscles tighten, how your breathing is, and any other personal reactions. Then sit, stand or lie down in Hook-Ups for two to five minutes. Notice the differences in muscle thightness, breathing and outlook after this time. The situation is the same, but the whole mind/body system is being used to handle it more efficiently.

Following is a sampling of other Brain Gyms that work for specific skills development.

LAZY 8'S FOR WRITING

The Lazy 8 for writing is a pencil and paper exercise specifically geared to improve written communication. Lazy 8's for writing are excellent for establishing the necessary rhythm and flow for good hand/eye coordination. To do a Lazy 8 you draw an infinity symbol (a sideways eight) on paper or chalkboard with a flowing continuous movement. Start at the middle, draw counterclockwise first: up, over and around; then clockwise: up, over, around and back to the midpoint. Five or more continuous repetitions are done with each hand and five or more with both hands together. This is best done large at first (but within the visual field), to stimulate large muscles, and on a surface to stimulate tactile awareness.[12] This action relaxes the muscles of the hands, arms and shoulders as well as facilitating visual tracking.

Figure 7.6: Lazy 8's For Writing

You can experience the integration this activity brings by thinking of something you need to communicate in writing. Notice how tightly you are holding the pen as you begin to write. How clear are your thoughts? Now write a few sentences and notice if the ideas flow easily or if there is effort in communicating what you want to say. Do the horizontal 8 as big as an $8\,^1/_2$ x 11 inch sheet of paper. Then write a few sentences again, noticing how tightly you hold the pen, how clear your thoughts are and if you are now able to communicate with ease.

Lazy 8's are very helpful to me when I get writer's block. Students also find them very helpful when taking a test. If they start to feel stressed and realize that their thinking has become homolateral, they simply do some Lazy 8's on their desk tops with their fingers and experience cross-lateral integration again. Then they can find the answers more easily.

LAZY 8'S FOR EYES

Lazy 8's for eyes are similar to the Lazy 8's for writing except that the focus here is on eye movements and improving hand/eye and eye/hand coordination. These Lazy 8's are done by training the eyes on a moving thumb as it describes an infinity sign in the visual field. To do this, hold either thumb at eye level in the mid-field of the body at approximately an elbow length from the eyes. For maximum muscular activation the movements should be slow and conscious. Holding the head still, but relaxed, and just moving the eyes to follow the thumb, move the thumb directly up the center of the mid-field to the top of the visual field and then counterclockwise out around and down to the left side. As the thumb reaches the lower mid-field of the visual field bring it back up the center and clockwise out, around and down the right side. This should be continued in an even flowing movement at least three times with each hand. Then both hands should be clasped with the thumbs forming an X. While focusing on the center of the X, again follow the clasped thumbs through the Lazy 8 pattern.

Figure 7.7: Lazy 8's For Eyes

This activity effectively strengthens the extrinsic eye muscles, assisting network development and myelination from the frontal eye field area for fine motor tracking. It also sets up learning patterns that coordinate hand/eye and eye/hand muscle alignment.

The Lazy 8 pattern can also be drawn in a three-dimensional field close to and away from the eyes. In this version of the exercise the plane of the figure 8 is shifted 90 degrees so that it is now perpendicular to the body. This exercise works the intrinsic muscles that hold the lens and determine pupil size. Starting at the midpoint, move the thumb up and away from your body as you circle the outer loop, then move up through the midpoint and toward your eyes as you circle the nearer loop. Again, this should be done in a free-flowing pattern with only the eyes and hand moving.

People with glasses might want to take them off so the visual field is not pre-empted by the rims of the glasses. If done right, you should feel maximal muscle movement, equally in both eyes. This means you may feel like you've been doing push-ups with your eyes if the muscles are a bit weak.

This is often difficult for people who have been under a great deal of stress. One student I worked with, who had been in a sexually abusive situation for years, could only do a few of these at a time without pain in the eye muscles. It had been impossible for her to read, because in her chronic state of stress her outer eye muscles had strengthened for peripheral vision and her inner eye muscles were very weak. In this condition she was unable to bring her eyes into focus for two-dimensional foveal focus or to track across a page of reading. With persistence, over a month's time, the muscular movements of her eyes became stronger and more balanced so she was able to achieve foveal focus and finally read.

Lazy 8's are an important activity for me after working on the computer. I can start to feel the eye strain setting in, which also causes my neck muscles to tighten and my shoulders to become sore. By doing the Lazy 8's for eyes, my eyes and shoulders relax and I'm able to continue with my work.

THE ELEPHANT

This is one of the most integrative of the Brain Gym activities. It is done by placing the left ear on the left shoulder, tight enough to hold a piece of paper between the two, then extending the left arm like a trunk. With knees relaxed, the arm draws a Lazy 8 pattern in the mid-field, again starting up the middle and out and around with eyes following the movement past the finger tips. For increased effectiveness, it should be done slowly three to five times on the left and an equal number of times with the right ear against the right shoulder.

The Elephant activates all areas of the mind/body system in a balanced way. The movement is mainly from the core muscles, activating the vestibular system, especially the semicircular canals. Hand/eye coordination is also involved, all orchestrated by the basal ganglion of the limbic system in conjunction with the cerebellum and sensory motor cortices of the cerebrum with emphasis on the frontal lobes. Visual input activates the occipital lobe and, if elephant sounds are added, the hearing mechanisms within the temporal lobes.

Figure 7.8: The Elephant

People who have experienced chronic ear infections find the Elephant extremely challenging, but see major results with improved balance and equilibrium within a few weeks. If done on a regular basis, the Elephant stimulates the whole vestibular system, re-establishing nerve networks that might have been damaged during ear infections. Elephants are highly recommended for people labeled ADD, as this exercise assists full activation of the Reticular Activating System, thus improving attention.

THE THINKING CAP

The Thinking Cap wake up the whole hearing mechanism and assists memory. It is done by unrolling the outer ears from top to bottom several times. It might be interesting for you to try this simple experiment: Close your eyes and listen for a few minutes. Are you hearing things equally with both ears? Does one ear seem bigger, or is it hearing more clearly than the other? Are any sounds muffled? If you are in a noisy environment, are you able to pick out individual sounds? Now, unroll your ears about three times on each side and close your eyes again. Notice the difference.[13]

Figure 7.9: The Thinking Cap

The link between hearing in the temporal lobe and memory in the limbic system appears to be very strong. My students at the University of Hawaii found the Thinking Cap to be very useful when needing to recall some technical information for an essay or exam. They also begin using this activity when I'd say "I want you to remember this information." Often, if I can't remember a person's name or the reference for an article, I do the Thinking Cap and the answer pops into my mind. Just the act of physically stimulating the tactile receptors in the outer ear, wakes up the whole hearing mechanism. (Acupuncturists identify over 148 points in the outer ear as corresponding to areas of the body, from the feet at the top of the ear to the head at the ear lobe.)

THE ENERGY YAWN

The Energy Yawn is done by massaging the muscles around the temporal-mandibular joint (TMJ). The TMJ lies right in front of the ear opening and is the joint where the lower jaw meets the upper jaw. Across this joint run trunks from five major cranial nerves that gain sensory information from all over the face, eye muscles, tongue and mouth and activate all the muscles of the face, eyes and mouth for mastication and vocalization.[14]

Figure 3.4 graphically depicts the large area of the sensory and motor cortices these nerves supply. When we are stressed, the jaw often tightens up and nerve function across this area decreases. The Energy Yawn relaxes the whole facial area so that sensory intake can more efficiently occur. It also facilitates more effective verbalization and communication.

Figure 7.10: The Energy Yawn

When children are having difficulties with reading, it may be because the eyes are not working well together. They also may not be hearing clearly due to stress. Tension in the TMJ may also make it difficult for them to verbalize, which is tied to thought processing. The Energy Yawn is remarkable in its effects with these children. By relaxing the muscles and facilitating full nerve function across the temporal mandibular joint, all the nerve functions to and from the eyes, facial muscles, and mouth are improved.

THE CALF PUMP

Stress can trigger a reflex, called the tendon guard reflex, that tightens and shortens the gastrocnemius and soleus muscles in the calf. The Calf Pump is a lengthening exercise that relaxes these muscles. In the process, cerebrospinal fluid flows more easily within the central nervous system, and communication becomes freer. The Calf Pump is done by lengthening the calf of one leg while bending the knee of the other leg. Hold the back of a chair, keeping the torso fairly upright and place one foot, (with the heel up) about twelve inches behind the other foot. Take a deep breath and as you exhale, lower the heel of the back foot to the ground and bend the front knee forward. The torso should remain upright, not leaning forward. These are the leg "stretches" often done by runners. Repeated several times, the Calf Pumps relaxes the gastrocnemius and soleus muscles and thus releases the tendon guard reflex. (The tendon guard reflex is discussed in detail in Chapter Twelve.)

Parents can assist the child in doing the Calf Pump. The child lays on her back and the parents place both hands on the bottoms of her feet, gently pushing the ball of each foot (the rounded broad part between the toes and arch) forward so that the calf lengthens. Many children love to push simultaneously with their feet against the parent's applied pressure, especially when goaded to "push me away," "push me really hard." The contraction during the push allows the calf to further lengthen in relaxation.[15] This relaxation has an interesting link to verbal skills, and greatly facilitates communication in speech-impaired and autistic children.

Figure 7.11: Calf Pump

THE ENERGIZER

The Energizer is a lengthening and deep breathing activity that increases oxygen, relaxes neck and shoulder muscles and assists in cerebrospinal fluid flow around the central nervous system. The Energizer helps to wake up the system, especially after a grueling session on the computer or sitting for a long time.

To do the Energizer, place your hands on the desk in front of you. Lower your chin to your chest, feeling the stretch in the back of the neck and the relaxed shoulders. Taking a deep breath, scoop forward with the head bringing it up and back, allowing the back to arch slightly and opening the rib cage. Then exhale, curving the back and bringing the chin back to rest on the chest.[16]

Figure 7.12 The Energizer

Taking an Energizer break after a ten or fifteen minute learning session, reactivates focus. The body has a chance to move in a way that activates the vestibular system, waking up the brain, relaxes the shoulders which improves hearing, and brings in more oxygen to assist in nervous system function. This is another activity that is indispensable to me at the computer. As its name implies, I feel activated, energized and ready to put ideas together again.

DENNISON LATERALITY REPATTERNING

Infant crawling has long been known to be crucial for activating full sensory functioning and learning. Crawling involves movements that cross the body's midline and use both sides of the brain in concert. Our cross-lateral movements help us to build the capacities that allow full sensory access (auditory, visual, proprioceptive) from both sides of the body. (Later on, walking incorporates all of our early stages of development from infancy to toddling.)

Dr. Dennison discovered that some people he worked with were unable to Cross Crawl but were proficient at homolateral movement (arm and leg on the same side of the body moving together). These people generally accessed brain hemispheres in a one-sided way, and suffered stress from lack of full sensory-motor functioning. Dennison also discovered a high correlation between the inability to Cross Crawl and the tendency toward learning difficulty.

Drs. Doman and Delacato coined the term patterning to describe the process of repeating a natural movement again and again to imprint it in the body's physiology even years after the developmentally appropriate time has passed.[17] In 1981, Dr. Dennison coined the term repatterning, meaning a return to the natural, integrated pattern imprinted within the nervous system during normal development. For many people, stress disrupts cross-lateral patterning. They must compensate for this disruption with less efficient patterns of movement, sensing and learning.[18]

Dennison Laterality Repatterning is a specific series of activities that reestablish efficient, integrated patterns among cross-lateral movements, vision and hearing. The Laterality Repatterning activities (some of which are homolateral, i.e., on one side only) are performed with the help of a trained instructor. This experience enables the learner to recognize the inefficiency of homolateral movement and homolateral sensory processing, which contrasts strikingly with the more efficient, integrated state as learning becomes easier. The transformation of the Down's Syndrome boy learning his numbers is a compelling example of this most elegant micro-intervention.

Though Dennison Laterality Repatterning is simple, it does require some training and a certain depth of understanding to successfully do it. Therefore, I will not attempt to provide instructions for it in this book.

Brain Gym, with its cross-lateral, fine motor movements activates balanced and equal muscles on both sides of the body. This is directly related to integrated and equal activation of the motor cortex of the frontal lobes of the cerebrum as well as the basal ganglion and cerebellum. Consistent, routine activation of the motor cortex elaborates nerve networks in the rest of the frontal lobe including the premotor and superior pre-frontal cortex.

Since these specific movements are activating nerve networks throughout the brain, in both hemispheres simultaneously, they help build the hardware needed to assure success for life-long learning.

Brain Gym is effective for everyone and optimizes learning and performance at every level in all cognitive endeavors — communication of ideas; creativity and performance in art, music, sports and dance; increased productivity in the workplace. Because the exercises relieve and manage stress, Brain Gym also contributes to overall health.

Schools and all other learning settings from preschool to corporate training classrooms are obvious places to use Brain Gym.

Indeed, I have never worked with an age group or type of individual that failed to learn more effectively as a result of using these exercises. They help the young to get ready to learn, and the elderly to maintain active thinking and memory. But perhaps the most profound improvements from Brain Gym that I have witnessed were with adults and children labeled "learning disabled," "Attention Deficit Hyperactive Disorder," "Emotionally Handicapped," Down's Syndrome. Brain Gym is drug-free, simple and highly effective. It maintains a fine-tuned mind/body system and assists global learning and comprehension for all.

8. ≈
What Goes Wrong?

Every child has inside him an aching void for
excitement and if we don't fill it with something
which is exciting and interesting and good for him,
he will fill it with something which is exciting and
interesting and which isn't good for him.
— *Theodore Roosevelt*

If movement is essential for learning and thought, then why aren't "hyperactive" people, who move all the time, thinking and learning? If people have all the necessary elements to take in the world sensorially, to process and integrate information, and to demonstrate the skill of thought, why are some people labeled "learning disabled"? If the drive to learn is intrinsic to the human body/mind from before birth to death, why do some people have "attention deficit disorder"?

In the United States alone there are between 1.5 million and 4.5 million school children, mainly boys, who are labeled ADHD (Attention Deficit Hyperactive Disorder). Every week, 15,000 American school children are being referred for assessment, and up to 80% of all American school children could be diagnosed as learning disabled.[1-2]

In my observation, based on years of work with schools and school children, the labels used for specific learning difficulties are generally arbitrary and non-pathological. These labels include: Hyperactive, Attention Deficit Disorder (ADD), Attention Deficit Hyperactive Disorder (ADHD), Learning Disabled, and Emotionally Handicapped. Efforts to help people with learning difficulties have often relied on the pigeonhole strategy: labeling a problem and thinking that greater understanding will follow from greater generalization. But more often than not, labeling leads to oversimplification and insensitivity to the very real, very unique people behind the label. Sadly, in some ways we have trapped these children — and adults — in a diminished view of themselves and their potential for learning.

In light of the amazing resiliency of the human body/mind system, I propose that we hold off such a judgement until a person has completed their learning, which will take a lifetime. How can we label someone who is still in the process of becoming, a process we all are engaged in until we die? Having said that, I hasten to agree that there are people with specific learning difficulties. However, if we must label them, why not label them according to the underlying core problems rather than just the symptoms? I suggest the label **SOSOH**: *Stressed Out, Survival-Oriented Humans*.

WHO ARE *SOSOH*?

What do I mean by stressed out, survival-oriented? I am referring to non-integrated, lopsided brain functioning, a tendency to operate reflexively and/or reactively from survival centers in the brain stem and the sympathetic nervous system. How does stress fit into the picture? Stress from various environmental, developmental, family and social influences is a trigger setting off events in the nervous system that produce and regulate survival-oriented behavior. I believe that chronic exposure to stress inhibits full brain development.

Stress necessitates an overemphasis on survival-oriented brain processing at the expense of rational, limbic and cortical functioning, especially within the frontal lobes. Consequently, stressed out, survival oriented humans have less opportunity to develop nerve nets into the frontal lobe and may exhibit learning difficulties as a result. In the next five chapters we will look at these detrimental effects of stress in greater depth. Here I wish to emphasize that stressors of various kinds, some obvious, some less visible, are causative agents for many learning difficulties.

As far as I can tell, my SOSOH label easily covers all the other labels we currently apply to learning problems. These familiar labels, including Fetal Alcohol Syndrome, have been attached to the following patterns of behavior:

Excessive activity — hyperactivity,

Difficulties in maintaining attention and focus on a task,

Disruptive behavior,

Learning difficulties,

Inability to control behavior in alignment with social norms,

Marked discrepancy between seemingly high verbal skills (constant talking) and the ability to communicate effectively,

Erratic, non-graceful, unbalanced or poorly controlled movements.

All these behaviors fall within the realm of frontal lobe functioning. The frontal lobes control fine motor movement, inner speech, self-control, and reasoning. I believe that people who exhibit these behaviors, my SOSOH group, have been exposed to stressors which require them to be concerned more with survival than reason. Because of this, they lack integrated nerve-net development and myelination into the frontal lobe area of the cerebrum.

HYPERACTIVITY AND THE FRONTAL LOBE

A study by Alan Zametkin and colleagues at the National Institute of Mental Health graphically demonstrated the frontal lobe / hyperactivity connection. Zametkin studied 25 hyperactive adults of childhood onset (who also had hyperactive children of their own). Using PET scans to measure these adults' cerebral glucose metabolism while engaged in an auditory-attention task, researchers found 8.1% less brain activity in the hyperactive group as compared to a normal control. The area of the brain with reduced function was the frontal lobe.[3]

Hyperactivity (and ADD or ADHD) is characterized by a lack of fine motor coordination, and constant, erratic, non-graceful adrenalin-initiated movements. Constant external chatter is also characteristic, pointing to a lack of inner speech development that controls social behavior.

The largest reduction of brain activity in the Zametkin study was found specifically in the premotor cortex and superior prefrontal cortex of the frontal lobes.[4] (See Figure 5.2, the four lobes of the neocortex.) These areas of the brain are crucial for the self-talk which controls behavior and planning, for fine controlled movement and for integrative thought. The prefrontal cortex, with its connection to Broca's area on the left side for motor control of speech, affects focused attention, motor activity and the ability to think before acting.[5]

When fully developed, in late adolescence or even adulthood, the frontal lobe takes all the information from the rest of the brain and synthesizes it into thought and action. These areas of the frontal lobe light up on PET scans when a person is thinking, and they link to the motor cortex which facilitates appropriate action in relationship to reasoning.[6] (See figure 5.3 which schematically represents the brain areas involved in thinking) Jay Giedd implicates malfunction in the frontal lobes and smaller frontal areas of the corpus callosum in ADHD. A smaller frontal corpus callosum may reflect communication problems between the two brain hemispheres.[7]

What Inhibits Learning

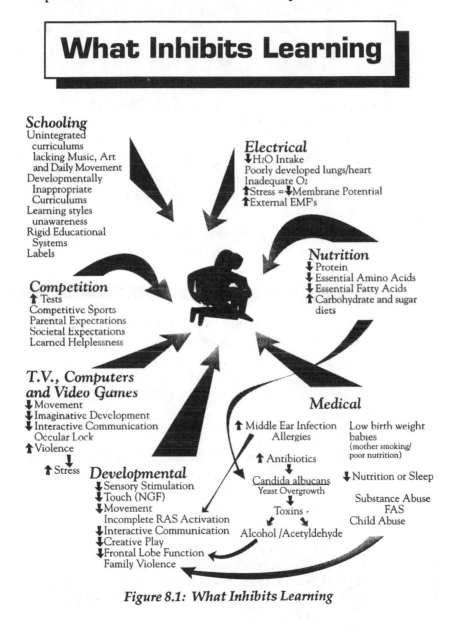

Schooling
Unintegrated
  curriculums
  lacking Music, Art
  and Daily Movement
Developmentally
  Inappropriate
  Curriculums
Learning styles
  unawareness
Rigid Educational
  Systems
Labels

Electrical
↓H₂O Intake
Poorly developed lungs/heart
Inadequate O₂
↑Stress = ↓Membrane Potential
↑External EMF's

Nutrition
↓ Protein
↓ Essential Amino Acids
↓ Essential Fatty Acids
↑ Carbohydrate and sugar
  diets

Competition
↑ Tests
Competitive Sports
Parental Expectations
Societal Expectations
Learned Helplessness

**T.V., Computers
and Video Games**
↓Movement
↓Imaginative Development
↓Interactive Communication
  Occular Lock
↑Violence
  ↓
  ↑Stress

Developmental
↓Sensory Stimulation
↓Touch (NGF)
↓Movement
  Incomplete RAS Activation
↓Interactive Communication
↓Creative Play
↓Frontal Lobe Function
  Family Violence

Medical
↑ Middle Ear Infection
  Allergies
  ↑ Antibiotics
  ↓
  Candida albucans
  Yeast Overgrowth
  ↓
  Toxins -
  ↙ ↘
Alcohol /Acetyldehyde

Low birth weight
babies
(mother smoking/
poor nutrition)

↓ Nutrition or Sleep

Substance Abuse
FAS
Child Abuse

Figure 8.1: What Inhibits Learning

So what are some of the stressors people face in their lives that limit frontal lobe development? I will attempt to categorize what I believe are the main stressors. Many are interlinked:

Developmental—lack of sensory stimulation, lack of movement, lack of touch (diminished Nerve Growth Factor), lack of interactive creative play and communication, unbalanced or incomplete RAS (Reticular Activating System) activation.

Electrical — inadequate water consumption, inadequate oxygen, excessive exposure to external EMF's (electromagnetic fields).

Nutritional — inadequate amounts of proteins, lack of essential amino acids and fatty acids, high carbohydrate and sugar diets.

Medical — low birth weight babies, chronic middle ear infections, allergies, medications, yeast overgrowth, inadequate diet or sleep, substance abuse, child abuse, poor vision or hearing.

TV, computers and video games—violence, decreased imaginative development, less interactive communication, ocular lock.

Competition—inappropriate expectations (at home, school, work and self-imposed), pressures towards social conformity, competition in sports and in the arts, learning in a winner/loser rather than cooperative framework.

Rigid educational systems — developmentally inappropriate curricula, constant low-level skills testing, lecture/writing formats for quiet classrooms, unawareness of or inattention to unique learning styles.

Most of these stressors overstimulate the survival centers of the mind/body system. They cause nerve activity to be centered in the sympathetic nervous system and brain stem, with little activation of the rest of the brain, especially of the frontal lobe.

A review of the research shows strong evidence for a variety of effects of stress on SOSOH people. I will go into greater detail in coming chapters, but one more example may suggest the significant, complex links that neuroscientific research is establishing between stress and brain function. The hippocampus of the limbic system, key to memory and learning, is profoundly affected by stress. In research on rats, Solomon Snyder found that enkephalins, chemicals produced in the brain during stress to numb pain, also increase hyperactivity and decrease memory.[8] In addition, the stressed rats lost more hippocampal cells (involved in memory) than the non-stressed ones. Furthermore, only the stressed rats lost cells in the part of the hippocampus that suffers selective damage in Alzheimer's disease in humans.[9] These results are thought to apply directly to humans, stress and aging. Adrenalin output rises during aging, rendering the hippocampus more vulnerable to neurological insults like seizures and strokes, especially in the presence of stress.

Many sources of stress can interfere with the learning process. In earlier chapters I have discussed the impact of various developmental factors on brain functioning and learning capacities. In the chapters ahead, I will do my best to address the rest of the list. Some, like malnutrition are well known inhibitors of learning and health. Others, like TV, competition and educational expectations exert less visible but no less serious influences on learning. We will take a look at them all. Armed with greater knowledge we can help ourselves and our children avoid situations and influences that pose a danger to brain development and to learning. That is why I have called the second part of this book, *Nurturing and Protecting Our Learning Systems*.

Nurturance and protection of the young are the primary roles of every family and every society. But as we look at our children, our schools, and our future, concerns mount that somewhere along the line we have gotten dangerously off track. We may be accepting far higher levels of stress than we can possibly manage and dissipate. In the following pages I hope to point us in a better direction.

9. ≈
Basics for the Brain:
Water and Oxygen

How do we nurture and support the complex development, organization and reorganization of the learning-thinking process? What are the essential elements necessary to protect our mind/body system throughout life? How do we assure full, efficient functioning of these massive networks with their boundless potential for learning? How do we responsibly care for Control Central so it will take care of us?

Aside from giving the body and mind something new and exciting to work on regularly, we must also provide them with the fuel and safeguards they need in order to thrive. Fortunately, some of the most important building blocks of high performance are readily available. But we have to know what they are, and why they are so important. In this chapter, we'll begin with the most basic: water and oxygen, and their connection with the electrical systems within our mind and body.

COOL, CLEAR, WATER

For a substance that is so essential to life, water seems remarkably unremarkable: colorless, odorless, tasteless and ubiquitous. Yet, it is the magic elixir for learning, the "secret potion" if you will.

Water is one of the most important and most abundant inorganic substances in the body. It makes up from 45% to 75% of our total body weight. Lean people have a greater proportion of water to total body weight because fat has very little water, while muscle has a lot. Water comprises more of the brain (with estimates of 90%) than of any other organ of the body, with muscles next at 75%, and then kidneys.[1] Under normal conditions, it is recommended a person drink one third of an ounce of water per pound of body weight (about a quart per hundred pounds of body weight) each day, with that amount doubled or tripled in times of stress. Why is water so essential to learning, and to life? To answer that question we need to look at the crucial roles it plays in electrical activity within the body, in the distribution of oxygen, and in nutrition.

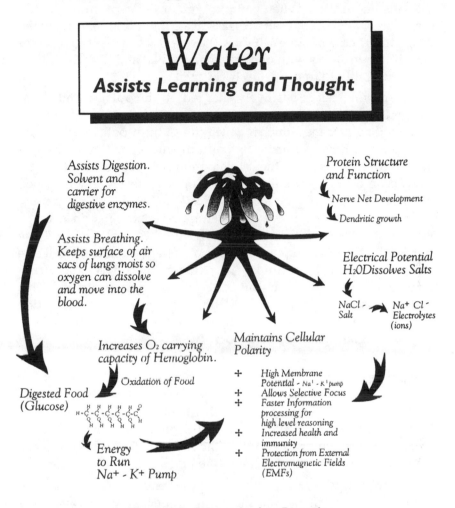

Water
Assists Learning and Thought

Assists Digestion. Solvent and carrier for digestive enzymes.

Assists Breathing. Keeps surface of air sacs of lungs moist so oxygen can dissolve and move into the blood.

Increases O_2 carrying capacity of Hemoglobin.

Oxidation of Food

Digested Food (Glucose)

Energy to Run Na^+ - K^+ Pump

Protein Structure and Function

Nerve Net Development

Dendritic growth

Electrical Potential H_2O Dissolves Salts

NaCl - Salt → Na^+ Cl^- Electrolytes (ions)

Maintains Cellular Polarity

+ High Membrane Potential - Na^+ - K^+ pump
+ Allows Selective Focus
+ Faster Information processing for high level reasoning
+ Increased health and immunity
+ Protection from External Electromagnetic Fields (EMFs)

Figure 9.1: Water Assists Learning

WATER AND THE BODY ELECTRIC

Our bodily systems are electrical. Ultimately, it is the electrical transmissions within the nervous system that make us sensing, learning, thinking, acting organisms. Water, the universal solvent, is essential for these electrical transmissions and for maintaining the electrical potential within our bodies.

The membranes of our nerve cells (and of all our cells) are polar (have a charge) due to the interplay between positively and negatively charged atoms called electrolytes. The electrolytes (ions), such as sodium (Na^+), potassium (K^+), and chlorine (Cl^-) come from the salts in our diet. When you put regular table salt into water, it dissolves. Water causes salt to disassociate into the atoms that make it up. In the case of table salt (NaCl), water will cause it to disassociate into two atoms with unequal charges: Na^+ and Cl^-. These then have the ability to transmit electrical current.

A living cell is positively charged on the outside and negatively charged on the inside thanks to a molecular process occurring at the cell membrane, which is called the sodium-potassium pump. This pump actively transports sodium ions (positively charged atoms) to the outside of the cell leaving large, nondiffusible negatively charged ions (organic phosphate, protein and chlorine) trapped inside.[2] The polarity of the cell is called the resting membrane potential. A resting nerve cell membrane maintains an average voltage of -70 mv (millivolts) inside. This implies a voltage of +70 mv outside.[3] (It is more difficult to measure voltage outside the cell due to dilution within tissue fluids.) This differential between the -70 mv on the inside and the +70 mv outside is the membrane potential. This potential is commonly indicated by referring only to the inside charge: -70 mv. The greater the differential (for example -80 mv / +80 mv), the higher the membrane polarity.

Optimal nerve and muscle function depend on proper membrane potential (polarity). The water/electrolyte balance is so critical to the living system that if the membrane potential within the cells drops to -30 mv and remains there, death will ensue. This can occur through radical dehydration or malnutrition. Even under normal circumstances, the polarity across the membrane can decrease just from inadequate levels of water in the body.[4]

High cellular polarity (membrane potential), raises the threshold of sensitivity at the cell membrane, effectively increasing the integrity of the cell membrane by lowering its sensitivity to outside stimuli. Surrounded as we are by a world of stimuli, high membrane polarity gives us a choice. It takes more of a stimulus to activate a nerve impulse, so we can choose what stimuli we wish to focus our attention on and not be distracted by irrelevant stimuli. As we will see, this enhances selective focus for increased learning, strengthens immunity and health, and protects against the effects of external electromagnetic fields.

The sodium-potassium pump uses ATP (adenosine triphosphate), as its energy source to actively transport the positively charged atoms to the outside of the cell. ATP is formed as the food we eat (mainly carbohydrates) is broken down by oxygen (oxidation) to release energy. The released energy is trapped in the ATP molecule and carried to the sodium-potassium pump as its energy source.[5]

A CLOSER LOOK AT A NERVE IMPULSE

At the microscopic, cellular level all the activities by which we define and know ourselves depend on tiny electrical impulses which occur through the movement of electrolytes in and out of the cell. Though minute and executed in a flash, they profoundly affect our ability to learn, remember, feel, think and physically act in our lives.[6] How do they work?

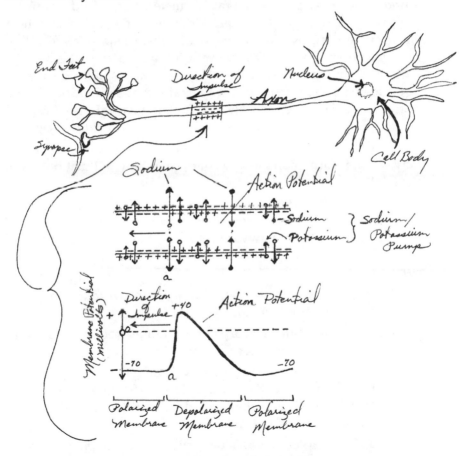

Figure 9.2: Membrane Polarity and Neuron Impulse Transmission

In its polarized state, the nerve cell has an action potential, the means to respond to a stimulus. When a strong enough stimulus activates an area on the nerve cell membrane, the sodium-potassium pump shuts down at that spot, allowing sodium to rush from the outside to the inside. With basically equal amounts of positive and negative ions on the inside, the membrane is no longer polar: it is depolarized. The sodium-potassium pump next to this spot is deactivated, and a wave of depolarization moves, like falling dominos, down the entire length of the nerve cell as an action potential. Action potentials measure about 100 millivolts in amplitude, are one millisecond in duration and can be generated at 200 per second.[7]

Depolarization waves move at 100 meters per second, sending a message from sensory organs to the brain or from the brain to muscles and glands. This is similar to the alternating (+ to -) current found in electrical circuits. But at 100 meters per second, the nerve transmits messages at less than 1 millionth the speed at which electrical signals move on a copper wire.[8] Even at that relatively slow rate, your brain takes only a few milliseconds to arrange a specific pattern of millions of signals, which is then instantly dissolved, never to be repeated that same way again. The sodium-potassium pump immediately reestablishes its functioning, thus repolarizing the cell membrane again so it is ready to send the next message.

With the nervous system's ability to process one thousand new bits of information every second, examining all that occurs in the mind/body system in this simple example would take volumes, if not a library, to explain.[9]

To put that last paragraph in perspective, I'd like you to do an experiment, and notice how long it takes. "Move your left big toe." The following is a very basic sketch of what is happening in that simple act:

1. Your eyes are moving, picking up the words on the page, "move your left big toe."

2. This activates sensory nerve endings (rods and cones) in the retina at the back of the eye.

3. Waves of depolarization travel down the sensory neurons to the synapses in the Central Nervous System where neurotransmitters bridge the gap and activate the Great Intermediate Net, Control Central.

4. The nerve networks are activated to decipher the command, connecting the visual stimuli with words, memory

and sensations in the association areas of the occipital, parietal and temporal lobes of the brain.

5. The brain then discriminates between right and left, and determines "big" compared with "little." It must then pull out a physical memory of "toe."

6. Then it activates nerve impulses to the motor cortex of the right frontal lobe of the brain which connects with the left big toe muscles, the basal ganglion for movement orchestration and the cerebellum for gross motor movement.

7. Through branching neural pathways of association neurons, the appropriate motor neurons are activated sending a wave of depolarization down the myelinated axons of the nerves.

8. At some point, either in the brain or spinal cord, the motor neurons cross to the left side, and travel along nerve pathways in the sciatic nerve.

9. The impulses travel down the left leg to the muscles of the big toe causing them to contract.

10. Another message is instantly sent from proprioceptive sensors in the big toe to the sensory cortex of the parietal lobe of the brain to tell you that you have just moved your left big toe.

And it took you how long? Theoretically you could move your left big toe 200 times a second, because the system has the potential to generate new impulses at that rate.

The smooth functioning of this system is highly dependent on water, oxygen and nutrients with water taking first place as the most necessary ingredient.

COFFEE, TEA OR BRING ON THE CHOCOLATE!

Certain chemicals, called diuretics, dehydrate the body. Indiscriminate use of these chemicals may actually decrease learning potential. These include alcohol and caffeine, as in coffee, tea, some carbonated beverages and chocolate.

The body naturally attempts to maintain a balance between salt and water. Have you ever eaten a whole bag of salty potato chips only to find you are very thirsty? All those fiendishly tasty potato chips drive the salt level in the body way above the water level. To compensate, the thirst centers in the hypothalamus are activated, making you thirsty. If you obey that signal and drink water, the water is absorbed into the blood and carried to the kidneys which monitor salt/water balance. Certain hormones in the kidney, like Antidiuretic Hormone (ADH), facilitate reabsorption of water back into the blood, so it is not lost as urine. This way the water level increases until the salt and water are in balance again.[10]

Coffee, tea, chocolate and alcohol are all diuretics. They inhibit the reabsorption of water in the kidneys, causing more water to be lost in urine. You may have noticed that you urinate more when drinking these substances. With this loss of water from the system, optimal polarity and membrane potential can't be maintained in the nervous system. As you lose the water, a salt/water imbalance occurs. As available water levels decrease from drinking these dehydrating substances, the thirst centers in the hypothalamus of the brain are stimulated to send out an "I'm thirsty" call. So, we drink another of the same which dehydrates us more and makes us even more thirsty. Remember that "cotton" mouth feeling the morning after? Bars even supply free salty peanuts and popcorn to intensify the thirst call, and then make their money on the drinks.[11]

These diuretic substances are also implicated in headaches, as they dehydrate the brain by decreasing cerebrospinal fluid production through vasoconstriction of blood vessels to the brain. The cerebrospinal fluid's job is to surround and bathe the brain, keeping it hydrated. To make matters worse, when the water levels in the body are low, less fluid is available to produce this protective cerebrospinal fluid. Incidentally, I have heard that the best way to avoid a hangover and headache after a night of too much alcohol is to drink lots of water before going to bed. It makes sense.

Interestingly, when people are the most dehydrated, they are not thirsty. The body loses its alertness to dehydration. Your lips may be dry, your tongue may be sticking to the roof of your mouth, but you don't recognize that you are thirsty. That is the result of ignoring the body's thirst message for so long.[12]

Incidentally, fruit juice, soda and diet soda are not so good for you either. These drinks are high in sugars and salts which bind up water in the body, depleting the supply available for maintaining electrolyte levels in the nerves. The body treats these as food, and though they eventually supply metabolic water, initially water must be taken from other parts of the body to form digestive juices to break down these high sugar drinks.[13]

The most sensible drink is water. Having water available in handy one quart bottles makes regular sipping easy and keeps the system hydrated and working at optimal efficiency. If this simple, but very healthful habit is new to you, it might take a little getting used to. During the first week of increased water intake, the kidneys will need to adjust, thus more bathroom breaks may be necessary.

WATER, MALNUTRITION AND THE NERVOUS SYSTEM

As we have seen, anything that decreases membrane polarity damages the functioning of the nervous system. Decreasing membrane polarity is, in fact, one of the effects of malnutrition. From the point of view of brain development and learning, it is one of malnutrition's most dangerous and insidious consequences.

Proteins in our diet form albumins which hold water in the blood, preventing it from seeping out just anywhere, and assuring that it will arrive where it is most needed, usually the brain. If protein intake is very low or incomplete (missing any of the ten essential amino acids), there are not enough albumins formed. This causes water to seep into body cavities (a process called third-spacing) instead of being distributed adequately to the brain and nervous tissue. We have all seen this sad outcome in pictures of malnourished children with large bellies and thin arms and legs.[14] It is also seen in people with anorexia nervosa and bulimia, or in pregnant women with preeclampsia (toxemia) where edema is very evident. For the developing fetus, it inhibits proper development, resulting in premature and low birth weight babies.[15]

The fluid/electrolyte balance is so delicate that during malnutrition, water intake may be harmful until albumin levels rise. I was discussing the importance of water with a group of Russian psychologists when one woman mentioned that medical doctors in Russia were telling pregnant women not to drink much water. I was astounded until a doctor explained that, due to meat rationing (one pound of protein per person per month) many pregnant women suffered from toxemia. If they were to drink lots of water, it would carry other essential nutrients and salts away in their urine, possibly causing death.

People with syndromes such as inappropriate ADH secretion or psychogenic polydipsia (compulsive water drinking) might have to be careful not to drink too much water. However, for the vast majority of people, albumin levels are adequate, and drinking at least four eight ounce glasses of water daily is essential.[16]

We know that oxygen is as essential for learning as it is for life. It is essential because it breaks down food to release the energy needed for mind/body functioning. The energy that is provided by oxidation of food is so essential to the system that death occurs within only a few minutes after ceasing to breath.

The brain makes up only one fiftieth of the body's weight and yet it uses an amazing one fifth of the body's oxygen.[17] The first artery coming out of the heart carrying freshly oxygenated blood, the carotid, goes directly to the brain. The whole system tends to take care of the brain's needs first.

Water again enters the picture as a crucial player in assisting oxygen distribution to the brain. It keeps the surface of the air sacs of the lungs moist so oxygen can dissolve and move into the blood. Researchers at the National Institute of Diabetes and Digestive and Kidney Disorder have also discovered that increased water intake increases the capacity of hemoglobin to carry oxygen by one hundred to one thousand times.[18] Hemoglobin is the iron-bearing pigment in red blood cells that carries oxygen. Similarly, water assists digestion of foods in the digestive tract by dissolving them so enzymes can easily break them down producing the end products needed for oxidation.[19]

Once the oxygen has reached the cell, it oxidizes food there, releasing energy for production of ATP:

$$C_6H_{12}O + 6O_2 \Rightarrow 6CO_2 + 6H_2O + ATP \text{ (Used for Na}^+\text{K}^+\text{ Pump)}$$

(glucose) (oxygen) ⇨ (carbon dioxide) (water) (energy)

ATP traps energy from food and makes it available to structures within the cell, such as the sodium-potassium pump. Interestingly, a group at the Oregon Health Sciences University have provided evidence that ATP tends to be low in patients with depression and Alzheimer's disease.[20] This ATP deficiency may be due in part to inadequate oxygen uptake and distribution to the cells, caused in turn by low levels of water in the system.

It takes a physically fit body to supply the massive oxygen needs of the brain. Movement is not only essential for nerve net development and thought, but also for adequate heart and lung development to support brain function. Unfortunately, however, according to an alarming recent national study only 36.3% of school children in America have daily physical education classes. And added to that, the American Academy of Pediatrics found that 40% of all children in the United States, between ages five and eight, have at least one risk factor for heart disease. Also, fewer than half of all school children get enough exercise to develop healthy hearts and lungs.[21]

Movement has also greatly decreased in adult populations in the United States. Robert Dustman found that getting inactive men and women in their fifties and sixties, on a four-month brisk walking program increased their performance on mental ability tests by 10%. William Greenough and James Black found that active rats had 20% more blood vessels in their brains than sedentary rats.[22] Movement facilitates the development of increased blood vessels that carry learning-essential water, oxygen and nutrients to the brain.

Clean air is also important. Smoking during pregnancy is implicated in low birth weight babies and a higher percentage of children with learning disabilities. Preschool children whose mothers smoked heavily (ten or more cigarettes daily) during pregnancy scored significantly lower (an average of 9 points) on standardized IQ tests than kids whose mothers did not smoke. Also smoke-exposed children may not reach their full intellectual potential. Cigarette smoke contains an estimated 2,000 to 4,000 chemicals, some of which could damage new developing nerve cells.[23]

THE EMF CONNECTION

Our bodies produce low frequency electromagnetic fields (EMFs) from the electrolyte action and polarity across each of our cell membranes. Aside from being part of the communication system within our nerves, these low-frequency electromagnetic fields provide the body with a specific rhythm of vibration. We can measure these EMFs in the brain with the EEG (Electroencephalogram), or across the heart with the EKG (Electrocardiograph). We can even study the body's structure and function by polarizing the body in an electromagnetic field to obtain organ resonance with an MRI (Magnetic Resonance Imaging).[24]

Our EMFs are specific and delicate. Much research has been done in the past ten years about the effects of external EMFs on the human body. The research has mainly focused on possible links with fatal disease like cancer. But some of the more subtle effects may be far more important to our learning potential.

As we look at our present environments, it is very apparent that the external electromagnetic fields we are dealing with today are different from those twenty years ago. Reach back to a memory of your home twenty years ago. What were the electrical appliances and machines you had then compared to now? Today we are dealing with external fields not only from high tension wires, but satellite discs, cable TV, microwave ovens, fluorescent lights, computers, VCRs, all-electric kitchens, laundry rooms and heating, cellular phones, fax machines, answering machines, analog clocks and clock radios, hair dryers, safety alarm systems and electric blankets.

The earth's geomagnetic field at the middle latitudes is a thousand times more intense than the magnetic field generated by appliances in an average American home, but it is static and the human body has evolved in homeostasis with it. We now live in quite a different electromagnetic environment.

The EMFs in our homes are not static but possess alternating current producing a magnetic field that easily passes through the human body. In America, the alternating electric current goes through a complete cycle 60 times per second (60 hertz) and the associated magnetic field changes direction 120 times per second. The standard measurement of magnetic fields is in milligauss (mG) units.[25] The average background level of EMFs in a home, school or office may be 0.5 mG. When a person stands close to wiring or other conduits in the walls or floors, the levels of exposure can be 10 mG. Close to electrical devices or appliances, it can be even higher.[26]

Examples of milligauss readings on some basic appliances at a distance of 10 inches are: refrigerators average 2.6 mG, color TVs 7 mG, computers 7 mG, electric ranges 9 mG, fluorescent lights 10 mG, analog clocks and clock radios 14.8 mG, and microwave ovens 36.9 mG. These fields drop rapidly with distance. A refrigerator's EMFs drop to 1.1 mG at 2 feet and roughly 0.4 mG at 4 feet.

Many studies, like those from the Electric Power Research Institute (EPRI), are being done on the effects on human health of these increased nonstatic electromagnetic fields.[27] A thorough occupational study done in Canada and France was recently released. The study examined more than 4,000 cases of cancer occurring over a twenty year period among some 220,000 male electric utility workers. The workers were carefully monitored for daily EMF exposure. Interestingly, those exposed to the strongest magnetic fields showed no overall increase in cancer risk. But 50% of those exposed to **average** fields of 1.6 mG or more show a twofold increase in the risk of developing a type of adult leukemia called acute nonlymphoid leukemia.[28]

My interest lies in the effect of these weak (average) EMFs on our ability to learn. Closer to home, then, it is not high frequency EMFs but the ELFs (extremely low frequency electrical fields) in the above study and in our appliances that prove most harmful because they are closest to our own EMFs. According to researchers at the Medical College in Milwaukee, Wisconsin and Sci-Con Associates in Flagstaff, Arizona, effects of EMFs appear to relate to a combination of field intensity and frequency, therefore "less is not necessarily better." They suggest "prudent avoidance" of EMFs, especially with children.[29]

It seems that the technology on which our culture heavily depends gives us a big head start in developing the SOSOH traits we spoke of in the last chapter. Dr. Dee Coulter cites research showing that more newborns in technologically advanced cultures are exhibiting an "excited" state — almost a state of shock at birth. They lack the natural rhythm and coordination that, in previous generations, was established in the womb.[30] The fetus lies in amniotic fluid, a fluid/electrolyte bath that easily transmits external EMFs to the fetus. Outside EMFs may interfere with the fetus' own natural EMFs. If we consider the constant bombardment of EMFs that many pregnant women are exposed to, we can understand why babies are born "excited" and may remain that way throughout life.

The fetus normally learns rhythm and vibration through the mother's heartbeat and breathing as well as from the constant electrical impulses and EMFs being given off by these organs. This is one of the functions of the vestibular system, which fully develops and myelinates by five months in utero. Frequent exposure to external EMFs may interrupt those maternal rhythms, and may affect the baby's learning of rhythmic patterning. Babies born without this sense of internal rhythm cannot calm themselves with self-generated rocking, crooning or sucking. Instead, they just fret.[31]

There is a greater likelihood that these natural rhythms may be disrupted if the mother spends hours a day at a computer, in a highly electrified office with fluorescent lights, near electrical appliances, ironing, blow drying other peoples' hair in a beauty parlor, or sleeping under an electric blanket.

Stanford University chemists noted the ability of weak external EMFs to disrupt lipid membranes such as those that serve as the gatekeepers for chemicals entering or exiting cells (for example, the sodium-potassium pump). This would not only affect cellular function in a developing embryo/fetus, but would also affect that child's later learning skills (all of which are dependent on proper functioning of sodium-potassium pumps in the nervous system).[32] I wonder what are the effects of sonograms and fetal monitors, routinely used, often as early as the fourth or fifth month when the vestibular system is developing?

Awareness and prudent use of electricity in our living and learning environments might achieve a lot. In my own experience in the classroom, I have observed the remarkable effect of just turning off the fluorescent lights. There is often a physical sigh from the students, and the excited energy decreases markedly. Today, schools are often built with no windows (so students won't be distracted) and banks of fluorescent lights that emit EMFs. As a result, children may have to work extra hard to overcome the unbalanced EMFs from the fluorescent lights, with little energy left over to concentrate and learn.

Natural lighting, and even incandescent lights have a great advantage over fluorescent lights. Sunlight is easier for the eye to process, and does not increase the ambient EMFs in the work or school environment. In Russia, classrooms have a wall of large windows and very few light bulbs. And in Denmark, it is mandated by law that every school child and working adult be able to see nature from their seat or work space. Every building in Denmark is full of windows.

When I have spent the day working on my computer, I can definitely sense a major energy drain. If I don't take the time to get out in nature and walk, I have just barely enough energy to drag myself onto the couch to be zapped by more external EMFs from the TV.

Bone and fat (low water content tissues) are less affected by external EMFs than high water content tissues like the brain, muscles and kidneys. Considering that the brain is approximately 90% water, external EMFs must have some effect on its efficiency.

The importance of drinking water in order to maintain adequate, balanced electrolyte concentrations for high polarity across all the cellular membranes, cannot be overestimated. Water is an essential ingredient in maintaining the body's natural EMFs against these external fields.

10. ≈
Basics for the Brain: Nutrition

We all know that good, balanced nutrition is important to learning, but what does that mean? It means making sure the raw materials for healthy bodies, and especially the nervous system, are available. These include protein, carbohydrates and fats. It also means being careful not to weaken the body's ability to protect and restore itself by eating the wrong things, notably sugar.

Proteins and fats provide the major building blocks for the membranes of all the cells in our body. Specifically, they form the structure of the dendrites and developing nerve networks. Proteins also form the structure of the sodium-potassium pump to maintain polarity and assure proper nerve transmission throughout our system. In addition, they are involved in the hemoglobin structure (which enables blood to transport oxygen), in the contractile elements in muscle fibers, and serve as antibodies, hormones and enzymes.

Proteins are made up of long chains of amino acids that are assembled according to our DNA code. As proteins form, they fold on to themselves to create characteristic crystalline structures that facilitate their specific functions. Water plays an essential role in the building of the protein molecule. Proteins trap water as they crystallize, with water accounting for 27% to 77% of the crystal's volume. This allows water to influence and maximize the fine-scale structure and function of the protein.[1-2]

Our diets must be balanced to include all ten essential amino acids necessary for the synthesis of proteins. These amino acids cannot be synthesized by the human body from molecules present in the body. Animal products — meat, dairy, eggs — inherently provide the essential amino acids. Vegetarians must be very careful to combine foods in such a way that all essential amino acids are included in their diets.[3]

Pregnant women should be eating approximately 70 grams of protein a day to provide the building blocks for the developing fetus. Children especially need extra protein, as they form 90% of the nerve cells and dendritic extensions in their bodies before age five. They also need more proteins and fats to provide the membranes of new growing cells all through their growth years. The diets of children with learning difficulties are often deficient in protein. Just having a child eat an egg in the morning, instead of cereal, and providing snacks of cheese yogurt, or nuts, will go far towards giving them the needed building blocks to learn.[4]

Carbohydrates, which consist of long molecular chains of sugars, provide the main energy source for our bodies. They are the primary ingredients of grains, fruits, vegetables and dairy sugar. Each of these sources contains two simple sugars, one of which is a molecule of glucose — the main source of energy for the brain. This is the molecule that is broken down (oxidized) by oxygen to yield energy that is then trapped in ATP, leaving carbon dioxide (CO_2) and water, which are exhaled to be recycled by plants back into more food. Carbohydrates are essential, but they must be balanced with proteins and fats.

SUGAR AND THE SOSOH PERSON

When I speak at schools, I am often asked what I would do immediately to assist learning. My answer always begins with three items: First, ban TV and video games before the age of eight to give imagination a chance to develop. For older children, reduce viewing time and monitor the programs watched to cut out a major source of violence and adrenalin producing stress in the learner's life. (I've already discussed TV in Chapter 4, and will again in Chapter 12.) Second, institute a daily integrative movement program such as Brain Gym for every learner, to assure optimal learning readiness and frontal lobe activation. And third, decrease or, better yet, eliminate simple sugars in peoples' diets. If glucose is essential for brain function, why do I make this statement?

This recommendation actually encompasses more than sugar. Sugar is one player in a whole cycle of stress, disease, and immune system factors that contribute to learning problems. The whole cycle probably starts with stress and increased adrenalin, leading to low-ered membrane potential and polarity. This in turn leads to vulner-

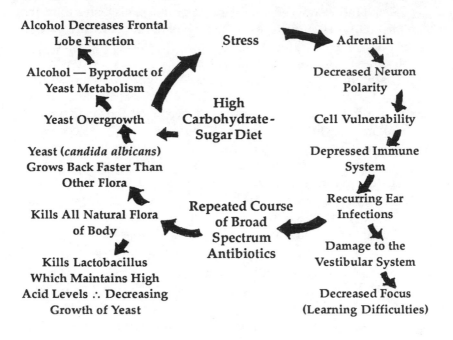

Alcohol Decreases Frontal
Lobe Function

Alcohol — Byproduct of
Yeast Metabolism

Yeast Overgrowth

Yeast (*candida albicans*)
Grows Back Faster Than
Other Flora

Kills All Natural Flora
of Body

Kills Lactobacillus
Which Maintains High
Acid Levels ∴ Decreasing
Growth of Yeast

Stress

High
Carbohydrate-
Sugar Diet

Repeated Course
of Broad
Spectrum
Antibiotics

Adrenalin

Decreased Neuron
Polarity

Cell Vulnerability

Depressed Immune
System

Recurring Ear
Infections

Damage to the
Vestibular System

Decreased Focus
(Learning Difficulties)

Figure 10.1: The Stress-Infection-Antibiotic-Yeast-Sugar-Toxins Cycle

able cells, food sensitivities (usually milk, wheat and corn) and a depressed immune system, which of course leads to infections, particularly respiratory disorders and ear infections.[5] Persistent, recurring ear infections (discussed in Chapter 11) are seen in 94% to 97% of children with learning disabilities. These chronic infections damage the vestibular system and inhibit maximal stimulation to the reticular activating system. This decreases the brain's ability to stay alert, focus and learn.[6]

Persistent, recurring ear infections also lead to long term, repeated treatments with broad spectrum antibiotics. Antibiotics do nothing for viral infection. Waickman notes that "Sixty percent of illnesses which take children to doctors are viral. Yet, many of these viral illnesses are treated with antibiotics."[7] Broad spectrum antibiotics alter all the natural flora of the body, decreasing the beneficial lactobacillus organisms which produce acid that holds down the growth of yeast and other organisms. Antibiotics can also interfere with the ability of the immune system to limit fungal (yeast) infections by decreasing the ability of white blood cells to destroy (phagocytize) yeast organisms.[8]

Since the yeast (*candida albicans*) grows back faster than the lactobacillus, yeast flourishes in the system. It then thrives and reproduces on excess sugars in the body supplied by diets rich in carbohydrates and sugars. This reproduction causes a yeast overgrowth situation. Yeast utilizes sugars as its main food source, releasing toxins (acetaldehyde and alcohol).[9] These toxins further adversely affect the immune system by decreasing the availability of essential omega-3 and -6 fatty acids. These fatty acids are necessary for the formation of prostaglandins, which stimulate T-lymphocyte function to resist allergies and infections.[10] T-lymphocytes, produced in the thymus gland, are key elements in the immune system.[11] With fewer T-lymphocytes, the body becomes overly sensitive and reacts to other foods (chocolate, cola, citrus, eggs), and to environmental allergens, chemicals and other stimuli.

This oversensitivity to environmental stimuli from the stress-infection-antibiotic-yeast-sugar-toxins cycle often manifests itself in fears and phobias prevalent among dyslexics. Harold Levinson identifies heightened sensitivity to fluorescent lights and photophobia as consequences of ear disorders from childhood infections and high sugar diets which result in yeast overgrowth.[12] It makes sense that children with reduced sensory acuity, poor hearing and balance due to infections, don't fully experience their environments. It seems likely that these children could develop fears and phobias leading to even greater stress.

Greater stress would, again, lead to infections as the cycle continues. With high sugar consumption thrown in, yeast overgrowth and the ensuing toxins could lead to over-sensitivity. External, low frequency electromagnetic fields might also exacerbate this whole cycle as they disrupt and weaken cellular membranes.

The toxins released by yeast overgrowth include alcohol. Dr. Waickman found that 60% of the population has some yeast in the alimentary tract capable of producing some alcohol in the stomach.[13] With diets high in carbohydrates and sugars, the conditions are right for further yeast overgrowth and alcohol production. Alcohol is easily carried directly into the blood from the digestive system, and primarily affects the frontal lobes of the brain. Within the frontal lobes, it inhibits nerve net growth and proper development and function. The symptoms show up as decreased attention span, behavior problems, disruptive conduct, irritability, increased sugar cravings, hyperactivity, depression and autistic behavior.[14-15] This is dramatically seen in Fetal Alcohol Syndrome.

The effects of alcohol in the system can be far-reaching, particularly in the frontal lobes, because they are responsible for fine motor coordination, high level formal reasoning and inner speech to control one's behavior. If you have had a "bit to drink," what do you notice about your fine motor coordination? How about your high level formal reasoning? And what does alcohol do to your ability to control your behavior in alignment with social norms? These are the same symptoms I have noticed consistently in SOSOH people. One hundred percent of the SOSOH people I've known and worked with have had high dietary sugar and carbohydrate intake.

In the past fifty years, sugar has become more readily accessible to the general public and its use has skyrocketed. Between 1957 and 1977, dairy product consumption declined by 21%, while sugar consumption increased dramatically: soft drink consumption up 80%, cookies, pies and desserts up 70%, and snacks up 85%. TV has contributed to this trend, familiarizing children with sugar more than any other kind of food.[16]

One way to stop the yeast overgrowth/alcohol cycle is to cut out sugars in the diet. It is important to note that all carbohydrates are simply chains of sugars and that fruits are very high in sugars. Sugar also means brown sugar, honey, molasses, maple syrup, fructose sugar, and corn syrup. So even such an ordinary meal as breakfast cereal with sugar and fruit is a real sugar whammy.

Reading food labels is essential in any sugar reducing effort. Very important is a balanced diet, rich in protein (meat, eggs, nuts, yogurt, cottage cheese, beans), vegetables that supply calcium, magnesium, Vitamin C and the B complex, chromium, zinc and essential fatty acids. I would love to see vending machines in schools that provide nuts, apples, yogurt, cottage cheese or vegetables in place of the usual fare. SOSOH children and adults I have worked with have commented that their sugar cravings have decreased when they drink more water.

The same symptoms of SOSOH occur in Fetal Alcohol Syndrome, which is believed to cause frontal lobe damage in utero that then can affect learning the rest of the child's life.[17] A genetic predisposition to alcoholism has also been found to be connected with hyperactivity.[18] If you have been around alcoholics, you've probably noticed that they gravitate to sugars when they are "on the wagon." The bottom line is that with stress and high dietary intake of sugars, anyone can produce their own alcohol, which will affect frontal lobe functioning. Even as "teetotalers," we have children and adults that are producing their own alcohol from the stress/sugar/ yeast cycle.

We should be aware of one additional and remarkably adverse characteristic of yeast in our system: they have receptor sites for cortisol, which means that yeast produce cortisol. As we will see in our consideration of stress in Chapter 12, while cortisol serves a valuable purpose for the mind and body on alert for danger, it decreases learning and memory function.[19]

11. ≈
The Vestibular System and Learning Disorders

All learning in the first fifteen months of life is centered around vestibular system development. Balance, locomotion, coordination of vision with movement, all of these fundamental abilities which we learn early and rely on the rest of our lives depend upon the proper functioning of the vestibular system. Additionally, the vestibular system maintains the all important arousal state (through the reticular activating system) necessary to be alert and responsive.

HOW THE VESTIBULAR SYSTEM GETS DAMAGED

Disturbance to the vestibular system causes major learning difficulties. Researchers Frank and Harold Levinson found that 94% to 97% of children with dyslexia and learning disabilities showed two or more abnormal neurological or ENG (electronystagmographic) parameters indicating a cerebellar/vestibular system dysfunction.[1-2] All of these children had experienced trauma to the cerebellar/vestibular system in the form of ear infections, allergies, or trauma such as having been "shaken" as infants.

As we saw in Chapter 10, yeast overgrowth has also been implicated in cerebellar/vestibular system dysfunction. Degeneration of the vestibular system due to keeping the head still for long periods of time (as with watching TV) has also been implicated in acquired dyslexic symptomology.[3-4] Damage can occur even before birth. A study of seasonal birth patterns showed that viral infections (influenza, measles) during the second trimester of pregnancy (when the vestibular system is developing) are contributing causes of hyperactivity and mental retardation, as well as of autism and schizophrenia.[5]

In these unfortunate conditions cerebellar/vestibular damage shows up in several ways. Unbalanced activation of muscles which control the movement of the eyes (extraocular muscle dysmetria) causes them to overshoot or undershoot their position of optimal effectiveness when reading. The dyslexic must concentrate so much on moving his eyes that cerebral input for comprehension or retention is limited. Another sign of damage is a defective waking state in the cerebrum, which leads to hypo- or hyper-vigilance with difficulty in maintaining attention, concentration or focus. In this condition, the child "flickers" in and out of consciousness, unable to maintain focused attention.[6]

VESTIBULAR SYSTEM DAMAGE AND LABELED BEHAVIOR

In children identified as ADD (Attention Deficit Disorder), Hyperactive or ADHD (Attention Deficit Hyperactive Disorder), stress and semicircular canal damage may cause low or erratic RAS function. These children may flicker in and out of wakefulness, especially if there is no stimulation via movement. They tend to lose their balance easily and have more playground accidents. They often invade other people's space without knowing it, exhibiting an incomplete understanding of spatial relationships in their environment. They can't stand still, but they can run, since running is more like a propelled fall and doesn't demand as much balance as standing. They likewise can swim or ride a bike because their body is then supported. They "noodle" in their desks because the back and neck muscles haven't been adequately trained to hold their bodies upright against gravity.[7]

If these children are not given full freedom and encouragement to move and practice balance when they are little, there may be too little vestibular activation to assist in repair of the damage. Without the stimulation and new nerve-net development in the vestibular system, difficulties from middle ear trauma are exacerbated. This lack of stimulation can occur when children spend long periods of time in front of TV or video games.

Children truly want to be "good." In order to "stay alert" where there has been vestibular damage, they must move, wiggle and constantly turn their heads. Often this is precisely how they first get tagged with the ADD, Hyperactive or ADHD labels. Teachers become frustrated with their constant movement and tell them to "sit still." Wanting to stay alert, the children's next strategy is to activate their balance centers by tilting their chairs so that only the back two legs of the chair are supporting them. The teacher's response is to demand that they "sit up right and pay attention." But this is a contradiction for these children. If their heads and bodies are still, there will be reduced activation of their brains. These children are also the ones asked to stay in during recess to complete work—when the best thing for them would be to go outside and move.

When children move, damaged tissue in the vestibular system can be overridden as new nerve nets develop and myelinate. As we saw in Chapter 3, the benefits of cerebellar vestibular stimulation — movement — on cognitive growth during infancy are well established.[8] Gross motor and cognitive retardation in deaf children can be eliminated by stimulating the semicircular canal system through movement.[9] First graders who engaged in physical exercise periods that emphasized movement requiring maximum cerebellar/vestibular system control sharply reduced their rates of academic failure.[10] Another study reports that movement and stimulation of balance greatly assist attentional disorders and improve reading.[11]

HOW BRAIN GYM HELPS THE SYSTEM HEAL ITSELF

Brain Gym activities specifically stimulate and develop the cerebellar/vestibular system. The Cross-Crawl, done very slowly while moving the head, requires balance, thus activating the vestibular system. So does the Elephant, which also involves the core muscles of the torso, and strengthens hand/eye coordination. Brain Buttons bring attention to the core muscles in relation to the vestibular system and visual areas within the occipital lobes of the brain. Simply placing the hand on the navel assists balance and brings attention to the gravitational center of the body.

Brain Gym, with its cross-lateral and balanced fine motor movements, activates large areas of the motor cortex and frontal eye field area of the frontal lobes. Consistent, frequent activation of the motor cortex and frontal eye field area through Brain Gym movements, affects nerve-net elaboration into the rest of the frontal lobe including the pre-motor and superior pre-frontal cortex.

12. ≈

Fight or Flight
The Stress Effect on Learning

The highest priority of all living organisms is, simply, to live. From the moment we are born, food, oxygen and water are essential to daily life maintenance. No less critical for survival is the capacity to sense and avoid danger. Nourishment and protection from danger are so essential that a whole range of instinctive drives and automatic processes have evolved in the human body/mind system to insure that these fundamental requirements are satisfied. Of course, hunger and thirst are familiar experiences to everyone. Less evident perhaps are the self-protective instincts that our mind/bodies trigger whenever we sense threatening circumstances in the environment.

Stress is a reaction to perceived threat. The stress response prepares the individual to mentally and physically take protective action. In times of real danger, these survival instincts are invaluable. They heighten our sensitivity to the environment. They intensify muscle strength, blood flow and oxygen distribution. But the stress response does not make us smart, creative or rational. In fact these instinctive processes are largely carried out in the brain stem and sympathetic nervous system with little activation of the rational areas of the brain.

Living with chronic stress has detrimental, far reaching consequences. The American Medical Association contends that over 90% of illness is stress related. In this chapter we will explore the dynamics of stress, its impact on our nervous and immune systems, and its effects on our health and capacity to learn.

WHAT HAPPENS WHEN WE GO ON ALERT

When we are confronted with a threat, one of our body's responses is to send out powerful chemical messengers which put our entire systems on high alert for danger. Among the most well known of these substances is adrenalin (norepinephrine), one of the more than fifty currently known neurotransmitters (chemical messengers which transmit nerve impulses). Adrenalin elicits the survival response of fight or flight.

Though everything in our life is simply an event, our creative mind determines how we will perceive it. If we perceive something as a threat, adrenalin is secreted to protect us from danger. Threats come in many forms and degrees, depending on our unique perceptions of our world. How do you feel about taking a test, meeting someone new, giving a speech, handling a business deal, being on a plane, being in an airless room with smokers, work or school deadlines, having a party, getting married, dealing with death, or even taking some quiet time alone? The possibilities are endless. As long as we continue to perceive a situation as a threat, we secrete adrenalin into our system.

The survival response is orchestrated by the brain stem, with adrenalin being secreted at the nerve endings of the sympathetic nervous system and the adrenal medulla of the adrenal glands. The sympathetic nervous system — a part of the autonomic nervous system — usually operates without conscious control and regulates the activities of smooth muscles, cardiac muscle and certain glands. The sympathetic branch is concerned with processes involving the expenditure of energy, particularly during perceived danger, and sets up the fight or flight response. Adrenalin reinforces the body's primary defenses by increasing blood flow to the heart, lungs and large muscles, especially of the arms and legs, away from the digestive system and the brain. This blood flow insures a greater dispersal of electrolytes to the membranes of these muscles so they can contract — preparing us to fight or flee.[1]

That's probably the original reason why we are warned not to swim directly after we eat. If you feel that swimming is dangerous, your fear can cause adrenalin to be released, which in turn moves blood away from the digestive system to the big muscles. This causes stomach cramps. So if you perceive swimming as dangerous, swimming immediately after eating might indeed be dangerous.

This overall bodily dispersal of electrolytes causes cell membrane potential throughout the body to decrease from the normal of -70 mv to -60 mv or lower. It's like turning on all the faucets in an apartment building — everybody gets some water but the pressure is low. Every cell gets some electrolytes, but because of more widespread dispersal, the levels are lower, thus lowering the membrane potential.

When the membrane potential is lower, it requires less stimuli to activate the defense systems throughout the body. Our sensory apparatus becomes hyper-sensitive, alert to everything that is happening in the environment so we know where danger lies. Even the eyes move peripherally and the pupils dilate to better take in every aspect of our environment that might pose a threat. Meanwhile, as muscles contract in preparation for fight or flight, they generate heat. To protect delicate internal organs from this heat, the body sweats, thus increasing water loss and decreasing cell membrane polarity further by -16 mv or more, from the average of -70 mv to -54 mv, or less.[2] Lower membrane potential, while making us more alert to smaller stimuli, disables our capacity to selectively focus and control our thinking. At such times, learning is very difficult.

Adrenalin release is a graded response dependent on the level of threat to the system. However, once adrenalin is released at the nerve endings and into the blood from the adrenal glands, it takes a while to break it down. The liver must detoxify all the adrenalin before we feel completely calm again. We all know the experience of going to a scary movie, and returning home only to find it takes a while to relax.

During stress, the cortex of the adrenal glands also secretes a group of hormones called the glucocorticoids. Cortisol (hydrocortisone) is the most abundant of these hormones, responsible for about 95% of all glucocorticoid activity. Cortisol increases blood sugar levels to provide the needed energy for efficient muscle function. Cortisol also constricts blood vessels to the surface of the body, which increases blood pressure to the core of the body and the muscles, to protect the surface of the body so it will not lose valuable fluids if wounded.[3] (Cortisone cream, widely used as an anti-inflammatory, causes swelling to go down by constricting blood vessels and reducing fluids to an injured area.)

Research at McGill University concluded that increased cortisol correlated with decreased learning and memory as well as attention problems.[4] When we are under stress, we normally remember less than we otherwise would, and this relates directly to increased cortisol in the system. No wonder it is difficult to focus and remember under stress!

When we are on alert, geared up to fight or flee, the entire system is very sensitive to any and all external stimuli — a flash of movement, a pencil dropping, someone whispering, etc. The brain waves become faster (in the higher Beta range), and we react.[5]

Any or all of the stressors mentioned in the chart "What Inhibits Learning" in Chapter 8, can be perceived by a child as a threat rather than a learning experience or healthy challenge. Children in situations they perceive as stressful react with scattered attention, "climbing the walls" and fighting. This is a normal response to stress. And yet we label these children "ADD — Attention Deficit Disorder," "ADHD — Attention Deficit Hyperactive Disorder," "Hyperactive" or "emotionally handicapped" rather than seriously addressing the stressful situation.

THE TENDON GUARD REFLEX

Another example of the mind/body's profound and intricate reaction to stress can be found at the muscular level, in the "tendon guard reflex." This reflex, an automatic process triggered by stress, shortens the calf muscles and locks the backs of the knees, thereby preparing the body to stand and fight or run from danger. The tendon guard reflex is a feedback mechanism that protects tendons and associated muscles from excessive tension. It causes the muscles associated with the Achilles tendon (gastrocnemius) to contract while antagonistic muscles (tibialis) relax, thus shifting movement to the toes.[6]

When the back of the knees lock and the body moves forward onto the toes during stress, the rest of the body must align to maintain balance. The muscles of the lower back and neck contract to keep us straight and balanced. The tendon guard reflex is meant to occur only for a short time as we prepare to fight or run. But with such high levels of stress in our society today, many people end up with their knees, lower backs and necks almost perpetually locked. This immobility of the spine also decreases natural cerebral spinal fluid flow around the brain. And back muscles can be pulled so tight that people end up with lower back problems or herniated discs between the vertebra — all due to stress.

Shortened calf muscles, as evidenced by "toe walking" often show up in autistic and speech-impaired people. These people may be exhibiting an exaggerated tendon guard reflex in response to intense stress. From the work I've done with autistic and speech-impaired children, I believe there may be a link between shortened calf muscles (gastrocnemius) and the inability to speak. In a perpetual state of stress, the calf muscles naturally tend to shorten, and at the same time speech is inhibited. Paul Dennison observed this same correlation of symptoms in his work with children.[7]

The potential significance of the link between the tendon guard reflex and speech was first suggested to me by my experience with an autistic eight year old boy who had never spoken. He was placed in the hearing-impaired class at his elementary school, where he would sit in the corner and rock all day. His teacher, a specialist for the hearing-impaired, used Brain Gym activities she had learned from me at a Hawaii State Teachers Association conference. Calf lengthening activities were among the Brain Gym activities she used three to four times a day. After about two weeks he began participating in some of the activities in a limited way. Two weeks later he uttered his first words which grew into sentences within that week. The teacher contacted me to talk to the excited and joyful parents.

In my subsequent personal work with autistic and speech-impaired children, I have continued to use Brain Gym activities which consciously bring neural attention away from the survival response, and relax and lengthen the calf muscles.[8] The results have included dramatic success with speech development. All the autistic children I have worked with who had never spoken before were able to speak within weeks after doing these lengthening exercises. This link with relaxed calf muscles and speech is profound and should be more closely investigated.

CHRONIC STRESS

In a tight spot, the survival response is more compelling than formal reasoning. We can afford to give up some focus and rationality once in a while to get out of a jam fast. But the cost quickly mounts when stress is pervasive. Perpetually responding to a stressful world with survival-oriented (SOSOH) behavior takes its toll on the nervous system. Because the nerve net development and myelination is focused in the survival areas, nerve net development into the limbic system and neocortex is limited. People who live with a great deal of stress may inadequately develop the neural pathways that form the foundations for new learning, reasoning and creativity.

Chronically stressed out, survival-oriented people are often unaware of how stressed they are, because for them it has become a way of life. Hans Selye calls that unawareness the General Adaptive Syndrome (GAS), a complex physiological mechanism designed to permit the body to adapt continually to stress. If this mechanism is functioning normally, the body and mind are able to adapt successfully to a wide range of stresses and assaults.[9] Adaptation, however, does not necessarily include higher thinking skills and creative functioning.

Consider some of the seemingly ever-present stressors in our technological society: projected fear of violence or death (perpetuated by the news media and by TV programming with an average of twelve acts of violence every hour), insecurity about the future with unstable home, school and work situations, competition at school or the job market, the fast pace of life. Without effective stress management, we limit our ability to be creative, productive, learning individuals throughout life.

COMMUNICATING STRESS TO CHILDREN

Our stress response may start early in life, even as early as the womb. Fetuses can be affected by their mothers' adrenalin levels. Pregnant women, when they feel stressed, often notice a difference in their babies' in-utero movements compared to times when they feel peaceful and relaxed. Since the womb is such a profound place of learning, mothers might look at ways to lower stress levels during pregnancy.

Infants are highly sensitive to the emotions of their caregivers (parents, family and friends). They can immediately sense the fears and tensions around them, and become stressed themselves. This is often apparent in first babies, especially boys.[10] Because boy babies are developmentally about two to three weeks behind girl babies at birth, their digestive systems aren't as well developed as girls'. They need to eat more often, urinate more often, thus they sleep less and cry more. If the parents become overly tired or concerned, their fears and anxiety can be perceived by this child whose primary focus is survival and it may become colicky. Aside from teething, parental anxiety is possibly the main cause of fussiness in healthy babies whose basic needs have been met.

Twenty percent of new mothers suffer from postpartum depression.[11] They tend to be anxious and feel their lives are out of control. Their babies are more likely to be small (low birth weight), also more likely to be drowsy as infants, cry a lot, and show tension by squirming and arching their backs. As toddlers, they tend to be especially emotional and later on exhibit a variety of behavior problems, many of which last into adolescence.[12]

SOSOH AND THE FAMILY

The family is where all the important first modeling of behavior occurs. Organized, peaceful and safe home environments help to shield children from many of the factors that lead to SOSOH. Alternatively, if parents and other caregivers live highly stressful, disruptive lives, their children may imprint that training onto their own nervous systems.

Many home based factors can promote SOSOH behavior. Poorly performing students are often from low socioeconomic families. They may have experienced poor nutrition, lack of early sensory enrichment and high family stress, even violence.[13] When children are heavily stressed in dysfunctional homes, they suffer. They may not get support and attention. The essence of who they are may never surface. In their efforts to be OK in the face of their models, the SOSOH pattern develops. The symptoms develop from the instinct for survival and the need to be accepted, not from conscious understanding. With survival as their primary goal, the higher centers of thought and regulation may just not develop, though the full potential is there.

Sharon Wegschneider Cruise's portrait of the "Mascot" survival role fits a majority of SOSOH people. According to Cruise, Mascots tend to play the clown, vying for either positive or negative attention. This serves two purposes: to be recognized, and to siphon off family or social tension by their actions. They are caught in a painful contradiction: what they experience in their lives is chaos, but they are told everything is fine. Because they trust what is being said to them, Mascots become unable to trust their own intuition and may have the illusion of being crazy. They feel fragile, insecure and anxious, thus exhibiting a lack of confidence and self-esteem. Their actions are geared to gain attention at any cost. Sometimes, if they push, they get this attention in the form of physical abuse, but at least it provides the basic human need for touch.[14-15]

Scientific findings show that children are more highly susceptible to their environment than was previously believed. Such stressful experiences as witnessing domestic violence and undergoing abuse activate hormones that impair normal cerebral development. These hormones can actually damage the brain cells that control later learning ability and can lead to intellectual and behavioral problems in adulthood.[16]

As a counselor, working with variously labeled SOSOH children in grades K-8, I found about 95% of them assuming the Mascot survival role. Realizing that survival is the priority of each of these children, it is incongruous to ask them to do high level deductive reasoning and to control their behavior rationally.

The importance of caregiver modeling cannot be overstated. Putting more attention on supportive, effective early family relationships may reap more benefits with SOSOH people than anything else. In my experience, the most eloquent evidence for this point is the noticeable absence of SOSOH people in African villages where every adult is an important caregiver, and every child is valued as a unique and integral part of the clan.

Training adult caregivers to manage stress effectively and control their own behavior, and then teaching their children these techniques, is at least as effective, if not superior to Ritalin. Good learning and good problem solving require active involvement and persistence by the model caregivers.[17]

Children must also learn to take responsibility for their actions. If caregivers play the Family Hero or Enabler role, always doing everything for their children, the youngsters will not learn and gain confidence in their ability to take responsibility and be in control of their lives.[18-19] Caregivers can assist children in developing responsibility, starting before the age of two, by modeling and then allowing and encouraging them to take care of their toys, pets and other people.

STRESS AND VULNERABILITY TO DISEASE

Stress has enormous health consequences as well. Because adrenalin and other stress-induced neurotransmitters lower cell membrane polarity, stress puts the very health of the cell at risk. The bacteria and viruses (pathogens) which prey on cells are essentially scavengers, searching for the vulnerable cells in an organism. They mostly attack cells with lowered membrane polarity.

George W. Crile graphically demonstrated this connection with an experiment in which two electrodes with the same charge (either positive or negative, but not both) were placed approximately four inches apart on a person's forearm. A charge was generated for a short time, and then the area on the forearm was carefully studied. Within a day, a lesion had formed on the site. Cultures were then taken from both forearms to assess the extent of bacterial and fungal growth. The lesion showed no greater concentration of bacteria and fungi than the untreated forearm. Within days, however, the lesion became densely populated with disease-causing organisms. These ever-present organisms on the skin did no damage until the integrity of the skin cells was destroyed by lowering the membrane polarity.

The lowered membrane polarity left the cells vulnerable and open to pathogenic attack.[20]

We are most vulnerable to disease in times of increased stress. Increased stress leaves the body more open to disease by decreasing the integrity and polarity of cell membranes. The opportunity for illness is always present. We are constantly breathing in pathogens and some (such as viruses) live in our body for long periods of time. When stress levels rise, disease organisms can finally enter cells and cause sickness.

With all the stressors in our world today, it is little wonder that infants exhibit elevated adrenalin levels and are more vulnerable to chronic ear infections. Harold Levinson discovered that over 90% of children with learning difficulties had ear infections as infants.[21] Nature apparently intended the stress response to be short lived, getting the body out of danger in a life-threatening situation and then going back to normal. To maintain high stress and adrenalin levels for long periods of time leaves the body open to disease, such as chronic ear infections in children.

The way we choose to perceive and process our experiences determines whether we handle them calmly or allow them to trigger the stress response. The human mind is very active and can create stress-inducing future scenarios that cause us to worry and live in fear. This fear takes a definite toll on our health. Type A personalities, who are highly vulnerable to heart disease, workaholics and other Super-types who strive to meet unrealistic personal or societal expectations are prime candidates for the stress response.

EMOTIONS AND HEALTH

The immune system is regulated by the limbic system, the area of the brain that processes emotions. In the 1980's, researchers at the National Institute of Mental Health discovered receptor sites for limbic system neuropeptides and neurotransmitters on cells of the immune system, particularly monocytes. Monocytes, a type of white blood cell, are key players in the immune system that migrate to areas of infection and destroy the pathogenic organisms of disease. Damage or lesions to the hypothalamus (part of the limbic system) will cause changes in monocyte and other white blood cell activity, and therefore in the immune system.[22]

The close association of neuropeptides and neurotransmitters with both the emotions and the immune system suggest that emotions and health are deeply interdependent. If being happy, sad, thoughtful, and excited triggers the production of neuropeptides and neurotransmitters in our limbic system, then the immune cells must also be affected when we are happy, sad, thoughtful and excited.[23]

With the nervous and immune systems inextricably linked chemically, our emotions naturally affect the whole body. The heart, traditionally designated as the seat of emotions and love, has recently been downgraded in that role in favor of other organs. And yet, the heart is chemically linked directly to emotions. The atrium area of the heart produces a hormone (Atrial Natriuretic Factor - ANF) that dramatically affects every major organ of the body and operates in response to a strong emotion from the limbic system, whether it be anger or love. Therefore ANF plays a key role in our emotional state, immune system function, memory and learning.[24] It impacts the thalamus and its dynamic with the pituitary, the master endocrine gland for body regulation. It also influences the hypothalamus and pineal gland, regulating the production and action of melatonin which affects circadian rhythm and mood swings.

Our growing awareness of the emotion/immune system link underscores the importance of responsibly expressing our emotions. The responsible expression of emotion requires an integration of all parts of the mind/body system at the time the emotions are felt. This facilitates the linking of insight and reasoning with emotion. Learning this process begins with limbic brain development around fifteen months of age. If the emotions that are expressed by the child are listened to seriously, in a safe, supportive environment, the child will learn to express them responsibly. By the age of five, the child is able to connect reason (from the neocortex) with the emotions; and by age eight, adds insight (from the frontal lobes) to refine the emotions. Over time the responsible expression of emotion becomes a valuable tool, absolutely essential to a healthy person — and a healthy society.

When strong emotions, especially fear, anger or rage cannot be, or are not expressed, they remain unresolved. These unresolved emotions end up being relegated to the sympathetic nervous system, where they can build over time into fear and may eventually explode as violence, or manifest internally as disease. In either case, the stress response is stimulated, leaving the system vulnerable to disease and inhibiting the learning process.

Research shows, for example, that sexually abused people, who have been unable to express their emotions about the abuse, produce high levels of adrenalin and endorphins and exhibit weakened immune systems. Frank Putnam of the National Institute of Mental Health and Martin Teicher of Harvard Medical School found that chronically high adrenalin levels can kill neurons in brain areas crucial for thinking and memory. They found that sexual abuse arrested growth of the left hemisphere, hampering development of language and logic, and increased levels of an antibody that significantly weakened the immune system.[25] The link between sexual abuse and emotions is dramatically shown in research conducted by Dr. Lenore C. Terr. She found that sexually abused people showed an indifference to pain, a lack of empathy, an inability to define or acknowledge feelings, and an abhorrence of emotional intimacy.[26]

In contrast to the stress reaction, when we are able to responsibly express and resolve our emotions, or feel positive, exhilarated, excited, getting the AhHa's of learning, we actually boost our immune system. When we are relaxed, genuinely happy, elated, joyful, there is an increase in interferons and interleukins, which are secreted at the cellular level. Interferons and interleukins increase membrane polarity, making cells invulnerable to pathogenic organisms. Adrenalin, interferons and interleukins are all life-protecting chemicals: adrenalin for acute survival, and interferons and interleukins for health and longevity.[27]

WHY TOUGHING IT OUT MAY MAKE YOU WEAKER

Men die earlier in our society than women, the main natural cause of death being cardiovascular disease. It now appears, contrary to the old Hollywood stereotype, that a stout heart is not one that is indifferent to emotion, and a "broken heart" may be more than a metaphor for what happens when love is not expressed, or the emotional needs for love and connection are not met. And yet, despite all the evidence that disease is stress-related and that it is healthy to express emotions, thereby releasing stress, society continues to promote a non-emotional model to our youth, especially males.

Recent research demonstrates intriguing correlations between the ways males and females conduct relationships, their sense of self-esteem, and ultimately their health. In a study of people ages 14-28, females turned out to have a very different basis for their self-esteem than males did.[28] Girls with high self-esteem tend to be cheerful, assertive, emotionally open, warm and able to work well with others. Boys with high self-esteem tend to be stern, humorless, unemotional and lacking in social skills. This study asserts that relating to others well fosters self-esteem in females, whereas managing one's anxiety with an unemotional attitude significantly aids male self-esteem. Not surprisingly, males in this study showed higher stress levels and hyperactive ratios than females. Where do these notions of male- and femaleness come from? We have only to look as far as the TV sitcoms and our mass media in general to find them.

Adequate expression and resolution of emotions helps to mitigate stressful situations. How we experience and express our emotions, particularly negative ones, largely determines whether we secrete adrenalin or other neuropeptides. When such intense negative emotions as anger and grief are responsibly expressed rather than suppressed, adrenalin is released in minimal amounts, or not at all. Expressing the emotion prevents the stress associated with it from becoming chronic. When we can truly express grief, we can also deeply express joy. Then life becomes a rich, alive, passionate adventure of learning and health.

TV, THE NOT SO HIDDEN STRESSOR

There is a growing realization that excessive TV and TV violence may be linked to learning difficulties. By 1977 more than one hundred published papers representing fifty laboratory and field studies and other experiments involving ten thousand children and adolescents from every conceivable background all showed that TV violence affects viewers. They demonstrated that TV violence makes children more willing to harm others, more aggressive in their play and more likely to select aggression as the preferred response to conflict situations.[29]

Consider some of the disturbing trends in our society's viewing habits: American pre-school children ages 2-5 years watch over 27 hours per week.[30] Approximately one half of American parents have given up setting limits on what children watch.[31] 24% of American households keep a TV in the child's bedroom and 25% of American adults cannot conceive of a large enough amount of money to persuade them to stop watching TV.[32]

In 1994, there were an average of twelve acts of violence per hour on the TV, sixteen acts per hour in children's programming, and eight acts per hour in adult programming. A recent study found that the average American child watches 3 hours of TV a day with one fourth watching more than 6 hours of TV a day. By age 13, children will have seen an estimated 18,000 violent murders on TV.[33] An extensive, fifteen year longitudinal study in the United States, Canada and South Africa, showed long-term childhood exposure to TV as a causal factor behind approximately one half of the homicides, rapes and assaults committed in these countries.[34]

Cartoon violence is carefully and deliberately used to lure the child to watch, and to attract the largest possible audience for the purpose of selling products. Violent cartoons have been found to be the easiest means of attracting the entire 2 to 11 year age group. The most serious and widespread effect of this marketing scheme is desensitization and the development of thick-skinned, detached, cynical human beings.[35]

HOW TV CAUSES STRESS

Dr. Byron Reeves of Stanford University conducted studies of TV viewers' electrical brain activity. Their brains responded to movements on the TV as if they were actually real, causing the nervous system to prepare for a physical response.[36] Our brains are very sensitive to quick movements, sudden noises, and color changes that might signal danger, so we prepare for fight or flight to protect ourselves. TV programers know and use this to keep us watching, even when we may not want to. You can confirm this for yourself by counting all the lighting changes that occur during a TV show and commercials. Because there is a natural physical reaction to danger, and there is no outlet for the impulse when watching TV, the watcher may develop overactivity, frustration or irritability that can affect other areas of his life.[37-38-39-40]

The brain is geared to insure the care and longevity of humans so the whole species will survive. During limbic system development, we begin to learn about relationships, emotion and bonding for species survival. When young children see people being harmed or killed on TV, it triggers their innate concern for species survival. Anything that goes against species survival during those first four years could precipitate the stress reaction.

At the same time, children have an instinctive desire to imitate observed behavior without reasoning whether it ought to be imitated or not. They mimic anything, including destructive and anti-social behavior.[41] Infants as young as fourteen months of age demonstrably observe and incorporate behavior seen on TV.[42]

Up through age four, children cannot distinguish between truth and fiction when they view TV. For preschoolers, TV is a source of entirely factual information about how the world works. TV violence, though stimulating the survival response, can become a commonplace, daily thing. It seems that the innate species survival sense can be dulled, and replaced by an impression of the power and allure of violence. In later years, under severe stress, adolescents and adults revert to their earliest impression of what violence is and its role in society. Much of this impression could have come from TV.[43] This shows up dramatically in a study of male felons imprisoned for committing violent crimes (homicide, rape and assault). 22% to 34% admit to consciously imitating crime techniques learned from TV, usually successfully.[44]

Hyperactivity is exhibited in boys eight times more often than in girls.[45] Boys are given very vivid models through male violence on TV. They are given strong messages to be tough and "play it cool" in the face of violence. With no acceptable way to release or express the stress they feel, adrenalin pumped into their muscles may lead to a hyperactive state where excess energy causes them to constantly move or fidget. The next step is a SOSOH label — Hyperactive, ADHD, ADD, or Emotionally Handicapped.

THE MORPHINES IN OUR HEAD

There are other neuropeptides secreted in response to high levels of stress and pain. These neuropeptides, the body's natural painkillers, are called enkephalins and endorphins and are located in the thalamus, hypothalamus and parts of the limbic system. First discovered in 1974 by Candace Pert and Solomon Snyder at John Hopkins University, these natural opiates (morphines) are a throwback to the time when immediate pain relief meant that animals could flee from an attacker without delay.[46]

The marathon runner offers a good example of how these pain killers operate. There is a point at which the balanced exercise of running starts to become painful. At this point the body sends messages to the brain that it's time to stop before major tissue damage occurs. Runners refer to this as The Wall. If the runner ignores the body's message and continues to run, the brain receives the message that this is a life-threatening situation and that it is essential to keep moving. At that point, the brain secretes endorphins to block the pain sensation to the brain so that the runner can get his body out of danger.

The runner experiences a sense of euphoria because the pain has stopped. But by not listening and responding to the body's message to stop, and masking the body's distress with chemical signals that the body is still in imminent danger, runners end up with unnecessary injuries. With the competitive push today, I wonder if we haven't developed a society of endorphin addicts that are getting high on their own morphine. This may be an attempt to block out the pain in their over-stressed lives.

I have also seen increased endorphin response in children who "space out" at school, leaving the pain of their world behind. That pain may include trauma and abuse at home, a highly painful experience in school, or in many cases, both. Again the system is all too quick to label these children Hyperactive, Emotionally Handicapped, and ADD.

Balanced aerobic activity, where we don't go beyond our bodies' messages and secrete endorphins, increases oxygen intake so important to learning. Aerobic exercises such as swimming, walking, running and cycling that use the large muscles of the body, mainly legs, are healthful activities that keep the heart rate up. The President's Council on Physical Fitness and Sports recommends a minimum of half an hour per day for physical and intellectual health.[47] Doctors and psychotherapists dealing with stress in patients are now recommending exercise, particularly walking (the Cross Crawl), as a highly effective stress-management therapy.[48]

Non-competitive, co-operative physical education programs that encourage student input are fun for everyone. They decrease the stress and, therefore, increase learning power. Taking the unnecessary competition out of our lives will render them less painful and decrease the need for endorphins.

In addition to acting as pain blockers, endorphins effect our health in another critical way: when produced in response to emotional stress, they suppress the activity of T-Cells, thus lowering our resistance to pathogens, cancer and autoimmune disease. T-Cells, also called T-lymphocytes, are white blood cells from the thymus gland that are especially effective in destroying bacteria, viruses, fungi, and cancer cells. The disease AIDS greatly decreases T-lymphocytes in the blood. Though many people have the AIDS virus, the ones that manifest the disease may be dealing with emotional stressors that increase endorphin levels in the system.[49]

THE GREAT GABA

There is a great deal more to be learned about the effects of stress on the complex chemistry of the mind/body's learning processes. And there is a great deal that is known that is beyond the scope of this book. But there is one more neurotransmitter that deserves special mention for its role in learning, and illustrates how well the body's systems work together to facilitate learning.

To learn, actively reason and remember new information it is essential for the brain to block out non-important stimuli and maintain attentive focus. GABA (gamma-aminobutyric acid) blocks out unimportant stimuli by hyperpolarizing the membranes of post-synaptic neurons, increasing the membrane's polarity (to more than -70 mv inside) to the point that it will respond only to specific chosen stimuli.[50-51] We activate neurons that secrete GABA when, for example, we are reading a highly absorbing book. We choose to become unaware of our environment and the passage of time, so the brain is not distracted as it maintains complete focus. We also intentionally secrete GABA at night in order to block out light, sounds and the feel of the bed on our bodies so we can go to sleep. With GABA, the system can choose its focus rather than react, as it does with adrenalin, to all the stimuli around it.

We consciously choose which membranes to hyperpolarize with GABA. For example, when I was a new mother, I could block out the DC-10's that flew over our house at night, but if my daughter made the slightest whimper, I was awake immediately. My daughter's welfare was my conscious intention. So while raising the threshold of awareness to aircraft noise, I lowered the threshold in areas of the nervous system associated with awareness of my daughter's well-being. Similarly, during a learning session, we use GABA to block out irrelevant stimuli such as the sounds of a pencil dropping, kids giggling, or street noises. This gives us the ability to focus our attention.

GABA gives us the control to be fully present, mentally and emotionally, thus overriding the adrenalin reaction. We learn to secrete it through practice, in an environment with good models, where quiet, focused time is encouraged. People who have not acquired this highly important mind/body skill, are among those likely to be labeled "hyperactive." They tend to take in and react to all the stimuli around them, but cannot selectively choose when it is appropriate to ignore certain stimuli. They haven't fully developed the ability to calm and focus their own system. I have found that Brain Gym can be very helpful to these people. The areas of the brain that house the neurons which secrete GABA are associated with movement, particularly fine, coordinated movements. It would seem, therefore, that doing fine coordinated movements, like Brain

Gym, would increase the stimulation and proliferation of dendrites from those neurons, thus increasing the availiabilty of GABA in the system to bring about focused attention.

Managing stress means using the whole body/mind system in a more efficient and healthful way. It takes consciously moving the focus and nervous energy of the mind/body system away from the survival centers, and distributing it in a balanced manner to all areas of the system. We can't expect ourselves, our children, or people of any age to learn optimally under the shadow of stress. The ability to manage stress in every part of our lives opens the door for all meaningful learning.

13. ≈

Mis-Education and
The Labeling Game

Because of the infinite variation in the way individuals are assembled, it must be assumed that the sentient properties of any one person, like his or her fingerprints, could never be identical with those of another. It is probable, therefore, that there does not exist or ever will exist one person exactly like another. If uniqueness were an indispensable requirement for an evolving society, every person would be indispensable.

— *Paul MacLean*[1]

Competition is so pervasive in our society that even school children are afflicted by the omnipresent pressures that lead to stress. School itself is a big source of stress, even more so for those children whose academic performance is poor. Inevitably, school is a defining experience for nearly everyone. Self-esteem, choice of career, expectations in life are greatly influenced by the grades and rewards we receive in school. Poor performance in school brings out a lot of negative emotions which lead to fear and perceptions of threat. That is stress. As we have seen, stress further disables the learner, setting off a vicious cycle that sends grades spiralling downward.

It does not have to be this way. If instead each student felt valued and supported, a great deal of stress could be eliminated from learning situations. A lot of poor school work is attributable to educational practices, particularly in schools which do not accomodate for learning differences. People learn differently, yet school is set up to favor certain styles of learning and school work focuses on certain kinds of tasks.

On the whole, school teaches, tests and values logic brain

tasks. Logic, sequence, computation, categorization, verbal skills are all highly prized abilities in school. Intuition, emotion, vision, humor, rhythmic movement, image formation, and other gestalt brain capacities are not practiced, tested or particularly valued at school. It is only in the real world, outside of the classroom, where success depends upon entrepreneurship, imagination and insight, that we begin to appreciate the importance of the gestalt brain. School is very lopsided, and many students suffer and end up exhibiting SOSOH behavior because of this bias.

OUR INNATE LEARNING STYLES

We are all uniquely wired. Our specific life experiences shape our perceptions, the way we learn and in essence, who we are. Some of our neuronal wiring, (our nerve networks), however, are determined by innate factors. For instance, we all show a preference for one hand over the other, one eye over the other, even one ear over the other. We also exhibit a preference for one brain hemisphere over the other.

Our wiring is also determined by the specific way we choose to take in sensory information and our dominant sense's connection to our preferred hemisphere. This wiring constitutes our unique learning style, and is neither good nor bad. It is merely a leaning toward certain types of perception and a preference for and ease with certain kinds of tasks. However, when the learning experiences you encounter, in school for instance, never match your preferences or bring out your strengths, you may begin to feel that your learning style is indeed inferior.

THE DENNISON DOMINANCE PROFILES

In recent years several systems for analyzing and identifying learning styles have been developed by educators and psychologists. Dr. Paul Dennison developed a method to gauge and characterize individual learning styles that yields very useful results. His approach is to determine basal dominance profiles that identify the lateral dominance of eyes, ears, and hands in relation to the dominant brain hemisphere. This assessment provides a deep insight into how individuals process information and experience.[2]

Dominance profiles give information about our preferred learning styles, but they also give us a clear understanding of our initial (basal) response in moments of stress. When we are under stress, we rely most on our dominant senses and our preferred ways of processing.

In less stressful situations, our dominance profiles can fluctuate. As we meet changing situations which require new learning and adjustments throughout our lives, we depart from our basal dominance profile, assuming adaptive dominance profiles. These adaptive profiles reflect self-designed learning strategies that work for us. However, under stress we react by immediately returning to our basal profile. Under stress, only one hemisphere, either the gestalt or logic brain, is efficiently functioning, and we have less effective use of the senses that do not feed into or are not expressed through that dominant hemisphere.

The basal dominance profile gives important information as to how we most easily take in and process new learning, especially when it is challenging. It is the road map of our specific base learning style. When we are confronted with a new learning situation, we will access information most easily through our dominant senses (eyes or ears), and express (either verbally, with gestures or in writing) with our dominant hand.

Eyes, ears and hands are of course the primary sense organs, the means by which we take in information. Because of our innate neural circuitry, the left hemisphere controls movement and receives sensory information from the right side of the body. The right hemisphere controls movement and receives sensory information from the left side of the body. Figure 13.1 presents a dominance "bug," a schematic drawing that will help you to visualize the dominance profiles. A darkened area of the bug, indicates dominance in that hemisphere, hand, eye or ear.

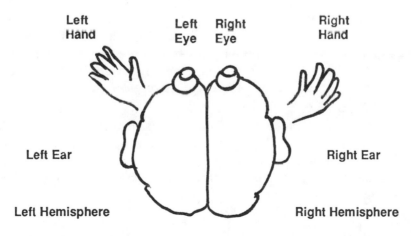

Figure 13.1 Dominance Bug

The efficiency of sensing depends upon whether or not the dominant eye, ear or hand is on the side opposite the dominant brain hemisphere. For example, visual input is most efficient when the dominant eye is opposite the dominant brain hemisphere. If the left brain and right eye are dominant, then vision is facilitated. The left brain controls the muscular movements of the right eye, thus optimizing the efficiency of  three dimensional and two dimensional focus, tracking and peripheral vision. The same would be true for the right brain/left eye dominance.

If however, both the left eye and left brain are dominant (**homolateral**), then vision is less effective because the dominant brain is not controlling the muscular movements of the dominant eye. Homolateral refers to the dominant eye, ear, or hand being on the same side as the dominant brain, decreasing efficiency, especially under stress  when the functioning of the non-dominant hemisphere is limited. I will refer to homolateral profiles as **limited**.

The eyes facilitate seeing and visual interpretation of our world. The ears facilitate hearing, listening and memory. Interestingly, hearing is processed in the temporal lobes which are closely linked to the limbic system's memory areas. The hands facilitate communication: oral, written and gestural. The left hemisphere initiates language (both verbal and written) expression in the right hand. The right hemisphere initiates expressive movement and physical manipulation in the left hand. When both the left hemisphere and left hand are dominant, communication becomes limited. The same is true if the right hemisphere and right hand are dominant. These are simplistic explanations that only touch on the high degree of complexity these profiles represent.

The following is a chart of basal profiles, giving an idea of how the hemispheres, eyes, ears and hands work together. Some people have cross-lateral profiles for specific senses, and some have homolateral profiles for specific senses. These can also be mixed in any combination, for example, a person may be cross-lateral for eyes and homolateral for ears.

Cross-lateral Profiles

DOMINANT SENSE	DOMINANT HEMISPHERE	PREFERRED LEARNING STYLE
Right eye	Left	Visual
Left eye	Right	Visual
Right Ear	Left	Auditory
Left Ear	Right	Auditory
Right hand	Left	Verbal
Left hand	Right	Kinesthetic

Homolateral Profiles

DOMINANT SENSE	DOMINANT HEMISPHERE	LEARNER STYLE
Right eye	Right	Visually limited
Left eye	Left	Visually limited

Visually limited learners prefer to learn through their other senses. They may close their eyes or look away to concentrate on information they really want to learn or express.

Right ear	Right	Auditorially limited
Left ear	Left	Auditorially limited

Auditorially limited learners may tune out when people talk too much, as in lectures.

Right hand	Right	Communication limited

Communication limited learners see the whole image and may have difficulty breaking it down to the pieces of language to express their understanding.

Left hand	Left	Kinesthetically limited

Kinesthetically limited learners may have difficulty manipulating objects in the learning environment to communicate their ideas.

Figure 13.2: Dennison Dominance Profiles

The Dennison dominance profiles became a valued addition to my counseling work with Special Education and Emotionally Handicapped students. Used in Individualized Educational Programs (IEP's), the profiles informed and supported each child's understanding of his or her unique way of learning. (IEP's are usually year long educational goals, set up for each individual child and agreed upon by the teacher, counselor and parent of the child.) The dominance profile also gave the parents and teachers an understanding of how to approach and honor each child's learning style. Some teachers even began using it in regular classrooms as part of student self-understanding and self-esteem programs.

DOMINANCE PROFILES AND EDUCATIONAL LABELING

After using this dominance profile assessment in many schools with many students, I began to see certain patterns emerge. I noticed, for example that many of the students who were gestalt brain dominant and/or sensory limited were also the ones who had been labeled as having learning difficulties. In 1990 I undertook a more formal study to compare dominance profile types with schools' systems of labeling students.[3]

Using the basal dominance profiles, I collected data from a random sample of 218 students attending Denver, Colorado and Kona, Hawaii schools. The dominance assessment was done using muscle response checking — a diagnostic method used by doctors, kinesiologists, chiropractors, and other health professionals — while bringing the subject's attention to each arm, each eye, each ear, and each hemisphere of the brain. The students were also identified by the following labels established by assessment criteria in these schools:

GT = Gifted and Talented (children chosen for this program excelled academically and had high SAT scores, thus succeeded at language and math skills)

N = Normal (children doing OK in the regular classroom)

R = Remedial (includes children in Chapter 1 and children with specific reading difficulties)

X = Special Education/Emotionally Handicapped (children labeled with learning disabilities and Attention Deficit Hyperactive Disorder - ADHD).

HSR = High School Redirection (an alternative high school for students who had previously dropped out of other schools)

The following graph shows my findings with percentages of each group checked. (The columns representing logic and gestalt for each group total 100%.)

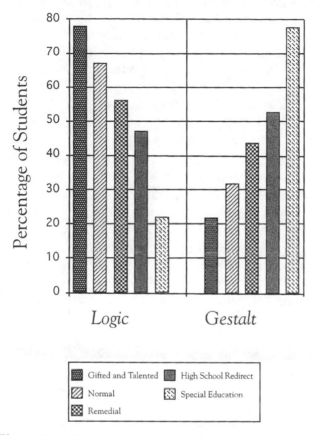

Figure 13.3: Hemisphere Dominance in a Random Sample of 218 Students Attending Denver, Colorado and Kona, Hawaii Schools

HOW RIGHT BRAINERS ARE WRONGED

The first thing that struck me profoundly was the contrast between the label applied to 78% of the logic dominant students and the label assigned to 78% of the gestalt dominant students. In the schools I studied, students with high verbal abilities and logic brain processing were more often labeled gifted and talented. Those with gestalt processing and low linear verbal skills were more frequently labeled as learning disabled/Special Education.

As is well known (and as I explained in Chapter 5), logic

dominant processors, usually called left brained, focus on the details: specifically, in language, on the words, syntax, and sentence structure. In math they are more able to use linear detailed processing in problem solving. They are also more adept at learning the details of technique in art, music, dance and sports. In music, they tend to do well with note reading, timing and specific technique in holding or playing the instrument. Since music is generally taught in a linear fashion, starting with notes, timing and technique, left brain processing is useful at the beginning. But if logic brained music students do not adequately develop gestalt brained capacities, they may have difficulty accessing the image, passion, rhythm and flow necessary to make their music come alive.

As the chart shows, students with logic brained talents are more often positively reinforced with the Gifted and Talented label by the educational system. They are more likely to have high self-esteem and experience less stress, because school work is geared toward their competencies. This allows them the confidence to explore gestalt avenues of learning. (But only if they are not overly stressed by competition and the pursuit of ever higher grades). With less stress in the long run, they have a better chance of obtaining more integrative learning strategies, nerve-net development and myelination across the corpus callosum.

Gestalt processors, usually called right brained, are able to take in the big image, feel the emotional connections, access intuitive understanding and need to learn kinesthetically through movement. In art, music, dance and sports they access the passion, movement and big picture — all elements which are crucial to creativity. They prefer to approach music as a whole, exploring, playing and singing what they hear and feel.

If they are not adequately using their left brains (in times of stress for instance) they will have difficulty managing details and linear processing. Gestalt learners more than logic learners are affected by the early push, between ages 5 and 7, to learn linear functions both in language and math. These children begin to judge themselves as "dumb" and develop "learned helplessness."

A study comparing brain wave activity in "learning disabled" and "normal" children discovered a major difference. "Learning disabled" children, exhibited 1) less overall left-hemisphere activation, even with verbal tasks, and 2) significantly fewer shifts from one hemisphere to the other when tasks required different processing strategies.[4] I believe this directly relates to stress in these children. Due to stress in the learning environment, they end up depending only on their dominant hemisphere (gestalt), the brain stem and sympathetic nervous system. They become unable to explore and adequately access their logic hemisphere. Thus they are trapped in a vicious cycle. The stress of schooling heightens their inability to learn in a logical way, diminishing myelination and easy access between both hemispheres. Gestalt learners in our society have been strongly discriminated against!

Gestalt learners have to struggle to make it through our educational system. I believe Albert Einstein was a gestalt learner. His early academic failures are legendary, and he frequently referred in later life to his reliance on visual imagery rather than linear logic. "The words of the language," he said, "as they are written and spoken, do not seem to play any role in my mechanisms of thought. The psychical entities which seem to serve as elements in thought are certain signs and more or less clear images which can be voluntarily reproduced or combined."[5] Fortunately, he sought out holistic learning situations that fed his curiosity and lust for understanding. As a world we have been blessed with his incredible insights, all of which were more intimately bound to his internal images and feelings than to strictly linear processing.[6]

Our educational system does little to encourage holistic, intuitive, image-based (as opposed to verbal-based) thinking. But where would we be without these capacities? Gestalt learners have talents that are too frequently undervalued in school. If as a result, gestalt learners undervalue themselves we run the risk that they stop contributing in significant ways. We must strive to understand and facilitate the learning process of gestalt learners so we do not lose this valuable resource.

HOW THE EDUCATIONAL SYSTEM FAVORS FULL SENSORY ACCESS

Our educational system favors students that can process linearly, take in information auditorially and visually, look at the teacher, and restate pieces of information in a logical, linear fashion. In my study these students are listed as "full sensory access" (in general they are left brained, right eyed, right eared and right handed). They make up, on average, only 15% of the test population. Those labeled "gifted and talented" are the largest segment of this full sensory access group.

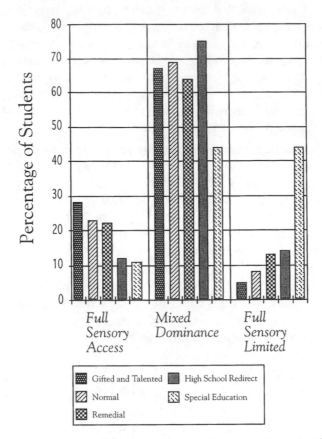

Figure 13.4: Sensory Access Patterns in the Same Sample of 218 Students

These students usually do well on the verbal and mathematical skills tests commonly given in our schools, including the Scholastic Assessment Tests (SAT's), which despite their limited scope, are considered in the United States to be reliable assessments of intelligence. You will notice that this profile is highly dependent on logic brain functioning. But if these learners are not encouraged to use gestalt brain processing, they may not adequately develop some very important abilities like: seeing the big picture, feeling the emotional implications of ideas or spontaneously generating new ideas. Yet the whole system is geared to teaching predominantly logic processing skills.

Let's examine some of the other implications of this study. In Figure 13.5, note the column marked auditorially limited. When the dominant ear is on the same side of the body as the dominant hemisphere, auditory functioning is less effective and the person might not easily hear what is being said. In my study, the auditorially limited profile represents an average of approximately 52% of the population. Yet lecturing is our primary way of teaching. A typical lecture, then, is likely to be missed by over half of the audience. Thinking Caps (discussed in Chapter 7) are excellent at tuning up listening capacities when done prior to a lecture.

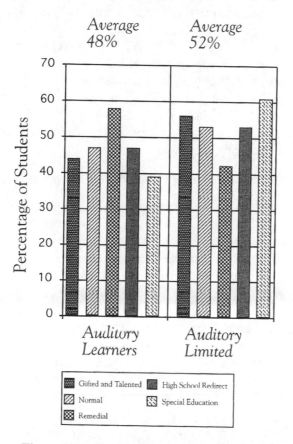

Figure 13.5: Ear/Hemisphere Dominance Patterns in the Same Sample of 218 Students

Also notice that a high percentage of both the "gifted and talented" and the "special education" students were auditorially limited. Here is an interesting and seemingly paradoxical commonality which can be explained when you consider that the vast majority of "gifted and talented" students are logic dominant and therefore verbal. So even though they are auditorially limited and may not hear what is being said, they talk — and so are believed to be more intelligent. The opposite is true for the Special Education students, mainly gestalt dominant, who are not verbal. Our society equates verbal skills with intelligence, and therefore labels those who speak well as Gifted and Talented. Less verbal students are more likely to be labeled Special Education.

In this same study, among the students with cross lateral profiles for hands and hemispheres, 22% of the Gifted and Talented group were kinesthetic and not verbal compared to 89% of the Special Education group. We highly value linguistic ability in our traditional educational system. Our SAT tests reflect this by testing the linguistic and logical/mathematical intelligences. As Howard Gardner has observed, this bias ignores at least five other intelligences, including the kinesthetic, visual/spatial, musical, interpersonal and intrapersonal. Many students sitting in classrooms are kinesthetic learners, yet the typical school curriculum offers very few if any kinesthetic learning techniques.

WHEN LOOKING AT THE TEACHER MEANS NOT PAYING ATTENTION

We also tend to believe that people are learning only if they are looking at us when we are teaching. Being a teacher for so long, I know it does feel good to have people looking at me when I talk. But, notice in Figure 13.6 the column marked visually limited. This represents any profile where the dominant eye is on the same side as the dominant hemisphere. With only 27.8% of the GT group compared to 72.2% of the special education group being visually limited, there might be an overemphasis on visual learning in the classroom. If concepts are new and difficult to understand, visually limited people may need to look away or shut their eyes in order to take in the information more easily through their dominant senses. Unfortunately, this is often construed as inattentiveness.

A 15 year old girl was sent to me because she was failing math. She was left brained, right handed, right eared and left eyed, therefore her basal profile showed visually limited, logic dominance with full auditory and communication access. Auditory learners with logic brain dominance usually do well at math. So I decided to sit in on the class. The teacher had put her in the front of the room, directly in front of him. Every time he read or wrote a math problem  on the board she would close her eyes and turn her right ear toward him. She was doing her best to optimize her preferred sense (hear-

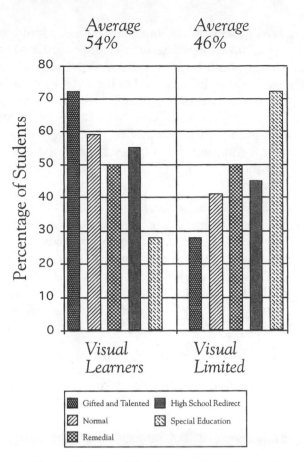

Figure 13.6 Eye/Hemisphere Dominance Patterns in the Same Sample of 218 Students

ing) in what had become a stressful situation for her. He immediately said "look at me, look at the board!" As soon as she had to look at the teacher or the board, she lost her auditory concentration and her optimal ability to learn.

All three of us learned a lot from this observation. As a result, the teacher put her in the third row on the left side of the room. She had full right ear access. He was no longer disturbed by her seeming lack of attention. Meanwhile, she began doing Brain Gym daily to enhance her preferred auditory sense and get her vision activated. Within a month she was getting straight A's on her math work

I had a similar case in an Anatomy and Physiology class I taught at the University. A woman came back to school after 25 years of practical nursing to get her bachelors degree in nursing. She sat in the back of the room and knitted during the whole class. She never took a note and very seldom looked at me. She got one of the highest grades in the course and knitted nine sweaters that semester! She was an auditory learner and did not need to look at me or the board to learn. And by using both hands in knitting, she was accessing both hemispheres and keeping them equally activated. In European schools, children knit as part of their skills training. This is an excellent activity for facilitating development of fine motor coordination, frontal lobe functioning and hemispheric integration for ease of learning.[7]

The visually limited profile also affects ease of reading, especially in stressful circumstances. Under stress, the eyes will react by moving peripherally and the dominant eye muscles will not receive full motor function from the dominant brain. This makes foveal focus and tracking across a page of reading difficult. Integrated sensory input will also be minimized. Lazy 8's for Eyes (discussed in chapter seven) help the eyes work together for maximal visual intake of information.

ARE LEFT EYED READERS BETTER OFF IN CHINA?

The left eye dominant trait also sheds an interesting light on learning. We are not truly binocular. That large protuberance between your eyes — your nose — interferes with complete binocular vision. So, we have one main tracking eye. The other eye follows. The right eye naturally tracks from left to right while the left eye naturally tracks from right to left.

The learner with a left eye dominant pattern will want to look at the right side of the page first and then move to the left. In languages that are read from right to left (Hebrew or Chinese), left eyed students would have the edge. Perhaps they would be the "gifted and talented" students, reading easily and therefore gaining acclaim.

Notice that in my study, the remedial students have the highest percentage of left eye dominance. Eighty-one percent of these students were also left eyed/right handed. Since the eye naturally wants to track from the right to the left, it will also guide the hand from the right to the left which may cause writing difficulties or letter reversals. This would also indicate a connection with hand/eye coordination and difficulty with writing. These are the children in Chapter 1 programs who reverse letters and numbers and have difficulty with beginning reading. They simply need a bit of reme-

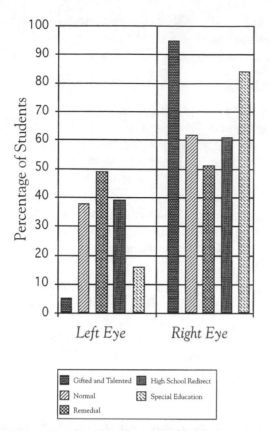

Figure 13.7: Eye Dominance in the Same Sample of 218 Students

diation to facilitate ease of tracking in the opposite direction. The vision training, taught by Dr. Dennison, strengthens the right eye function by activating tracking in all directions while holding specific accupressure points. Brain Gym activities for eyes, especially the Lazy 8's, facilitate tracking and foveal focus to assist with both reading and writing.

HOW ABOUT THE TEACHERS?

My study also profiled the teachers in the subject schools. Fully three out of four, 75% of them, were logic dominant, right handed, right eyed, and auditorially limited.  Under stress, people with this profile tend to talk about the details, not listen, and expect students to look at them. Of course teachers are as stressed out as anyone else, maybe even more so. With crowded classrooms and SOSOH children acting out in class, teachers may revert to their own basal dominance profiles. Stress creates a circle of frustration for everyone concerned.

THE PROFILE OF A DISADVANTAGED GROUP

The most disadvantaged group of learners are those who are full sensory limited, especially when they are gestalt brain dominant. Figure 13.4 presents a comparative graphing of this group in the column marked full sensory limited. Only 5% of the Gifted and Talented students are fully limited compared to 44% of the Special Education group. People that are fully gestalt limited (right brained, right eyed, right eared, right handed) have difficulty taking in sensory input during times of stress. They withdraw and process through internal images, movement and emotions, unable to explain themselves verbally.

It is important for them to have quiet time alone to process the situation. Again, in our very verbal society, we want people to articulate their thoughts and feelings. The gestalt fully limited learner, may see the big picture but have difficulty expressing it in language. In their frustration at not being able to verbalize, they may strike out emotionally. They may end up in fights or become emotionally volatile in the classroom, thus earning the label of emotionally handicapped.

Gestalt fully limited people can be assisted when several factors are included in the learning environment. These include: (1) moving to learn , (2) getting the whole picture first, then tieing in the details later, (3) starting linear processing at age 7-8, not before, (4) feeling secure in their emotions and relationships, and (5) taking quiet time out to process new learning in an intrapersonal way. With highly traditional crowded classrooms, mostly logic brained teachers, and curricula based on detail first, these limited learners spend a lot of time in survival mode. This can lead to "learned helplessness" and the astoundingly large numbers of gestalt learners in our expensive special education and emotionally handicapped programs.

MEMORIES OF A GESTALT LEARNER

My personal profile is the gestalt fully limited dominance pattern. I believe that is why Brain Gym and the successes from it have been personally important to me. I see myself in the children I have worked with. I know the system is stacked against them.

Personally, I had a great deal of difficulty with cognitive skills in school. I couldn't read until age 10. It was only after a tutor honored my developmental pace and learning style that reading finally clicked for me. Then I became a voracious reader. The weekly spelling tests left me numb from fear and it didn't take me long to believe I was "dumb." By the fifth grade, my self-esteem plummeted when I had to memorize times tables. Later I grew to hate math as I failed algebra two years in a row. It was frustrating, I could come up with the answers, but I didn't know how to go through the linear steps to demonstrate them. The more I struggled, the less I understood. A most humiliating day occurred when the teacher made me take the test in a separate room because she believed that my answers came by cheating. I simply had a learning style that didn't fit the system. If I were in grade school today, I would undoubtedly be in a special education class with a learning disabled label. I was fortunate that in my grade school in the 1950's they hadn't yet heard of special education.

In my grade school, there was a strong physical education program. Movement, art and music were daily integral parts of the curriculum. These subjects brought me enough excitement and success in school to keep me coming back each day, even with all my self-doubt and "retarded" cognitive skills. I also had the freedom to spend quiet time alone in nature with my imagination, and a curiosity that stimulated my life-long interest in biology. I am a successful educator, biologist, neurophysiologist and international lecturer, in spite of it all, though at times, those little voices of self-doubt from my school struggles creep back in.

I recognized this same frustration in my daughter as her joy of learning diminished with each advancing year of school. Though she struggled with the traditional system, she soared the six months she attended a Montessori school at age 7 and later at High School Redirection (an alternative school in the Denver Public School System) that accommodated her unique learning style.

As I worked with the wonderful children in the special ed and emotionally handicapped programs at various schools, I could see through their frustration to the unheralded intelligence inside each of them. I've found them to be spontaneous and to excel in kinesthetic, musical, visual/spatial and interpersonal intelligence. By honoring the arts, movement and interpersonal relationships more in our schools and society, these students may one day become our leaders.

Though our educational system espouses and rewards left hemisphere problem solving, the role of the right hemisphere in problem solving is gaining recognition. One researcher, Grayson Wheatley, has addressed an aspect of right brain problem solving which I recognize as my own specific way of processing math, particularly algebra.

According to Wheatley, the right hemisphere excels in tasks that are non-verbal, spatial and less familiar.[8] It grasps the whole and solves the problems at once. The left hemisphere processes the stimulus information so the stimulus can be described in language. In problem solving, it is important not to force children to use language as the vehicle for thought when imaging is more appropriate. Children can know without being able to state the thoughts in words. Bob Samples elaborates this thinking by noting that problem solving requires restructuring of elements, not just following rules.[9]

We are still leaning too heavily on algorithmic (linear, mathematical, rule oriented) learning, still expecting students to learn primarily through rote memorization, all the way up through college. Why? Memory and linear skills are easy to test and quantify. These kinds of tests give objective comparisons. But what do they measure? Facts and linear skills are useful acquisitions, but are they the most important part of a person's education? Shouldn't we be more concerned about thinking, creativity, application of knowledge to real life situations. The emphasis on low level skills and memory testing fosters an emphasis on low level thought processing — teaching to tests. Consequently, practice in high level thinking can be and often is shortchanged. As Herman Epstein has observed, "More than half the population in the United States never reach the Piaget stage of formal reasoning. We have knowers but few thinkers!"[10]

The stress of constant testing diminishes the ability to see problem solving in a larger context. It turns education into a numbers game where competition, rather than cooperation, is encouraged and information is not moved to applicability or creative thought. If we can advance to an education that balances memory and thinking, and honors each person's learning processes, agile learners with valuable thinking tools can emerge. Or, to put it more cerebrally, as Bob Samples does: "We discovered that if the right hemisphere functions are celebrated, the development of left hemisphere qualities becomes inevitable."

I've been in classrooms where math is being taught only from story problems. Students access images when they solve story problems and work from a three-dimensional, real life perspective. Sometimes the students themselves devise the story problems, making them emotionally relevant as well as accessing deeper imaginative thought. The problems are then solved in cooperative learning groups of three to four students. Though all the answers in the classroom may be identical, the way each group arrives at the answer may be unique. The groups then share their problem solving methods, and each student gains insight into the overall problem solving process.

In a university setting (for example, an economics course of 300 students), it makes much more sense to use a cooperative learning model than to simply lecture, which is bound to miss a large proportion of the students. (In my study 52% of students were auditorially limited.) Divide students into groups, give them guidelines and let them discuss, write, diagram, learn and anchor in personal experience with the information presented. The movement of putting their thoughts into language, writing or pictures, and gaining insights from each other will expand high level formal reasoning and move us toward a nation of thinkers.

McKim goes one step further in contending flexibility is the key to productive thinking. He believes it advisable to stop thinking consciously about a problem, relax, take a walk or sleep on it, allowing the thinking to proceed unconsciously without stress.[11] In school we must allow movement and integration time to insure high level problem solving.

Awareness of learning style differences has motivated teachers and whole school systems to be more innovative in their curricula. Programs such as those based on Howard Gardner's Multiple Intelligences and Bernice McCarthy's 4-MAT system derived from David Kolb's work, facilitate learning style differences and are gaining acceptance.[12-13] Gardner's rethinking of the definition of intelligence has contributed a great deal to reshaping educational theory and practice. In Gardner's view, intelligence: 1) is the ability to respond quickly to a new situation; 2) is of importance to a specific culture — it helps and supports that culture; 3) has to have its own developmental patterns; and 4) is of equal potential in everyone.[14]

Sandra Zachary, a third grade teacher in Hawaii, had her

students figure out their own dominance profiles at the beginning of the school year. She then had them organize themselves according to their easiest sensory access: visual learners in front; auditory learners in the next row with right ear dominants on the left side of the room and left ear dominants on the right side of the room; and the gestalt fully limited in the back of the room with clay or wax to manipulate kinesthetically during class. This facilitated understanding of and honoring of all the students resulting in high self-esteem for all.

Each day they did Brain Gym activities for five minutes at the beginning of the day, after recess and after lunch. At the end of six weeks, students were allowed to change seats, which they did with a deeper understanding of their preferential patterns and learning strengths. The stress levels in the classroom had become minimal and classroom management became a co-creative process for everyone. In the end, each student gained the highest academic success they had yet achieved in their schooling. This was a simple, commonsense way to honor each learner.

HONORING ALL STUDENTS

As long as we hold inflexible beliefs about what makes someone valuable, or intelligent or right, we promote the labeling and petty competition that can destroy our human diversity and potential. The SAT's and IQ tests with their highly linear, linguistic/mathematical orientation have set the criteria for intelligence in our society. A majority of teachers continue to believe that learning only occurs when a child is quiet, still, listening and handing in all their homework. Competition is so keen in the learning arena that parents are pushing cognitive skills on children much too early and then bragging about it to other parents. And, if their child is not performing at the same level or higher than the child down the block, parents are taking them for evaluation and diagnosis of learning disabilities. There are groups that will diagnose "learning disabilities" as early as one year old. Again, how can we judge someone who is just becoming?

Parental expectations seem to heighten as the child enters school and much pressure is put on teachers to make sure the child succeeds academically. Honor students are even being touted now on bumper stickers: "Proud parent of an honor student." If we truly "honor" our learners, we will be sensitive to their developmental and learning style needs and realize that every person is an "honor student." Tools like the dominance profile assist that process and help to bring understanding and compassion while eliminating the need for competition. Dominance profiles can also bring understanding to couples in conflict, during parent/child conflicts, or with conflicts in the work or play setting.

The health of our educational system depends on our nurturing and promoting the learning of all our citizens. We must relinquish judgments that lead to stress-provoking labels and competition. An appropriate thinking curriculum must be established that synthesizes whole mind/body processing through regular art, music and movement in conjunction with cognitive skills. We must give learners mind/body integrative tools, such as Brain Gym, that allow them to stop the stress cycle and activate full sensory/hemisphere access. Perhaps then we can fully realize the unique human potential that Paul MacLean invokes, in an evolving society where all people succeed at learning.

People learn instinctively, but what we learn and how we view ourselves as learners very often depends on how we are treated by instructors and other role models in our life. The following paragraphs are excerpted from a letter written by an Australian Aboriginal mother to her child's teacher. With very few words this eloquent woman expresses a universal parental yearning: honor my child.

Dear Sir/Madam

Before you take charge of the classroom that contains my child, please ask yourself what you are going to teach Aboriginal children....

You will be well advised to remember that our children are skillful interpreters of the silent language, the subtle, unspoken communication of facial expressions, gestures, body movement and the use of personal space. They will know your feelings and attitudes with unerring precision, no matter how carefully you arrange your smile or modulate your voice.

They will learn in your classroom, because children learn involuntarily. What they will learn will depend on you. Will you help my child to learn to read, or will you teach him that he has a reading problem? Will you help him to develop problem solving skills, or will you teach him that school is where you try to guess what answers the teacher wants? Will he learn that his sense of his own value and dignity is valid, or will he learn that he must forever be apologetic and "try harder" because he isn't white?

Can you help him acquire the intellectual skills he needs without at the same time imposing your values on top of those he already has?

Respect my child. He is a person. He has a right to be himself.

Yours very sincerely
An Aboriginal Parent[15]

14. ≈
Drugs and Hyperactivity

Man is so made, that whenever anything fires his
soul . . . impossibilities vanish.
                                    —*LaFontaine*

Our society has long had strong, but mixed feelings about relying on wonder drugs for the troubles that afflict us. Trust and dependence on magic bullet type cures alternate with suspicions about exaggerated claims of success and concerns about unintended, and unadvertised, side effects. In the treatment of behavior that adversely affects learning, the pendulum is now definitely swinging in the direction of recognizing the need for non-invasive, natural and common sense alternatives to drugs.

The drugs we use to treat hyperactivity are a good place to start. There are compelling reasons to question the continued practice of treating hyperactivity and attention deficit disorders with Ritalin and other such drugs.

First, ADHD (Attention Deficit Hyperactive Disorder) is just a label with no proven genetic or pathological background. The causal agents are most certainly environmental factors already delineated in the chart on What Inhibits Learning in Chapter 8. These complex environmental factors are headed up by lack of adult attention and non-stimulating learning environments. Peter and Ginger Breggin point out that when faced with an ADHD labeled child, adults have two divergent choices: transform themselves and then the education system, or suppress the child. Too often drug therapy seems the easier route. Children are naturally curious, active and dependent on parental attention for their learning. When children have something interesting to do, or when they are given a reasonable amount of quality attention, ADHD often disappears.[1]

Second, non-intrusive, child-centered, common sense methods work better in the long run. Suitably applied, these methods will allow children to be in charge of their emotions and physical energy, and give them tools to use throughout their lives.

And third, the risks of drug use usually outweigh the benefits. Drugs interact with the brain and the body in intricate, often undesirable ways. Valium, one of the most commonly used tranquilizers in our society today, gives us a warning. Valium competes with the neuropeptides responsible for causing feelings of anxiety (octadecaneuropeptides). The drug's calming effect confuses the nervous system as a whole, at the same time it preempts emotional release. Valium also acts on the monocytes (white blood cells that destroy disease organisms), thus directly affecting the immune system. The behavior of monocytes is delicate and vulnerable. Adding mood-modifying chemicals to the already complex chemical structure of the body and immune system seems very risky at a time when the incidence of life threatening diseases (cancer, AIDS, and heart disease) is rising.[2]

RITALIN AND THE BRAIN

The National Institute of Mental Health estimates that a million U.S. children are currently taking Ritalin.[3] Ritalin acts on the brain just like "speed" — neuropharmacologically, it has the same effects, side effects and risks as cocaine and amphetamines. The FDA classifies Ritalin in the high addiction category, Schedule II, with amphetamines, cocaine, morphine, opium and barbituates.[4]

Ritalin (methylphenidate), Dexedrine (dextroamphetamine) Cyleit (pemoline), and sometimes the tricyclic anti-depressants (Tofranil and Norpramine) used in the treatment of hyperactivity, may also have detrimental long-term effects on the immune system and the body in general.[5] These drugs affect the basal ganglion and corpus striatum — the brain areas responsible for increased motor control and sense of time.[6] All of these drugs modify the levels of neurotransmitters in the brain, particularly in the frontal lobes.

The frontal lobes control our ability to shift from a free association, open state to a detailed, focused state of awareness. This ability to shift from a broader, diffuse state to sharper, narrow focus is important for human thinking and problem solving. This is the way high level formal reasoning occurs as we easily move back and forth between the big picture (broad input) and the details. Drugs used in the treatment of hyperactivity, principally Ritalin, though they allow attention to repetitive school work, detail and rote memory, inhibit the ability to shift focus between open and focused consciousness.[7]

And there is no evidence that Ritalin improves learning or academic performance.[8-9]

One study of hyperactive adults that had been treated with Ritalin, showed nearly one-quarter failed to finish high school. Only one of the hyperactive boys, compared with eight of the control group, went on to obtain a graduate degree. Far fewer members of the hyperactive group held professional-level jobs compared to the control group. As adults, between one-third and one-half continued to experience ongoing hyperactivity.[10] Overall, this is not a great record for Ritalin.

PET Scan studies also show a marked decrease in dopamine in ADHD (Attention Deficit Hyperactive Disorder) labeled people. Dopamine is a neurotransmitter that plays a role in the control of movements. Nerve cell bodies containing Dopamine project axons widely into the prefrontal area of the frontal lobe as well as to subcortical structures including the basal ganglia.[11] These areas have to do with regulation and control of normal fine motor movements. Some medical conditions have been helped by treatment with dopamine. For instance, dopamine has been administered medically in Parkinson's Disease to control shaking and erratic movements.[12]

Ritalin is thought to activate increased dopamine production within the brain, causing a decrease in hyperactive movement. However, if the brain reacts to Ritalin as it does to other researched stimulants (Thorazine, endorphins, marijuana and cocaine), there may be long term side-effects.

Studies show a feedback mechanism in the brain that adjusts brain chemistry in response to these stimulants. The feedback mechanism will attempt to rid the brain of excess stimulant by reducing the amount of its own natural production. The mechanism is so overstimulated that when the stimulant is discontinued, the natural brain levels may be left even lower than before, exacerbating the situation. Though these studies did not include Ritalin, this same mechanism may be occurring.[13] Parents complain of children going into depression and showing even greater hyperactivity when taken off Ritalin on weekends. As an addictive stimulant, Ritalin can cause withdrawal symptoms which include depression and irritability. Unaware of this withdrawal reaction, parents may feel the child should be put back on the drug.[14]

Danger also lies in the long-lasting changes in brain chemistry that may result from long-term use. Since Parkinson's disease is related to low dopamine production, children who are medicated for hyperactivity may be more at risk of Parkinson's Disease in later life.[15]

Some of the precautions and adverse reactions stated for Ritalin include: loss of appetite, abdominal pain, weight loss, insomnia, tachycardia (irregular heart beat), nervousness and possible hypersensitivity, anorexia, nausea, dizziness, palpitations, headache, dyskinesia and drowsiness. There is a very specific statement in the Physicians Desk Reference (PDR) with regard to Ritalin: "When symptoms are associated with acute stress reactions, treatment with Ritalin is usually not indicated."[16]

This stress connection can be seen in a recent PET Scan study on the effects of Ritalin on adults labeled with ADHD. By the end of the study there was less restlessness and improved attention among subjects, but their brain activity still exhibited the stress reaction. From these results, David Shaffer concluded that adult ADHD is caused by unrecognized and untreated stress.[17] I feel strongly that my label— SOSOH — addresses the root cause, stress, of people having difficulties with maintaining attention and exhibiting hyperactivity. And so I agree with the PDR's recommendation regarding the stress reaction, that Ritalin is not indicated for use with ADHD.

Interestingly, no consistent brain abnormalities have been found in children labeled ADHD. However, ominously enough a study has found brain shrinkage in labeled ADHD adults who have been taking Ritalin for years.[18]

In my work with schools I have been shocked at the rising number of children on Ritalin. In one school I recently visited, almost one-half of the students in a particular classroom were on Ritalin, many on the insistence of the teacher or school administration.

ALTERNATIVES TO DRUGS

There are beneficial alternative strategies for helping people labeled hyperactive, ADD and ADHD. Dr. Eberhard Mann, a physician and Director of the Hyperactivity Clinic at Kapiolani Counseling Center in Hawaii, advocates a comprehensive treatment for ADHD. "By comprehensive treatment we mean a treatment program that deals with each problem that inhibits a child's learning potential and positive social interactions. Treatment components include special education, peer group counseling, self-control training, parent and teacher education, motivation and self-esteem building, anger management, and in some cases, `stimulant' medication like Ritalin."[19] He also points out that Ritalin does not improve specific learning deficits or reduce aggressive behaviors.

Brain Gym is also a non-invasive, common sense alternative to drug therapy. It appears to fit Dr. Mann's idea of a Comprehensive Treatment Program. It effectively assists self-control training, motivation, self-esteem, and anger management. Natural neurotransmitter production (GABA and dopamine) is stimulated when the whole brain is activated, as it is with Brain Gym. Hyperactive children and adults that I've worked with have been able, after doing the Brain Gym activities, to slow and coordinate their movements, shift easily between details and the broad picture, and focus on learning. With daily Brain Gym the person gains more and more control as the frontal lobe and basal ganglion are being activated regularly. And symptoms of ADHD greatly lessen or completely disappear in an amazingly short time.

GOING BEYOND THE SOSOH LABELS

Is there really attention deficit disorder? SOSOH people, or all of us for that matter, are much more easily engaged when the lessons and the learning environment are relevant and valued. If the project they are working on interests them, they are able to focus their attention and even lose track of time. Motivation is a key element in focused attention. As our studies of the brain have shown us, there is a close physiological link in the nervous system between the attention center (RAS) in the brain stem and the limbic system, seat of emotion, motivation and memory.

If learning, any learning, is valuable to the learner, the brain will be activated. All people are naturally curious, especially about themselves and the world they exist in. Given motivating and interesting challenges, each brain will comprehend and contribute in its own unique way. Albert Galaburda puts it succinctly: "The way dyslexics — or anyone else — use their brains is a critical factor in modifying them."[20] Even people with true dyslexia, where there may be deficits in the left hemisphere, do well with right hemisphere skills.[21] It's time to let go of our judgments, expectations and beliefs about what is "smart," and glory in learning and in each unique learner.

If there is any doubt about the efficacy of providing a safe, personally valuable learning environment and doing Brain Gym daily, I offer a list of the skills developed by all students labeled with learning disabilities in a matter of no more than six weeks. The learners I observed were able to:

1) relax and have fun in the classroom, enjoying the learning process,

2) carry on intelligent conversations and think about things that are important to them,

3) focus their attention on a task for a long enough period to complete it well,

4) show care and concern for other learners, teachers and themselves,

5) listen quietly and attentively as others shared their ideas,

6) work and play well with others (fights decreased dramatically),

7) come to an equitable understanding following a fight,

8) stand up for themselves in a confident, positive way when being abused by others,

9) confidently express their creativity in myriad ways, through music, art, poetry, dance and interpersonal relationships,

10) appropriately express anger as well as affection,

11) attain fine motor coordination and balance,

12) exhibit use of inner speech for deductive reasoning and control of their own behavior,

13) experience success and celebrate the success of others,

14) implant themselves within my heart as incredibly wondrous human beings and magnificent survivors.

Can any drug treatment offer these results? And my experiences are by no means unique.

It is time to see each child and every person as unique learners with their own specific time line and pace of learning. Understanding the stressors that lead to the SOSOH labels gives us a place from which to start in setting up optimal learning situations. And simple, natural drug-free tools like Brain Gym can assist us as we consciously undertake to eliminate all the SOSOH labels concealing the intelligent learner beneath them.

One boy, a third grader in a self-contained classroom for the emotionally handicapped, (he showed a gestalt, fully limited dominance profile) touched my life so deeply with his intelligence that I wrote this poem about him:

THE GIFT

I felt his sticky warmth as he clutched the back of the chair.
    "Lost child, hyperactive, L.D., ADHD, emotionally handicapped"
His bloody nose and caked hair covering the mud stained face
    and two white rivulets that coursed from his eyes
        to spill with anger on the floor.

Caught in the innate act of survival — the playground fight
    a desperate attempt to hold some dignity — some sense of
        humanhood against a peer's cutting words.
    Imprisoned in labels, chiseled on his delicate memory from birth.
        Child of light reduced to a psychological/linguistic profile
            carefully maintained and elaborated by each new caretaker.

These same lips that now quivered with frustration, had yesterday
    led me through his imaginative richness on a fantasy that left
        my reality behind in the wake of its intricate beauty.
    And these now bloody hands had drawn a man with 17 arms,
        each holding a uniquely carved cane, and walking his
        rainbow colored dog with fluorescent eyes.

And these legs, bruised and valiantly locked to hold up the
    sagging trunk of his body, knew their way expertly around
        a soccer ball and could effortlessly sprint his
        bare feet down a grass and lava playground.
    This child who knew too few hugs and kisses, this exquisite
    child with the future in his heart.

I was this child, many years ago — unable to explain my needs
        or voice in a logical way my frustration.
    Unable to know that the hole in my soul needed a hug,
        or someone to see me clearer than I did
            to connect me with me —
    Or show me how - a quick course in knowing and loving self,
        and believing it in the face of all the labels
        and limited, socially imposed images.

This moment and this child are a place to start to heal the wounds.
    His eyes, a reflection of the world — all sticky,
        bruised and filled with FEAR,
    deep and honest they don't allow me to turn away.
    He is my gift, my wake-up call — one more
        God given opportunity to learn LOVE.

15. ≈
Looking Outward for Models

> *It surprises me how our culture can destroy curiosity in the most curious of all animals — human beings.*
>
> — *Paul MacLean*[1]

To get a better sense of what makes learning successful, I believe it's time to look at what works — not only in our culture and educational system, but elsewhere in the world. I often think we misrepresent the truth by calling ourselves and our culture "First World," while labeling African villages high in the Lesotho mountains "Third World." The distinction may be apt only if we are referring to the proliferation of technology or economic affluence. But when it comes to learning, it is time for a major re-evaluation. I'm not suggesting we return to B.T. (before technology), but I do believe we have a lot to learn about learning from the insights and practices of other cultures.

INSIGHTS FROM THE THIRD WORLD

In the villages of Lesotho in Southern Africa, social values and communal practices support early childhood development much more effectively than ours do. The benefits for the children are substantial. An occupational therapist who heads an assessment group in Kuazulu, South Africa shared her interesting findings with me. Of the 10,000 children assessed for learning readiness prior to school entry each year in Kuazulu, the black rural children have consistently scored far superior to the white urban children on all but three of the fifty assessment tests. On two of these three they tested the same. On the third — which tested their foveal focus — they did poorly (for reasons I explored earlier in Chapter 6). The black children exhibit a high level of learning proficiency, body/mind integration and a strong motivation to learn.[2]

These cultures have much to teach us about valuing people,

early sensory-motor stimulation, encouragement of responsibility, language development, and interpersonal relationships. Children, and especially babies, are considered the treasures of the whole clan. In one tribal culture, a newborn baby spends its first six weeks with just its mother and immediate family to allow close bonding. During that time, the whole tribe is involved in clearing any grievances they have with one another. They wear leather aprons with long fringes. They tie knots in the fringe for each grievance they carry against another member of the community. It is their job to clear all the grievances and untie all the knots before the baby is presented to the tribe at the end of the six week period.

Since there are many babies born to this tribe, there is constant reconciliation. This custom guarantees a high degree of social harmony for the good of the young. Ideally, all children are to be brought into a fully loving, cooperative community that works together for the benefit of each child throughout its growth. Additionally, each adult in the tribe becomes responsible for the upbringing of every child. This is another socially cohesive practice which endows children with concern for the collective good, knowledge of the rules and boundaries, and entitlement to security and love.

Upon learning about this system, I realized why I have often felt overwhelmed as a single parent. I have tried to do for my daughter what is naturally handled by at least a hundred other people in a family clan.

In the clan structure, the first year of the baby's life is full of sensory-motor stimulation. This includes the constant touch and attention from everyone in the community, the baby's place in the family bed at night, the rich natural smells of home, family and friends, and continuous physical contact with the mother, even when she works. At work, a mother will firmly attach the baby to her back by a towel or blanket so the baby's ear is next to her heart. From this place, the baby rocks and sways to the mother's graceful dancing movements and feels the vibrations and rhythm of her song as she goes about her work. Babies are lovingly fed on demand. By meeting the basic survival needs for hunger, shelter, warmth, and stimulation, a pattern of safety and security is established. From this secure foundation babies feel free to confidently explore their new environment.

From its position on her back the baby is free to turn its head, strengthening its neck muscles in order to see and hear the vibrant life going on around it from a binocular and binaural perspective.

The infant's muscular development is rapid, giving the baby even more command over its sensory-motor input.

Figure 15.1: African Mother's Carrying Method Confers Many Benefits

When the mother is not working, she stretches out the blanket so the child may explore its environment from its belly or back. Core postural muscles strengthen as it wiggles, explores its appendages and finally learns to roll over, push up, crawl and sit. Its eyes gain acuity and recognition in a sensory-rich environment. The baby sees constantly moving shades of green as the leaves overhead catch a breeze, the brilliant blue African sky with its ever changing cloud patterns, a plethora of brightly colored birds full of song, and the bobbing, laughing faces of children and adults bringing creatively designed toys made from plants, stones, cardboard, and even plastic shopping bags. These babies are lifted, cuddled, tickled and hugged.

As they start to scooch and crawl, they are given full access to their environment. Their playground is the dirt floor of the rondovelle at night in the midst of dance, song and stories, or the dusty, rocky or rich fields during the day as the mother works. Core muscle movement, gravitational understanding and full shoulder/pelvic girdle function develop naturally before the child takes its first step.

Once walking, the child learns quickly to run to keep up with the other children who, in their bare feet, can traverse any terrain with grace. I vividly remember one little boy who could not have been walking long, who started running with the other children after our truck as we left his village. His sister grabbed his shirt to stop him but he pulled away from her, leaving her standing there, and followed us for a good mile, smiling and laughing at the chase as his little legs and bare feet pumped across the rocky dirt road.

Children are a part of the whole family/clan structure, often being cared for by grandparents after they are weaned. As the children grow older they take care of younger children, and by the age of six are responsible for gathering firewood or looking after a cow, sheep or horse. They are encouraged in carving, weaving, singing, dancing, story telling, painting and creative, imaginative play.

Figure 15.2: Children Begin Taking Responsibility At An Early Age

At night the families in a compound eat together amid animated talk of the day's adventures. You can hear them calling to each other across the valley and over the sound of drums as they close their work day. Then, instead of TV, there are the stories from family members or clan members who have come to visit and who speak another dialect or language. Children are multilingual, knowing two or three languages by the time they go to school. There is always song as the night closes softly over the final drum beats and the last strains of multipart harmony to fade and fill the African night with silence and a billion stars.

The strong tribal traditions I experienced have as their core the idea of *ubuntu* which means: "Because I am, we are; and because we are, I am." The clan structure is based on consensus government. The chief calls the clan together when communal decisions must be made. It may take days or even weeks to decide the outcome, all clan members having the right to state their opinion. The consensus decision is then embraced and upheld by every clan member. Respect for the elders of the clan, and anyone older than oneself is learned early.

What struck me the most was the children's curiosity, and strong desire to learn. They walked long distances to attend school, and did it with utmost willingness. Learning and wisdom are highly prized by all clan members.

A FIRST WORLD LEARNING PLAN FROM AFRICA

Through these African communities, I gained an understanding of the crucial developmental factors necessary for the elaboration of full learning potential. Having observed and been privileged to share their life, I offer this summary as my idea of a "First World" plan to support learning and brain development:

A. A rich sensory environment full of sound, touch, smell and visual stimuli.

B. Lots of movement and the ability to freely explore one's own body in space.

C. Security and basic needs gratification that fosters full exploration of the physical environment.

D. Parents or other adults available as listeners, consultants and interactive participants in each child's growth.

E. Plenty of time and practice for pattern recognition — of sensory-motor patterns, language patterns, rhythm and music patterns and human relationship patterns.

F. The establishment of responsibilities, boundaries, and respect for self and others.

G. Encouragement of imagination, art, music, communication and interactive play.

The learning process is supported and nurtured when these factors are present in the home and community during the earliest years of childhood. Equally important in these formative years is how the learning process is regarded in the child's formal education. I have also been fortunate in witnessing and experiencing formal education programs that truly honor the learner, are student centered and democratic, and — more importantly — have a history of effectiveness. Through community encouragement, these programs are being implemented in schools across America with varying degrees of success. They are certainly raising the consciousness of their communities and allowing them to shed practices that are too often ineffectual.

Some schools in the United States have gone out of their way to accommodate individualized learning. Arney Langburg developed one such program in the High School Redirection Program, an alternative school within the Denver Public School system that gives "last chance kids" another chance. The school was fashioned after a school Arney developed and ran in Evergreen, Colorado to accommodate his own children during their high school years.[3]

There are fourteen criteria each student must meet for graduation. These include: knowledge of inner resources; caring for self and others; sense of justice; ethics and integrity; risk-taking, self-challenge; ability to change; appreciation for richness of cultural diversity; persistence, commitment; long-term employability; entrepreneurship; basic cognitive skills. Upon entrance, each student does a self-assessment of the fourteen graduation expectations, thus determining where to concentrate with further in-depth work. School policy encourages all students to set their personal, academic and social goals. With the assistance of a mentor, each learner sets up a specific learning program.

High School Redirection, with over 300 students in 1992, claimed the lowest absentee rate in the Denver Public Schools. They do a wonderful job, successfully graduating self-directed students with personal integrity, marketable skills, and a solid base for life-long learning success.

THE DANISH PUBLIC SCHOOL SYSTEM

A larger scale model of excellent public education is the Danish system. Schools in Denmark are organized around wise, learner-centered educational policies. Learning proceeds at a more brain-friendly pace than in American schools, the curriculum more closely aligned with hallmarks of natural brain development. Students participate in curriculum planning, enhancing their motivation to learn. The school work emphasizes thinking and integration of knowledge. There is less emphasis on quantification of progress, hence less competition.

In the Danish public school system, students don't begin school until age 7 and are not tested until approximately age 14. These first tests measure only linguistic, scientific, technical and mathematical skills. These are considered basic skills with information processing and creative thought receiving the principal emphasis of the curriculum, rather than the other way around. The final exam, given at age 17 or 18, is not at all like the final exams you might remember from high school. The Danish final demands much more integrative formal reasoning.

Students choose when they will take their final exam. Each is given a piece of art and a piece of literature, poetry or prose (usually one of the classics). They have a period of time to write the exam, usually a couple of weeks to a month. They are expected to prepare an integrated dissertation tieing their assigned pieces to history, biology, physics, chemistry, language, mathematics, art and social sciences. This final exam is written in two languages and then presented to a committee that interviews the student to determine eligibility for graduation.[4]

An impressive level of problem solving and reasoning was evident in all the Danish classrooms I visited, in students ranging from age 7 through college. The lack of disciplinary problems was striking, though many classrooms contained thirty-five to forty-five students due to a recent influx of immigrants into Denmark. Students were honored for their thinking skills and imagination and were encouraged to work in groups to develop communication skills.

The curriculum was developed at the beginning of each nine week period in a democratic process to accommodate the specific interests of the students and teacher. Teachers asked their students which topics they were interested in studying. The selected topics were then explored, setting the curriculum for the core learning sessions for the next nine weeks. Students took responsibility for gathering resources, developing projects in cooperative groups, and sharing their study and information with the rest of the class.

Teachers and students learned together. Age appropriate skills were taught and directly connected to the student-determined curriculum to enhance and anchor it.[5]

Each class lesson in the Danish Folkskole was replete with art, music, movement and cooperative group work. Cooperative learning in the Danish schools encouraged students to interact, share their learning preferences, and listen to and learn from one another. Social interaction occurring in the course of all these educational activities honored individual differences and gifts, thus eliminating the labels and limitations to individual initiative and creativity.[6]

A study of selected secondary schools in the United Kingdom, the Netherlands, Germany and Denmark during the 1992-1993 academic year came up with some interesting findings on how these educational systems vary, particularly in the ways they prepare young people for their role as citizens. In Denmark, national law stipulates that the primary function of the Folkskole is to prepare students to be citizens in a democracy. Participation in decision-making at the classroom level begins in the first grade and continues throughout the students' schooling.

The quantitative findings of this study showed that Danish students more confidently communicated and listened to ideas. They showed the highest levels of political efficacy. They also believed their actions could make a difference in their world. The Danish classroom climate was perceived as most open with the greatest opportunity to explore diverse sides of issues. Teachers encouraged students to form and comfortably express their own opinions on issues, even when they disagreed with the teacher's or other students' opinions. Danish students indicated the highest level of support for women in government and for free speech for all people, no matter what their viewpoint.[7]

RETHINKING EDUCATIONAL GOALS

"In the over-eager embrace of the rational, scientific and technological," David Kolb observes, "we lost touch with our own experience as the source of personal learning and development. The learning process must be reimbued with the texture and feeling of human experiences shared and interpreted through dialogue with one another."[8]

A variety of individuals and organizations have been creatively rethinking educational goals in the United States. Among them is the National Learning Foundation (NLF), which has defined its mission as placing America at the forefront of the emerging learning societies of the 21st century. The NLF is a public/private initiative set up by the White House Task Force on Innovative Learning to prepare the workforce for the changing educational requirements of industry and commerce. The workplace has changed. The explosion of information in our technologic society places, and will continue to place, new demands on every worker. Our schools need to turn out more appropriately educated citizens, what the National Learning Foundation calls, Agile Learners.

The Agile Learner is not a passive sponge of information, but the master of information, capable of reflection and choice. According to the NLF, the agile learner will display significantly different attributes and skills from those rewarded today in our school systems. These include:

PERSONAL
Flexible
Creative
Introspective
Curious
Imaginative
Adaptable
Aesthetically aware
Ambiguity tolerant
Acts from integrity

INTERPERSONAL
Celebrates diversity
Altruistically motivated
Effectively interdependent
   - collaborator
   - team player

ESSENTIAL
Literacy/numeracy
Mastery of technology
Communication
Negotiation

PERFORMANCE
Systems thinking
Pattern detecting
Synthesizing
Analyzing
Experimenting
Problem solving
Decision making
Reflective thinking

The indicators of success with such an education would be love of learning, high self-esteem, body/mind congruity, self-rescription and community consciousness.[9] These are the very qualities I saw in the Danish Folkskoles, so I know this is a practical and feasible goal, especially since we have workable proven models to follow.

The National Learning Foundation accepted Brain Gym as one of the top technologies for the 21st Century Learning Society in their bid to develop new — not retooled — educational strategies that prepare learners for the global businesses of tomorrow.

Integrative movements like Brain Gym accommodate all learning styles, enhance myelination between the two hemispheres and balance the electrical energy and integrative processing across the whole brain. Their objective is to realize the learner's maximum potential by activating full brain function, and by supporting individual learning styles and learning pace. Brain Gym can act as a bridge between the current educational system and the educational systems emerging worldwide to ensure the development of the agile learner.

Learning itself is part of a totally fulfilling life, and should continue to occupy a central role from infancy to old age. So the attitudes and practices which favor learning should themselves be studied and cultivated. This is a lesson that is taught by many individuals in many cultures.

Integrative movements such as the Brain Gym exercises are an effective, profound, common sense, non-drug option which greatly facilitate lifelong learning. That is quite a claim for something that anyone can do, at any time, anywhere and without monetary expense. Once we begin using all the capacity of the mind/body system, the learning process becomes immeasurably more effective, rekindling the excitement and joy that come with discovering our world, our relationship to it and our infinite creative possibilities.

Movement, a natural process of life, is now understood to be essential to learning, creative thought and high level formal reasoning. It is time to consciously bring integrative movement back into every aspect of our lives and realize, as I have, that something this simple and natural can be the source of miracles.

Notes

2: NEURAL NETWORKS

[1] Stevens, Charles F. *The Neuron*. IN: *Scientific American*, Sept. 1979, p. 1.

[2] Tortora, Gerard J. & Nicholas P. Anagnostakos. *Principles of Anatomy and Physiology*. Sixth Edition. NY: Harper, 1990. pp. 426-445.

[3] Nauta, Walle J.H. & Michael Feirtag. *The Organization of the Brain*. IN: *The Brain, A Scientific American Book*. San Francisco: W.H. Freeman, 1979. p. 40.

[4] Tortora & Anagnostakos. *Principles ....* p. 238.

[5] Nauta, Walle J.H. & Michael Feirtag. *The Organization of the Brain*. p. 49.

[6] Tortora & Anagnostakos. *Principles ....* pp. 336-337.

[7] Tortora & Anagnostakos. *Principles ....* pp. 345-348.

[8] Chopra, Deepak. *Quantum Healing, Exploring The Frontiers Of Mind/Body Medicine*. NY: Bantam Books, 1989. pp. 26, 50.

[9] Snyder, Solomon H. *The Molecular Basis of Communication Between Cells*. IN: *Scientific American*, October 1985, p. 33.

[10] Diamond, Marian. *Enriching Heredity, The Impact of the Environment on the Anatomy of the Brain*. NY: Free Press, 1988. pp. 67-77.

[11] Lichtman, Jeff W., Rita J. Balice-Gordon & Lawrence Katz, et. al. *Seeing Synapses: New Ways to Study Nerves*. American Association for the Advancement of Science, Annual Meeting in San Francisco, February 1994.

[12] Stevens, Charles F. *The Neuron*. pp. 1-2.

[13] Chopra, Deepak. *Quantum Healing*. p. 50.

[14] Masland, Richard H. *The Functional Architecture of the Retina*. IN: *Scientific American*, December, 1986, pp. 131-147.

[15] Merzenich, Michael. *Brain Plasticity Origins of Human Abilities and Disabilities*. Sixth Symposium, Decade of the Brain Series. NIMH and the Library of Congress. Washington, DC, Feb. 7, 1995.

[16] Chopra, Deepak. *Quantum Healing*. p. 26.

[17] Golden, Daniel. *Building A Better Brain — Brain Calisthenics*. IN: *Life Magazine*, July 1994, pp. 63-72.

[18] Schrof, Joannie M. *Brain Power*. IN: *U.S. News & World Report*, November 28, 1994, p. 94.

3: SENSORY EXPERIENCE

[1] Damasio, Antonio R. *Descartes' Error: Emotion, Reason, and the Human Brain*. NY: Putnam, 1994. pp. 112-113.

[2] MacLean, Paul D. *A Mind of Three Minds: Educating the Triune Brain*. IN: *Seventy-Seventh Yearbook of the National Society for the Study of Education*. Chicago, 1978.

[3] Pearce, Joseph Chilton. *Evolution's End, Claiming the Potential of Our Intelligence*. San Francisco: Harper & Row, 1992.

[4] Schiefelbein, Susan. *Beginning the Journey.* IN: *The Incredible Machine.* Washington, DC: National Geographic Society, 1986. p. 36.

[5] Tortora & Anagnostakos. *Principles ....* p. 488.

[6] Ayres, A. Jean. *Sensory Integration and Learning Disorders.* Los Angeles: Western Psychological Services, 1972. p. 58.

[7] Tortora & Anagnostakos. *Principles ....* pp. 392, 483-490.

[8] Hendrickson, Homer. *The Vision Development Process.* Santa Ana, CA: Optometric Extension Program, 1969. p. 4.

[9] Schwartz, Eugene. *Seeing, Hearing, Learning:The Interplay of Eye and Ear in Waldorf Education.* Excerpts from Camp Glenbrook Conference of the Association for a Healing Education, June 14-16, 1988. 1990.

[10] Klivington, Kenneth. *The Science of Mind.* Cambridge, MA: MIT Press, 1989. p. 149.

[11] Ayres, A. Jean. *Sensory Integration and Learning Disorders.* p. 70.

[12] Hernandez-Peon, R. *Neurophysiology of Attention.* IN: P.J. Vinkin & G.W. Bruyn (eds.), *Handbook of Clinical Neurology.* Amsterdam: North Holland Pub., 1969.

[13] Tomatis, Alfred A. *The Conscious Ear, My Life of Transformation through Listening.* Barrytown, NY: Station Hill Press, 1991. pp. 208-215.

[14] Campbell, Don G. *The Roar of Silence.* Wheaton, IL: Quest Books, 1989.

[15] Schiefelbein, Susan. *Beginning the Journey.* IN: *The Incredible Machine.* pp. 36-39.

[16] Tomatis, Alfred A. *Education and Dyslexia.* Fribourg, Switzerland: Association Internationale d'Audio-Psycho-Phonologie, 1978.

[17] Lonsbury-Martin, Brenda. *Using the Sounds of Hearing.* (February 1993 meeting of the AAAS.) IN: *Science News,* February 27, 1993, (vol. 143), p. 141.

[18] Hopson, Janet L. *We May Follow Our Noses More Often Than Is Now Realized.* IN: *Smithsonian Magazine,* March 1979, pp. 78-85.

[19] Stiller, Angelika, & Renate Wennekes. *Sensory Stimulation Important to Developmental Processes.* Neuenkirchen, Germany: *Astrup,* 31, 1992, 2846.

[20] Hopson, Janet L. *We May Follow Our Noses More Often Than Is Now Realized.*

[21] Tortora & Anagnostakos. *Principles ....* pp. 427-433.

[22] Tortora & Anagnostakos. *Principles ....* pp. 336-337.

[23] Restak, Richard M. *The Mind.* NY: Bantam Books, 1988. p. 87.

[24] Levi-Montalcini, Rita. *Developmental Neurobiology and the Natural History of Nerve Growth Factor. Annual Review of Neurosciences,* 1982, 5:341-362.

[25] Ayres, A. Jean. *Sensory Integration and Learning Disorders.*

[26] Pearce, Joseph Chilton. *Evolution's End, Claiming the Potential of Our Intelligence.* p. 113.

[27] Pearce, Joseph Chilton. *The Magical Child Matures.* NY: Bantam Books, 1986.

[28] Penfield, Wilder & H.H. Jasper. *Epilepsy and the Functional Anatomy of the Human Brain.* Boston: Little Brown, 1954. p. 28.

[29] Sacks, Oliver. *The Man Who Mistook His Wife for A Hat, And Other Clinical Tales.* NY: Harper & Row, 1987. p. 43.

[30] Crum, Thomas F. *The Magic of Conflict:Turning A Life of Work into A Work of Art.* NY: Simon & Schuster, 1987. pp. 54-56.

[31] Suplee, Curt. *Neurology: Watching, Imagining and Doing.* IN: *Science Notebook, Washington Post,* Oct. 17, 1994, p. 2. (Summarized from *Nature,* October 13, 1994.)

[32] Tortora & Anagnostakos. *Principles ....* pp. 475-480.

[33] Kohler, Ivo. *Experiments with Goggles.* IN: *Scientific American,* 206(5), 1962, p. 62.

[34] Gregory, Richard. *Eye and Brain, The Psychology of Seeing.* NY: McGraw-Hill, 1966. pp. 204-219.

[35] Grady, Denise. *The Vision Thing: Mainly in the Brain.* IN: *Discover,* June 1993 (vol. 14:6), p. 58.

[36] Escher, M.C. *M.C. Escher, 29 Master Prints.* NY: Abrams, 1981.

[37] Thing, N.E. *Magic Eye: A New Way of Looking at the World.* Kansas City: Andrews and McMeel, 1993.

[38] Tortora & Anagnostakos. *Principles ....* pp. 476-477.

[39] Diamond, Marian. *Enriching Heredity, The Impact of the Environment on the Anatomy of the Brain.* NY: Free Press, 1988. pp. 9-62

[40] Thomas, Alexander & Stella Chess. *Temperament and Development.* NY: Brunner/Mazel, 1977. pp. 18-26, 93-107, 183-190.

[41] Thomas, Alexander & Stella Chess. *Genesis and Evolution of Behavioral Disorders: From Infancy to Early Adult Life.* IN: *American Journal of Psychiatry,* 141(1), pp. 1-9.

4: THE ROLE OF EMOTION

[1] Damasio, Antonio R. *Descartes' Error and the Future of Human Life.* IN: *Scientific American,* October, 1994, p. 144.

[2] Gelernter, David. *The Muse in the Machine, Computerizing the Poetry of Human Thought.* NY: Free Press, 1994. pp. 46-47.

[3] Gelernter, David. *The Muse in the Machine.* p. 35.

[4] Damasio, Antonio R. *Descartes' Error: Emotion, Reason, and the Human Brain.* NY: Putnam, 1994. pp. 205-223.

[5] Damasio, Antonio R. *Descartes' Error: Emotion, Reason, and the Human Brain.* NY: Putnam, 1994. pp. 205-223.

[6] Damasio, Antonio R. *Descartes' Error.* p. 199.

[7] Damasio, Antonio R. *Descartes' Error.* p. 170-173.

[8] Damasio, Antonio R. *Descartes' Error.* p. 200.

[9] Coulter, Dee Joy. *The Triune Brain.* Longmont, CO: Coulter Pub., 1985. Sound Cassette.

[10] Damasio, Antonio, et. al. *Brain Faces Up to Fear, Social Signs.* *Nature,* December 15, 1994. IN: *Science News,* December 17, 1944 (vol. 146), p. 406.

[11] Tortora & Anagnostakos. *Principles ....* pp. 400-401.

[12] Middleton, Frank A. & Peter L. Strick. *Brain Gets Thoughtful Reappraisal.* *Science,* October 21, 1994. IN: *Science News,* October 19, 1994 (vol. 146), p. 284.

[13] Meaney, Michael J., et. al. *Memory Loss Tied to Stress.* IN: *Science News,* November 20, 1993 (vol. 144), p. 332.

[14] Chopra, Deepak. *Quantum Healing, Exploring the Frontiers of Mind/Body Medicine.* Conference in Honolulu, Hawaii, February, 1991.

[15] deBeauport, Elizabeth. Tarrytown Newsletter. 1983.

[16] Restak, Richard. *The Mind.* NY: Bantam Books, 1988. p. 319.

[17] Lazarus, Richard S. & Bernice N. Lazarus. *Passion and Reason, Making Sense of Our Emotions.* NY: Oxford University Press, 1994. pp. 203-208, 290-297.

[18] Coulter, Dee Joy. *Children at Risk: The Development of Drop-outs.* Longmont, CO: Coulter Pub., 1986. Sound Cassette.

[19] Pearce, Joseph Chilton. *Evolution's End, Claiming the Potential of Our Intelligence.* San Francisco: Harper, 1992. pp. 44-51.

[20] Coulter, Dee Joy. *Enter the Child's World.* Longmont, CO: Coulter Pub., 1986. Sound Cassette.

[21] Coulter, Dee Joy. *Enter the Child's World.*

[22] Damasio, Antonio. *Descartes' Error.* pp. 112-113.

[23] Tulving, Endel, et. al. *Hemispheric Encoding/Retrieval Asymmetry in Episodic Memory: Positron Emission Tomography Findings.* IN: *Proceedings of The National Academy of Sciences,* Mar. 15, 1994, pp. 2016-2020. See also: *Brain Scans Show Two-Sided Memory Flow.* IN: *Science News,* Mar. 26, 1994 (vol. 145), p. 199.

[24] Kandel, Eric R. *The Principles of Neuroscience.* Third edition. NY: Elsevier Press, 1991. pp. 1024-1025.

[25] Pearce, Joseph Chilton. *Evolution's End.* p. 141.

[26] MacLean, Paul D. *The Triune Brain In Evolution, Role in Paleocerebral Functions.* NY: Plenum Press, 1990. pp. 559-560.

[27] MacLean, Paul D. *The Triune Brain in Evolution.* pp. 559-575.

[28] Trowbridge, Anthony. *Ecology of Knowledge Network.* Paper given at the Science and Vision Conference, Human Sciences Research Center, Pretoria, South Africa. January, 1992.

[29] Pearce, Joseph Chilton. *Evolution's End.* pp. 164-171.

[30] Healy, Jane M. *Endangered Minds, Why Children Don't Think and What We Can Do About It.* NY: Simon & Schuster, 1990.

[31] Moody, Kate. *Growing Up On Television.* NY: Times Books, 1980. pp. 37, 51, 53.

[32] Bryant, Dr. Jennings. IN: Jane Healy, *Endangered Minds.* pp. 201-202.

[33] Rosemond, John K. *Parents Ask Questions About School.* IN: *Hemispheres Magazine* (Delta Airlines), April 1994. pp. 105-106.

[34] Gachelmann, K.A. *Dream Sleep: A Risk For Heart Patients?* IN: *Science News,* February 6, 1993, (vol. 143), p. 85.

[35] Somers, Virend K., Mark E. Dyken & Allyn L. Mark. *Sympathetic-Nerve Activity During Sleep in Normal Subjects. New England Journal of Medicine,* February 4, 1993, (vol. 328), pp. 303-307.

5: MAKING CONNECTIONS

[1] Harvey, Arthur. *The Numbered Brain.* Louisville: Center for Music and Medicine, University of Louisville, School of Medicine, 1985. p. 7.

[2] Chopra, Deepak. *Quantum Healing, Exploring the Frontiers of Mind/Body Medicine.* NY: Bantam Books, 1990. p. 50.

[3] Penfield, Wilder. *The Mystery of the Mind, A Critical Study of Consciousness and the Human Brain.* Princeton: Princeton University Press, 1977.

4 Begley, Sharon, Lynda Wright, Vernon Church and Mary Hager. *Mapping The Brain*. IN: *Newsweek*, April 20, 1992, pp. 66-70.

5 Haier, Richard J. *Images Of Intellect, Brain Scans May Colorize Intelligence*. IN: *Science News*, Oct. 8, 1994 (vol. 146), pp. 236-237.

6 Tortora & Anagnostakos. *Principles* .... pp. 433-438.

7 Tortora & Anagnostakos. *Principles* .... p. 433.

8 Tortora & Anagnostakos. *Principles* .... p. 438.

9 Luria, Alexander R. *Language and Cognition*. NY: Wiley, 1981. pp. 103-113.

10 Tortora & Anagnostakos. *Principles* .... p. 403.

11 Montgomery, Geoffrey. *The Mind In Motion*. IN: *Discover*, March, 1989, pp. 61-64.

12 McCrone, John. *The Ape That Spoke, Language and the Evolution of the Human Mind*. NY: Avon Books, 1991. p. 65.

13 Kolb, David. *Experiential Learning, Experience As the Source of Learning and Development*. Englewood, NJ: Prentice-Hall, 1984. p. 47.

14 Kolb, David. *Experiential Learning*. p. 47.

15 Williams, Linda Verlee. *Teaching for the Two-sided Mind, A Guide to Right Brain/Left Brain Education*. NY: Simon & Schuster, 1983. p. 26.

16 Edwards, Betty. *Drawing on the Right Side of the Brain*. Los Angeles: Tarcher, 1979. p. 40

17 Coulter, Dee Joy. *Our Triune Brain*. Longmont, CO: Coulter Pub., 1986. Sound Cassette.

18 Pearce, Joseph Chilton. *Magical Child*. NY: Bantam Books, 1980. pp. 29-34.

19 Piaget, Jean. *The Grasp of Consciousness, Action and Concept in the Young Child*. Cambridge, MA: Harvard, 1976. pp. 208, 346-353.

20 Shaffer, David. *Attention Deficit Hyperactive Disorder in Adults*. IN: *American Journal of Psychiatry*, May 1994, pp. 633-638.

21 Harvey, Arthur. *The Numbered Brain*. pp. 7-8

22 Edu-K for Kids graphically illustrates this necessary integration for full mind/body functioning. See, for example, Dennison, Dr. Paul E. and Gail E. Dennison. *Edu-K for Kids*. Ventura, CA: Edu-Kinesthetics, Inc., 1985. On Brain Gym exercises, see below, Chapter 7.

23 Coulter, Dee Joy. *The Sympathetic Thinker in a Critical World*. Longmont, CO: Coulter Pub., 1991. Sound Cassette.

24 Coulter, Dee Joy. *Classroom Clues to Thinking Problems*. Longmont, CO: Coulter Pub., 1986. Sound Cassette.

25 Ministry of Education and Research, International Relations Division. *Characteristic Features of Danish Education*. Copenhagen, Denmark. 1992.

26 Henriksen, Spaet, Svend Hesselholdt, Knud Jensen, & Ole B. Larsen. *The Democratization of Education*. Copenhagen, Denmark: Department of Education and Psychology, The Royal Danish School of Educational Studies. 1990. pp. 1-39.

27 Seligman, Martin E. *Helplessness: On Depression, Development, and Death*. San Francisco: W.H. Freeman, 1975. pp. 37-44, 134-165.

28 Mandaus, George F., et. al. *Tests Flunk, Study Finds. Science News*, Oct. 24, 1992 (vol. 142), p. 277.

[29] Epstein, Herman T. *Growth Spurts During Brain Development: Implications for Educational Policy and Practice.* IN: J. Chall & A.F. Mirsky (eds.), *Education and the Brain.* Chicago: University of Chicago Press, 1979. pp. 343-370.

[30] Piaget, Jean. IN: Campbell, Sarah F. (ed.), *Piaget Sampler, An Introduction to Jean Piaget Through His Own Words.* NY: Wiley, 1976. pp. 15-16, 71-78.

[31] Coulter, Dee Joy. *Enter the Child's World.* Longmont, CO: Coulter Pub., 1986. Sound Cassette.

[32] Gardner, Howard. *Frames of Mind, The Theory of Multiple Intelligences.* N.Y: Basic Books, 1983.

[33] Luria, Alexander R. *The Role of Speech in the Formation of Temporary Connections and the Regulation of Behavior in the Normal and Oligophrenic Child.* IN: Simon and Simon, (eds.), *Educational Psychology in the USSR.* Stanford: Stanford University Press, 1968. p. 85.

[34] Healy, Jane M. *Endangered Minds, Why Children Don't Think and What We Can Do About It.* NY: Simon & Schuster, 1990. p. 101.

[35] Tomatis, Alfred A. *The Conscious Ear, My Life of Transformation through Listening.* pp. 201-218.

[36] Coulter, Dee Joy. *Movement, Meaning and the Mind.* Keynote Address, Seventh Annual Educational Kinesiology Foundation Gathering, Greeley, CO, July, 1993.

[37] Coulter, Dee Joy. *Children at Risk: The Development of Drop-Outs.* Longmont, CO: Coulter Pub., 1986. Sound Cassette.

[38] Blakeslee, Sandra. *Brain Yields New Clues on Its Organization for Language.* IN: *New York Times, Science Times,* Sept. 19, 1991. p. C-1.

[39] Tortora & Anagnostakos. *Principles ....* p. 403.

[40] Tortora & Anagnostakos. *Principles ....* p. 403.

[41] The Talking Fish activity from Vision Gym and the Energy Yawn from Brain Gym increase activation to the communication centers across the TMJ. These release the tension in the jaw and facial muscles, including eye muscles, so that verbalization and expression can occur together easily. See the Chapter 7 below and Dennison, Paul E. & Gail E. Dennison, *Brain Gym, Teachers Edition.* Ventura, CA: Edu-Kinesthetics, Inc., 1989. p. 29.

[42] Rankin, Paul T. *The Importance of Listening Ability.* IN: *English Journal,* (college ed.), 2 (Nov. 1981), pp. 623-630.

[43] Werner, Elyse K. *A Study in Communication Time.* Master Thesis, Unpublished. College Park, MD: University of Maryland, 1975.

[44] *American's Use of Time Project.* Ann Arbor, MI: Inter-University Consortium for Political and Social Research, 1993.

[45] Healy, Jane M. *Endangered Minds.* pp. 86-104.

[46] Brewer, Chris & Don Campbell. *Rhythms of Learning, Creative Tools for Developing Lifelong Skills.* Tucson: Zephyr Press, 1991. p. 31.

[47] Coulter, Dee Joy. *Children at Risk: The Development of Drop-Outs.*

[48] Fuster, Joaquin M. *The Prefrontal Cortex: Anatomy, Physiology and Neuropsychology of the Frontal Lobe.* Second Edition. NY: Raven Press, 1980. p. 255.

[49] McCrone, John. *The Ape That Spoke.* pp. 252-253.

[50] MacLean, Paul D. *The Triune Brain in Evolution, Role in Paleocerebral Functions.* NY: Plenum Press, 1990. pp. 559-562.

6: MOVEMENT

[1] Quoted in Restak, Richard. *The Brain.* NY: Bantam Books, 1984. p. 76.

[2] Gardner, Howard. *Frames of Mind, The Theory of Multiple Intelligences.* NY: Basic Books, 1985. pp. 207-208.

[3] Gardner, Howard. *Frames of Mind.* p. 210. Roger Sperry quoted in E. Ewarts, *Brain Mechanism in Movement, Scientific American,* 229 (July, 1973), p. 103.

[4] Middleton, Frank A. & Peter L. Strick. *Anatomical Evidence for Cerebellar and Basal Ganglia Involvement in Higher Cognitive Function. Science,* October 21, 1994 (vol. 266), pp. 458-461.

[5] Stiller, Angelika, & Renate Wennekes. *The Motoric Development Across the Body Midline.* Neuenkirchen, Germany: *Astrup,* 31, 1992, 2846.

[6] Olsen, Eric. *Fit Kids, Smart Kids — New Research Confirms that Exercise Boosts Brainpower.* IN: *Parents Magazine,* October, 1994, pp. 33-35.

[7] Brink, Susan. *Smart Moves, New Research Suggests that Folks from 8 to 80 Can Shape Up Their Brains with Aerobic Exercise.* IN: *U.S. News & World Report,* May 15, 1995, pp. 78-82.

[8] Albalas, Moses, quoted in Dennison, Paul E. and Gail E. Dennison. *Edu-Kinesthetics In-Depth, The Seven Dimensions of Intelligence.* Ventura, CA: Educational Kinesiology Foundation, 1990.

[9] Dennison, Gail E. *The Big Vision Book.* Ventura, CA: Edu-Kinesthetics, Inc., 1995. (In preparation.)

[10] Schwartz, Eugene. *Seeing, Hearing, Learning: The Interplay of Eye and Ear in Waldorf Education.* (Excerpts from Camp Glenbrook Conference of the Association for a Healing Education, June 14-16, 1988.) 1990. p. 12.

[11] Interviews with Occupational Therapists for Kwazulu schools and consultants with the Sunfield Home School, Verulum, South Africa. March, 1993.

[12] Pisani, T. du, S.J. Plekker, C.F. Dennis, & J.P. Strauss. *Education and Manpower Development, 1990.* Bloemfontein, South Africa: Research Institute for Education Planning, University of the Orange Free State. p. 17.

[13] Coulter, Dee Joy. *Enter the Child's World.* Longmont, CO: Coulter Pub., 1986. Sound Cassette.

[14] Brewer, Chris & Don Campbell. *Rhythms of Learning, Creative Tools for Developing Lifelong Skills.* Tucson: Zephyr Press, 1991.

[15] Coleman, H.M. *Increased Myopia in Schools.* IN: *Journal of American Ophthalmic Association,* (41) 1970, p. 341.

[16] Young, F.A. *Myopia Development.* IN: *American Journal of Ophthalmology.* (52) 1961, p. 799.

[17] Kelley, C.R. *The Psychological Factors In Myopia.* Unpublished Ph.D. dissertation. NY: New York School of Research, 1953.

[18] Streff, John W. *The Cheshire Study: Changes in Incidence of Myopia Following Program of Intervention.* IN: *Frontiers in Visual Science,* Proceedings of the University of Houston College of Optometry Dedication Symposium. Houston, March, 1977.

7: BRAIN GYM

[1] Coulter, Dee Joy. *Movement, Meaning and the Mind*. Keynote Address, Seventh Annual Educational Kinesiology Foundation Gathering, Greeley, CO. July 1993.

[2] McAllen, Audrey E. *The Extra Lesson, Exercises in Movement, Drawing and Painting for Helping Children with Difficulties with Writing, Reading and Arithmetic*. East Sussex, U.K.: Steiner Schools Fellowship Publications, 1985.

[3] Brink, Susan. *Smart Moves, New Research Suggests that Folks from 8 to 80 Can Shape Up Their Brains with Aerobic Exercise*. IN: *U.S. News & World Report*, May 15, 1995, pp. 78-82.

[4] Delacato, Carl H. *The Diagnosis and Treatment of Speech and Reading Problems*. Springfield, IL: Thomas, 1963.

[5] Masgutova, Svetlana. *Psychological Impact on Children of Catastrophe*. IN: *Psychological Problems*, 1990, pp. 86-92. (A copy of this document can be obtained through the Educational Kinesiology Foundation.)

[6] I am presenting only the tip of the iceberg with this work. Further information can be obtained from the Educational Kinesiology Foundation, P.O. Box 3396, Ventura, California 93006-3396, Phone: (800) 356-2109 or (805) 658-7942.

[7] Dennison, Paul E. and Gail E. Dennison. *Brain Gym, Teachers Edition*, Revised. Ventura, CA: Edu-Kinesthetics, Inc., 1994. p. 25.

[8] Tortora &. Anagnostakos. *Principles* .... p. 591.

[9] Olsen, Eric. *Fit Kids, Smart Kids*. IN: *Parents Magazine*, October 1994, p. 33.

[10] Dennison. *Brain Gym, Teachers Edition*, Revised. p. 4.

[11] Dennison. *Brain Gym, Teachers Edition*, Revised. p. 31

[12] Dennison. *Brain Gym, Teachers Edition*, Revised. p. 5.

[13] Dennison. *Brain Gym, Teachers Edition*, Revised. p. 30.

[14] Dennison. *Brain Gym, Teachers Edition*, Revised. p. 29

[15] Dennison. *Brain Gym, Teachers Edition*, Revised. p. 20.

[16] Dennison. *Brain Gym, Teachers Edition*, Revised. p. 14.

[17] Delacato, Carl H. *The Diagnosis and Treatment of Speech and Reading Problems*.

[18] Dennison, Paul E. and Gail E. Dennison. *Edu-Kinesthetics In-Depth, The Seven Dimensions of Intelligence*. Ventura, CA: Educational Kinesiology Foundation, 1990. pp. 113-114.

8: WHAT GOES WRONG?

[1] McGuinness, Diane. *Attention Deficit Disorder, the Emperor's Clothes, Animal Pharm, and Other Fiction*. IN: S. Fisher and R. Greenburg (eds.), *The Limits of Biological Treatment for Psychological Distress*. NY: Erlbaum, 1989.

[2] Wang, M.C. *Commentary*. *Education Week*, May 4, 1988.

[3] Zametkin, Alan J., Thomas E. Nordahl, et. al. *Cerebral Glucose Metabolism in Adults with Hyperactivity of Childhood Onset*. IN: *New England Journal of Medicine*, Nov. 15, 1990 (vol. 323:20), pp. 1365-1366.

[4] Zametkin, Alan J., et. al. pp. 1361-1363.

[5] MacLean, Paul D. *The Triune Brain in Evolution, Role in Paleocerebral Functions*. NY: Plenum Press, 1990. pp. 561-562.

[6] Thatcher, Robert W., M. Hallett, et. al. *Functional Neuroimaging*. NY: Academic Press, 1994. pp. 95-105.

[7] Giedd, Jay N. *Quantitative Morphology of the Corpus Callosum in Attention Deficit Hyperactive Disorder*. IN: *American Journal of Psychiatry*, 1994 (vol. 151:5), pp. 665-669.

[8] Snyder, Solomon, et. al. *Opiate Receptors and Opioid Peptides*. IN: *Annual Review of Neuroscience*, 1979, (2:35).

[9] Sapolsky, Robert. *Stress Exacerbates Neuron Loss and Cytoskeletal Pathology in the Hippocampus*. IN: *Journal of Neuroscience*, September, 1994 (vol. 14:9), pp. 5373-5380.

9: BASICS FOR THE BRAIN: WATER AND OXYGEN

[1] Tortora & Anagnostakos. *Principles* .... pp. 37-38, 861-866.

[2] Tortora & Anagnostakos. *Principles* .... pp. 339-342.

[3] Fischbach, Gerald D. *Mind and Brain*. IN: *Scientific American*, September 1992, p. 50.

[4] Tortora & Anagnostakos. *Principles* .... pp. 37-40, 861-862.

[5] Tortora & Anagnostakos. *Principles* .... pp. 788-789.

[6] Tortora & Anagnostakos. *Principles* .... pp. 37-38, 861-866.

[7] Koester, John. *Current Flow in Neurons*. IN: *Principles of Neuroscience*. Third Edition. NY: Elsevier Press, 1991. pp. 1033-1040.

[8] Fischbach, Gerald D. *Mind and Brain*. p. 50.

[9] Harvey, Arthur. *The Numbered Brain*. Louisville: Center for Music and Medicine, University of Louisville, School of Medicine, 1985.

[10] Goodman and Gilman. *The Pharmacological Basis of Therapeutics*. Eighth Edition. NY: Pergamon Press, 1990. p. 622.

[11] Wiggins, Phillippa M. *A Mechanism Of ATP-Driven Cation Pumps. Biophysics Of Water*. NY: John Wiley, 1982. pp. 266-269.

[12] Batmanghelidj, F. *Your Body's Many Cries for Water*. Falls Church, VA: Global Health Solutions, 1993.

[13] Tortora & Anagnostakos. *Principles* .... pp. 837-845.

[14] Ferris, Thomas F. *Pregnancy, Preeclampsia and the Endothelial Cell*. IN: *New England Journal of Medicine*, November 14, 1991 (vol. 325:20), pp. 1439-1440.

[15] Tortora & Anagnostakos. *Principles* .... p. 852.

[16] Harrrison, Tinsley Randolph. *Harrison's Principles of Internal Medicine*. Twelfth edition. NY: McGraw Hill, 1991. pp. 281-297.

[17] McCrone, John. *The Ape That Spoke, Language and the Evolution of the Human Mind*. NY: Avon Books, 1991. p. 17.

[18] Colombo, Marcio F.; Donald C. Rau & V. Adrian Parsegian. *Protein Solvation in Allosteric Regulation: A Water Effect on Hemoglobin*. IN: *Science*, May 1, 1992 (vol. 256), pp. 655-659.

[19] Tortora & Anagnostakos. *Principles* .... p. 38.

[20] Hollowell, Marguerite. *Unlikely Messengers: How Do Nerve Cells Communicate?* IN: *Scientific American*, December 1992, pp. 52-56.

[21] Olsen, Eric. *Fit Kids, Smart Kids: New Research Confirms That Exercise Boosts Brainpower*. IN: *Parents Magazine*, October-November, 1994, pp. 33-35.

[22] Olsen, Eric. *Fit Kids, Smart Kids.*

[23] Olds, David L., & Charles R. Henderson. *Prevention of Intellectual Impairment in Children of Women Who Smoke Cigarettes During Pregnancy.* IN: *Pediatrics,* February 1994 (vol 93:2), pp. 228-233. See also: Fackelmann, K.A. *Mother's Smoking Linked to Child's IQ Drop.* IN: *Science News,* February 12, 1994 (vol. 145), p. 101.

[24] Stuchly, Maria A. *Electromagnetic Fields And Health.* IN: *IEEE Potentials Journal,* April 1993, p. 38.

[25] Taubes, Gary. *Electromagnetic Fields.* IN: *Consumer Reports,* May, 1994, pp. 354-355.

[26] Stuchly, Maria A. *Electromagnetic Fields And Health.* p. 35.

[27] Raloff, Janet. *EMFs Run Aground.* IN: *Science News,* August 21, 1993 (vol. 144), pp. 125-126.

[28] Taubes, Gary. *Electromagnetic Fields.* p. 355-356.

[29] Hendee, William & John C. Beteler. *Another Way EMFs Might Harm Tissue.* IN: *Science News,* February 19, 1994, p. 127.

[30] Coulter, Dr. Dee Joy. *Movement, Meaning and the Mind.* Keynote Address, Seventh Annual Educational Kinesiology Foundation Gathering, Greeley, CO, July, 1993.

[31] Coulter, Dr. Dee Joy. *Movement, Meaning and the Mind.*

[32] Lee, K.Y.C., Jürgen Klinger, & Harden McConnell. *Electric Field-Induced Concentration Gradients in Lipid Monolayers.* IN: *Science,* Feb. 4, 1994 (vol. 263), pp. 655-658.

10: BASICS FOR THE BRAIN: NUTRITION

[1] Wilmanns, Matthias & David Eisenberg. *Three-Dimensional Profiles from Residue-Pair Preferences; Identification of Sequences with Beta/Alpha Barrel Fold.* IN: *Proceedings of the National Academy of Science,* February 15, 1993 (vol. 90), pp. 1379-1383.

[2] Luthy, Roland, James U. Bowie & David Eisenberg. *Assessment of Protein Models with 3-Dimensional Profiles.* IN: *Nature,* Mar. 5, 1992 (vol. 356), pp. 83-85.

[3] Tortora & Anagnostakos. *Principles ....* pp. 801-803.

[4] Insel, Paul M. and Walton T. Roth. *Core Concepts in Health.* Mountain View, CA: Mayfield Publishing, 1988. pp. 256-264.

[5] Crook, William G. *The Yeast Connection: A Medical Breakthrough.* NY: Random House, 1985. p. 201.

[6] Levinson. Harold N. *The Cerebellar-Vestibular Basis of Learning Disabilities in Children, Adolescents, and Adults; Hypothesis and Study.* IN: *Perceptual & Motor Skills,* 1988 (vol. 67).

[7] Crook, William G. *The Yeast Connection.* p. 102.

[8] Witkin, Steven S. *Defective Immune Responses in Patients with Recurrent Candidiasis.* IN: *Infections in Medicine,* May-June 1985.

[9] Crook, William G. *The Yeast Connection.* p. 378.

[10] Truss, C. Orian. *Metabolic Abnormalities in Patients with Chronic Candidiasis.* IN: *Journal of Orthomolecular Psychiatry,* 1984 (vol. 13, 2).

[11] Iwata, K., and Y. Yamamoto. *Glycoprotein Toxins Produced by Candida Albicans.* IN: *Proceedings of the Fourth International Conference on the Mycoses.* PAHO Scientific Pub. No. 356, June 1977.

[12] Levinson, Harold N. *Turning Around The Upside-Down Kids, Helping Dyslexic Kids Overcome Their Disorder.* NY: M. Evans, 1992. pp. 145-153.

[13] Crook, William G. *The Yeast Connection.*

[14] Prinz, R.J., W. A. Roberts, & E. Hautman. *Dietary Correlates of Hyperactive Behavior in Children.* IN: *Journal of Consulting Clinical Psychology*, 1988, 48:769.

[15] Horrobin, D.F. *Alcohol — Blessing and Curse of Mankind!* IN: *Executive Health*, June, 1981 (vol. XVII, no. 9).

[16] Mauro, Frank and Roberta Feios. *Kids, Food and Television, The Compelling Case for State Action.* New York State Assembly Publishers, 1977. p. 102.

[17] Burgess, Donna M., and M.P. Streisguth. *Educating Students with Fetal Alcohol Syndrome of Fetal Alcohol Effects.* IN: *Pennsylvania Reporter*, Nov. 1990 (vol. 22:1).

[18] Donovan, Bernard T. *Humors, Hormones and the Mind: An Approach to the Understanding of Behavior.* London: Macmillan, 1988.

[19] Feldman, David. et. al. *Steroid Hormone Systems Found in Yeast.* IN: *Science*, August 31, 1984 (vol. 225), pp. 913-914.

11: THE VESTIBULAR SYSTEM AND LEARNING DISORDERS

[1] Frank J. & Harold N. Levinson. *Dysmetric Dyslexia and Dyspraxia: Hypothesis And Study.* IN: *Journal of American Academy of Child Psychiatry*, 1973 (vol. 12), pp. 690-701.

[2] Levinson, Harold N. *Turning Around the Upside-Down Kids, Helping Dyslexic Kids Overcome Their Disorder.* NY: M. Evans, 1992.

[3] Frank, J. & Harold N. Levinson. *Dysmetric Dyslexia and Dyspraxia: Synopsis of A Continuing Research Project.* IN: *Academic Therapy*, 1975-1976 (vol. 11), pp. 133-143.

[4] Levinson, Harold N. *The Cerebellar-Vestibular Basis of Learning Disabilities in Children, Adolescents, and Adults: Hypothesis and Study.* IN: *Perceptual and Motor Skills*, 1988 (67), pp. 983-1006.

[5] Livingston, Richard. *Season of Birth and Neurodevelopmental Disorders: Summer Birth Is Associated with Dyslexia.* IN: *Journal of the American Academy of Child and Adolescent Psychiatry*, May 1993 (vol. 32:3), pp. 612-616. See also: *Science News*, May 1, 1993 (vol. 143), p. 278.

[6] Frank J. & H.N. Levinson. *Dysmetric Dyslexia And Dyspraxia: Hypothesis And Study.*

[7] Coulter, Dee Joy. *Movement, Meaning and the Mind.* Keynote Address, Seventh Annual Educational Kinesiology Foundation Gathering, Greeley, CO. July 1993.

[8] Korner, A. F. & E.B. Thoman. *The Relative Efficacy of Contact and Vestibular Stimulation on Soothing Neonates.* IN: *Child Development*, 1972 (vol. 43), pp. 443-453.

[9] Kaga, K., R.R. March, & Y. Tanaka. *Influence of Labyrinthine Hypoactivity on Gross Motor Development of Infants.* IN: B. Cohen (Ed.), International Meeting

of the Barany Society, *Annals of the New York Academy of Sciences*, 1981 (374), pp. 412-420.

[10] Kohen-Raz, R. *Learning Disabilities and Postural Control*. London: Freund, 1988.

[11] Mosse, H.L. *A Complete Handbook of Children's Reading Disorders, A Critical Evaluation of Their Clinical, Educational, and Social Dimensions*. IN: Human Sciences press, vol. 1 and 2. 1982.

12: FIGHT OR FLIGHT — THE STRESS EFFECT ON LEARNING

[1] Tortora & Anagnostakos. *Principles* .... pp. 455-457.

[2] Restak, Richard. *The Mind*. NY: Bantam Books, 1988. p. 39

[3] Tortora & Anagnostakos. *Principles* .... pp. 523, 526, 807.

[4] Diorio, Diane, Victor Viau & Michael J. Meaney. *The Role of the Medial Prefrontal Cortex (Cingulate Gyrus) in the Regulation of Hypothalamic-Pituitary-Adrenal Responses to Stress*. IN: *Journal of Neuroscience*, November 1993 (13:9), pp. 3839-3847. See also: *Memory Loss Tied to Stress* ... IN: *Science News*, November 20, 1993 (vol. 144), p. 332.

[5] McCrone, John. *The Ape That Spoke, Language and the Evolution of the Human Mind*. NY: Avon Books, 1991. pp. 216-217.

[6] Tortora & Anagnostakos. *Principles* .... pp. 365-366.

[7] Dennison, Paul. Personal communication with the author.

[8] Dennison, Paul E. & Gail E. Dennison. *Brain Gym, Teachers Edition*. Ventura, CA: Edu-Kinesthetics, Inc., 1989. p. 20.

[9] Selye, Hans. *General Adaptation Syndrome and Diseases of Adaptation*. IN: *Journal of Clinical Endocrinology and Metabolism*, 1946 (6), pp. 117-230.

[10] Freize, Irene, et. al. *Women and Sex Roles, A Social Psychological Perspective*. NY: Norton, 1978.

[11] Beardslee, William R., et. al. *Level of Social-Cognitive Development, Adaptive Functioning, and DSM-III Diagnoses in Adolescent Offspring of Parents with Affective Disorders; Implications of the Development of the Capacity for Mutuality*. IN: *Developmental Psychology*, 1987 (vol. 23:6), pp. 807-815.

[12] Field, T., D. Sandberg, et. al. *Pregnancy Problems, Postpartum Depression and Early Mother-Infant Interaction*. IN: *Developmental Psychology*, 1985 (vol. 21), pp. 1152-1156.

[13] Bower, Bruce. *Growing Up Poor, Poverty Packs Several Punches for Child Development*. IN: *Science News*, July 9, 1994 (vol. 146), pp. 24-25.

[14] Satir, Virginia. *The Satir Model: Family Therapy and Beyond*. Palo Alto, CA: Science and Behavior Books, 1991.

[15] Wegscheider-Cruse, Sharon. *Another Chance, Hope and Health for the Alcoholic Family*. Palo Alto, CA: Science and Behavior Books, 1989. pp. 137-49.

[16] Hamburg, David. *39 Million Poor Americans — If They Don't Know Their Place, They're Learning It*. Carnegie Corporation of New York Report. IN: *The Washington Spectator*, May 15, 1994 (vol. 20:10), pp. 1-2.

[17] Healy, Jane M. *Endangered Minds, Why Children Don't Think and What We Can Do About It*. NY: Simon & Schuster, 1990. p. 201.

[18] Wegscheider-Cruse, Sharon. *Another Chance, Hope and Health for the Alcoholic Family.* pp. 132-137.

[19] Satir, Virginia. *The Satir Model.*

[20] Crile, George W. *A Bipolar Theory of Living Processes.* NY: Macmillan, 1926. pp. 104-110, 180-184.

[21] Levinson, Harold N. *The Cerebellar-Vestibular Basis of Learning Disabilities in Children, Adolescents, and Adults; Hypothesis and Study.* IN: *Perceptual & Motor Skills,* 1988 (vol. 67).

[22] Ruff, Michael R., Candace B. Pert, Richard J. Weber. *Benzodiazapine Receptor-Mediated Chemotaxis of Human Monocytes.* IN: *Science,* September 20, 1985, (vol. 229), pp. 1281-1283.

[23] Chopra, Deepak. *Quantum Healing, Exploring the Frontiers of Mind/Body Medicine.* NY: Bantam Books, 1990. pp. 66-67.

[24] Cantin, Marc and Jacques Genest. *The Heart As An Endocrine Gland.* IN: *Scientific American,* February 1986, (vol. 254:2), p. 76.

[25] Putnam, Frank & Martin Teicher. Findings presented at American Psychiatric Association Meeting, Philadelphia, Spring 1994.

[26] Terr, Lenore C. *Adult Memories of Child Abuse.* IN: *American Journal of Psychiatry,* January 1991, pp.68-72.

[27] Chopra, Deepak. *Quantum Healing.*

[28] Block, Jack and Richard W. Robins. *Gender Paths Wind Toward Self-Esteem.* IN: *Child Development,* June 1993. See also: *Science News,* vol. 143, p. 308.

[29] Moody, Kate. *Growing Up On Television.* NY: Times Books, 1980. p. 81.

[30] A. C. Nielsen Company. *Nielsen Report on Television 1990.* Northbrook, IL: Nielsen Media Research, 1990.

[31] Gallup, G., Jr., and F. Newport. *Americans Have Love-Hate Relationship With Their TV Sets. Gallup Poll News Service,* 1990 (55:21), 1-9.

[32] Peter D. Hart Research Associates. *Would You Give Up TV for A Million Bucks?* IN: *TV Guide,* 1992 (40: 41), pp. 10-17.

[33] Pearce, Joseph Chilton. *Evolution's End, Claiming the Potential of Our Intelligence.* San Francisco: Harper & Row, 1992. p. 169-170.

[34] Centerwell, B. S. *Exposure to Television As A Cause of Violence.* IN: G. Comstock (editor), *Public Communication and Behavior.* Orlando, FL: Academic Press, 1989. Vol. 2, pp. 1-58.

[35] Moody, Kate. *Growing Up On Television.* pp. 83, 90.

[36] Healy, Jane M. *Endangered Minds.* p. 200.

[37] Liebert R. & J. Sprafkin. *The Early Window.* NY: Pergamon, 1988.

[38] Moody, Kate. *Growing Up on Television.*

[39] Mander, J. *Four Arguments for the Elimination of Television.* NY: Morrow, 1978.

[40] Buzzell, Keith A. *The Neurophysiology of Television Viewing: A Preliminary Report.* (Obtained through Dr. Keith A. Buzzell, 14 Portland St., Frysburg, ME 04037.)

[41] Meltzoff, A. N. *Infant Imitation After A 1-Week Delay: Long-Term Memory for Novel Acts and Multiple Stimuli.* IN: *Developmental Psychology,* 1988 (24), pp. 470-476.

[42] Meltzoff, A. N. *Imitation of Televised Models by Infants.* IN: *Child Development,* 1988 (59), pp. 1221-1229.

[43] Flavell, J.H. *The Development of Children's Knowledge about the Appearance-Realty Distinction.* IN: *American Psychologist,* 1986 (41), pp. 418-425.

[44] Heller, M. S., and S. Polsky. *Studies in Violence and Television.* NY: American Broadcasting Company, 1976.

[45] Biederman, J., S. Faraone, K. Keenan, E. Knee, & M. Twuang. *Family Genetic and Psychosocial Risk Factors in DSM-III Attention Deficit Disorder.* IN: *Journal of American Academy of Child and Adolescent Psychiatry,* 1990 (vol. 29).

[46] Tortora & Anagnostakos. *Principles ....* pp. 408-409.

[47] Olsen, Eric. *Fit Kids, Smart Kids — New Research Confirms That Exercise Boosts Brainpower.* IN: *Parents Magazine,* October, 1994, p. 35.

[48] Burks, Robert and S. Keeley. *Exercise and Diet Therapy: Psychotherapists' Beliefs and Practices.* IN: *Professional Psychology: Research & Practice,* 1989 (vol. 20), pp. 62-64.

[49] Ackerman, Jennifer Gorham. *The Healer Within.* IN: *The Incredible Machine.* Washington, DC: National Geographic Society, 1986. pp. 217-219.

[50] Restak, Richard M. *The Mind.* p. 40.

[51] Tortora & Anagnostakos. *Principles ....* pp. 349, 407, 409, 531.

13: MIS-EDUCATION & THE LABELING GAME

[1] MacLean, Paul D. *The Triune Brain in Evolution, Role in Paleocerebral Functions.* NY: Plenum Press, 1990. p. 575.

[2] Dennison, Paul. *Whole Brain Learning for the Whole Person.* Ventura, CA: Edu-Kinesthetics, Inc., 1985.

[3] Hannaford, Carla L. *Educational Kinesiology ("Brain Gym") with Learning-Style Discriminated K-12 Students.* Unpublished Ph.D. Dissertation, Columbia Pacific University. 1993.

[4] Mattson, A., et. al. *40 Hertz EEG Activity in Learning Disabled and Normal Children.* Poster presentation, International Neuropsychological Society, Vancouver, B.C. February, 1989.

[5] Albert Einstein quoted in Howard Gardner, *Frames Of Mind, The Theory of Multiple Intelligences.* NY: Basic Books, 1985. p. 190.

[6] Brewer, Chris & Don Campbell. *Rhythms of Learning, Creative Tools for Developing Lifelong Skills.* Tucson: Zephyr Press, 1991.

[7] *The Folkeskole. Education in Denmark.* Ministry of Education and Research. March, 1991. Department of Primary and Lower Secondary Education, Frederiksholms Kanal 26, DK-1220 Copenhagen K.

[8] Wheatley, Grayson H. *The Right Hemisphere's Role in Problem Solving.* IN: *Arithmetic Teacher,* 1977 (11), pp. 36-39.

[9] Samples, Bob. *Educating for Both Sides of the Human Mind.* IN: *The Science Teacher,* January 1975, pp. 21-23.

[10] Epstein, Herman T. *Growth Spurts During Brain Development: Implications for Educational Policy and Practice.* IN: J. Chall & A.F. Mirsky (eds.), *Education and the Brain.* Chicago, IL: University of Chicago Press, 1979. pp. 343-370.

[11] Myers, John T. *Hemisphericity Research, An Overview with Some Implications for Problem Solving.* IN: *Journal of Creative Behavior,* 1982 (vol. 16:3), pp. 197-211.

[12] McCarthy, Bernice. *The 4-MAT System.* Barrington, IL: Excel, Inc., 1986.

[13] Kolb, David. *Experiential Learning, Experience As the Source of Learning and Development.* Englewood, NJ: Prentice-Hall, 1984. p. 96.

[14] Gardner, Howard. *Frames Of Mind.* pp. 59-70.

[15] *Letter to a Teacher.* IN: *The Native Perspective,* (Perth, Western Australia) July-August 1977.

14: DRUGS & HYPERACTIVITY

[1] Breggin, Peter R. and Ginger Ross Breggins. *The War Against Children.* NY: St. Martin's, 1994. pp. 3, 62, 78.

[2] Chopra, Deepak. *Quantum Healing, Exploring the Frontiers of Mind/Body Medicine.* NY: Bantam Books, 1990. pp. 66-67.

[3] Breggin, Peter R. and Ginger Ross Breggin. *The War Against Children.* p. 4.

[4] American Psychiatric Association. *Treatments of Psychiatric Disorders, A Task Force Report of the American Psychiatric Association.* Washington, DC: APA, 1989. p. 1221.

[5] Johnson, Dorothy Davis. *I Can't Sit Still — Educating and Affirming Inattentive and Hyperactive Children.* Santa Cruz, CA: Education, Training and Research Association, 1992. pp. 153-154.

[6] Hartmann, Thom. *Attention Deficit Disorder: A Different Perception.* Novat, CA: Underwood-Miller, 1993. p. 73.

[7] Whalen, C., and B. Henker. *Hyperactivity Children.* NY: Academic Press, 1980.

[8] Breggin, Peter. *Toxic Psychiatry: Why Therapy, Empathy and Love Must Replace the Drugs, Electroshock and Biochemical Theories of the "New Psychiatry."* NY: St. Martin's, 1991. p. 15.

[9] Swanson, J.M., D. Cantwell, M. Lerner, K. McBurnett, L. Pfiffner, & R. Kotkin. *Treatment of ADHD: Beyond Medication.* IN: *Beyond Behavior,* 1992 (4:1), pp. 13-22.

[10] Mannuzza, Salvatore, et. al. *Adult Outcome of Hyperactive Boys: Educational Achievement, Occupational Rank, and Psychiatric Status.* IN: *Archives of General Psychiatry,* July 1993 (vol. 50), pp. 565-576.

[11] Fischbach, Gerald D. *Mind and Brain.* IN: *Scientific American,* September 1992, pp. 54-55.

[12] Winslow, W. and R. Markstein. *The Neurobiology of Dopamine Systems.* Second Symposium of the Northern Neurobiology Group, Leeds, U.K., July 1984.

[13] Hartmann, Thom. *Attention Deficit Disorder.* pp. 75-76.

[14] Breggin, Peter R. and Ginger Ross Breggin. *The War Against Children.* p. 85.

[15] Hartmann, Thom. *Attention Deficit Disorder.* p. 76.

[16] Arby, Ronald and William J. Gole. *Physicians' Desk Reference, 1995.* Montvale, NJ: Medical Economics, 1995. p. 897.

[17] Shaffer, David. *Attentional Deficit Hyperactive Disorder in Adults.* IN: *American Journal of Psychiatry,* May 1994 (vol. 151), pp. 633-638.

[18] Nasrallah, H., J. Loney, S. Olson, M. McCalley-Whitters, J. Kramer, & C. Jacoby. *Cortical Atrophy in Young Adults with a History of Hyperactivity in Childhood.* IN: *Psychiatric Research*, 1986 (17), pp. 241-246.

[19] Mann, Eberhard M. *The Ritalin Controversy.* Paper presented at the Attention Deficit Hyperactive Disorder Conference in Honolulu, Hawaii, March, 1994.

[20] Galaburda, Albert. *Ordinary and Extraordinary Brains: Nature, Nurture, and Dyslexia.* Address presented at the Annual Meeting of the Orton Dyslexia Society. Tampa, Florida, Nov. 1988.

[21] Vail, Priscilla. *Smart Kids With School Problems.* NY: Dutton, 1987.

15: LOOKING OUTWARD FOR MODELS

[1] MacLean, Paul. Personal communication.

[2] Interview with Occupational Therapists working with the Sunfield Home School, Verulum, South Africa, March, 1993.

[3] Langburg, Arney. Principal, High School Redirection, Denver Public School System, Denver, Colorado.

[4] Ministry of Education and Research, International Relations Division. *Characteristic Features of Danish Education.* Copenhagen, Denmark. 1992 p. 1-39.

[5] Henriksen, Spaet, Svend Hesselholdt, Knud Jensen, & Ole B. Larsen. *The Democratization of Education.* Department of Education and Psychology, The Royal Danish School of Educational Studies. 1990.

[6] Nielsen, Jorgen & Thomas Webb. *An Emerging Critical Pedagogy. Rethinking Danish Educational Philosophy in the Light of Changing Concepts of Culture.* Huanistisk Arbog Pub., No. 4, Roskilde Universitetscenter. 1991.

[7] Hahn, Carole L. and Paulette Dilworth. *Preparing Participating Citizens in the European Community.* Presented to the Comparative and International Education Society, San Diego, CA, March 21, 1994.

[8] Kolb, David. *Experiential Learning, Experience As the Source of Learning and Development.* Englewood, NJ: Prentice-Hall, 1984. p. 2.

[9] Messier, Paul, Barbara Given and Charlene Engel. *National Learning Foundation Mission Statement.* Presented in February 1994. National Learning Foundation, 11 Dupont Circle, N.W., Suite 900, Washington, DC 20036-1271.

Index

Myelin 20, 21, 22, 64, 79, 82, 89, 119, 159
Myopia 105

N

National Learning Foundation 212
Neck muscles 100, 124
Neocortex 31, 32, 35, 53, 65, 68, 71, **75**, 76, 81, 91, 92, 164, 169
Nerve Growth Factor 39
Neural networks 17-28, **23**, 30, 32, 57, 72, 83, 100, 158, 159,
Neural networks and Brain Gym 130
Neural networks and memory 62
Neural networks and mental rehearsal 44
Neural networks and movement 102
Neural networks and nutrition 151
Neural networks and stress 133, 164
Nervous system 25, 27, 145
Neurons 18, **19**, 22, 24, 25, 26, 71
Neuropeptides 173, 199
Neurotransmitter 22, 53, 175, 199, 200
Neurotrophins 102, 112
Nutrition 136, 139, 151

O

Occipital lobe 31, 62, 73, 74, **75-77**, 125
Ocular lock (staring) 67, 118
Olfactory area 75
Opiates (morphines) 173
Oxygen 112, 118, 128, 136, 138, 141, 143, 146, 152, 160, 174

P

PACE 117
Pain 53
Parents 57, 83, 91, 93, 165, 196, 197, 201, 209
Parietal lobe 39, 73, **75-77**
Parkinson's Disease 99, 200, 201
Penfield, William 42, 74
Peripheral vision 104, 107

Pert, Candace 173
PET scans 27, 62, 74, 77, 200, 201
Phobias 154
Phonemes 36
Physical education 146, 174, 193
Pituitary 53
Planning 54
Plasticity 17, 27
Play 27, 64, 66, 91, 95, 136, 208
Posture 34
Potassium 140
Pre-motor cortex 134
Preeclampsia 145
Prefrontal cortex 134
Pregnancy 145, 152, 157
Prenatal 32, 36, 96, 149, 155
Printing 85
Problem solving 86, 194, 199
Proprioception 19, 26, 33, 39, 42-44, 45, 46, 68, 73, 75
Proprioceptors **43**
Proteins 24, 145, 151
Putnam, Frank 170

R

Rapoport, Stanley 27
Rational 51
Reading 81, 83, 84, 101, 102, 104, 105, 106, 107, 124, 127, 159, 190
Reason 66
Reasoning 52, 53, 59, 65, 76, 80, 86, 91, 134, 135
Reeves, Byron 172
Reflex 31
Relationships 56, 60, 61, 78, 80, 82, 91, 172
Remedial students 182, 190
Reptilian brain 31, 39, 53, 58, 68, 82, 120
Responsibility 208
Reticular activating system (RAS) 35, 41, 118, 136, 153, 157, 158, 202
Retina 46, 47, 104
Rhythm 149
Ritalin 167, 198, 199, 200, 201
Rods 47, 104
Rote memory 86, 194, 199

S

Salts 140, 143, 144

Scholastic Assessment Tests (SAT's) 186, 188, 196

Schools 105, 130, 150, 177, 211, 212

Self-control 134

Self-esteem 166, 170, 177, 182, 184, 196

Semicircular canals **33**, 34, 35, 125, 159

Sensation 26, 29, 48, 53, 54, 57, 73, 96, 100, 192

Sensory areas 75, 92

Sensory cortex 41, **42**, 76, 120, 125

Sensory learning 209

Sensory neurons **19**, 39, 76

Sensory-motor functions 78

Sensory-motor growth 41

Sensory-motor memory 75

Sensory-motor response 36

Shoulder muscles 124

Sign language 87, 92

Skills 23, 26, 27, 44, 75, 82, 87, 89, 98, 190

Skin 30, 39, **40**

Sleep 32, 36, 53, 68

Smell 26, 38, 61, 62, 68, 72, 73, 75, 76, 78, 82

Smoking 147

Social behavior 53, 82, 95

Social relationships 57

Sodium 140

Sodium-potassium pump 140, 141, 146, 150, 151

Somesthetic Association Area 75

Sonograms 150

Sound 26, 72, 74

Special education 107, 182, 187, 188, 192, 193

Speech 75, 82, 87, 89, 90, 91, 92, 99, 164

Speech-impaired 128

Sperry, Roger 98

Spinal cord 19-22, 71, 163

Sports 45, 64, 79, 82, 87, 88, 116, 120, 184

Steiner, Rudolf 97, 112

Stress 13, 14, 160-165

Stress and disease 152-154, **153**

Stress and dreaming 68

Stress and learning 109, 130, 133-137, **135**

Stress and memory 137

Stress and TV 172

Stress and vision 106, 124, 190

Stress and water consumption 139

Stress management 121, 130, 196

Stretching, legs 127

Stretching, neck and shoulders 128

Stroke 18, 27

Substance abuse 136

Substantia nigra 51, 54, 89, **90**

Sugar 144, 151, 152, 154, 155

Superior pre-frontal cortex 134

Survival 31, 52, 53, 54, 56, 57, 58, 60, 62, 66, 82, 160, 161, 166, 172

Survival centers 120

Survival response 164

Survival-oriented-stressed-out-human (SOSOH) 133, 155, 164, 166, 167, 178, 201, 202, 203

Sympathetic nervous system 133, 161, 169

Synapse 22, 24

T

T-Cells 174

Taste 26, 61, 68, 75, 76, 78, 82

Tay-Sachs disease 22

Teaching 41, 44, 56, 68, 81, 84, 86, 93, 99, 126, 158, 187-189, 191, 192, 195, 196, 201

Teicher, Martin 170

Television 14, 48, 66, 90, 93, 101, 136, 150, 152, 157, 158, 165, 171, 172, 173

Telodendria 22

Temporal lobe 62, 73, 74, **75-77**, 125, 126, 180

Temporal-mandibular joint 92, 126

Tendon guard reflex 127, 163

Tension 124, 127

Tests 122, 194

Thalamocingulate ganglion 95

Thalamocortical system 73

Thalamus 32, 53, 73, 76, 173

Thinking 79, 83, 98, 99, 107, 131, 135

Thinking Caps 125, **126**

Carla Hannaford, Ph.D., is a neurophysiologist and educator with more than twenty-eight years of teaching experience, including twenty years as a professor of biology and four years as a counselor for elementary and intermediate school children with learning difficulties.

Since 1988 she has been an internationally recognized educational consultant, making more than five hundred presentations worldwide on the neural basis of learning and educational kinesiology. She was selected as a guest educator with the AHP-Soviet Project in 1988, has been recognized by Who's Who in American Education, and has received awards from the University of Hawaii and the American Association for the Advancement of Science for outstanding teaching of science.

She lives in Hawaii and Montana.